ARTIFICIAL PERSONS

ARTIFICIAL PERSONS

THE FORMATION
OF CHARACTER IN
THE TRAGEDIES OF
SHAKESPEARE
BY J. LEEDS BARROLL

UNIVERSITY OF SOUTH CAROLINA PRESS

COLUMBIA, SOUTH CAROLINA

Copyright © 1974 UNIVERSITY OF SOUTH CAROLINA PRESS

First Edition

Published in Columbia, South Carolina,
by the University of South Carolina Press, 1974

Manufactured in the United States of America

Library of Congress Cataloging in Publication Data

Barroll, John Leeds, 1928–
   Artificial persons.

   1. Shakespeare, William, 1564–1616—Tragedies.
2. Shakespeare, William, 1564–1616—Characters.
I. Title.
PR2983.B28   822.3′3   73–13991
ISBN 0–87249–294–X

To the memory of Maurice Levine, M.D., Professor and Director of the Department of Psychiatry, the University of Cincinnati College of Medicine.

CONTENTS

P R E F A C E

M uch of the material in the early chapters was first presented in the "Perhaps" seminars sponsored by the Department of Psychiatry at the University of Cincinnati College of Medicine in 1967. The interaction there from old and valued friends, counselors, and university colleagues greatly contributed to the development of the study.

The W. H. Taft Fund, through the kind and repeated generosity of the University of Cincinnati, made possible the inevitable travel and time for research. *Cum ab nobis crimen removeres volemus, aut in rem aut in hominem nostri peccati causam conferemus.*

J. LEEDS BARROLL
Columbia, South Carolina
June 5, 1973

PART I

MAN'S RAGE
FOR IMAGE

Psychology and Psychiatry in Renaissance England

The conventions of stage performance do not usually allow for passages such as those we are more likely to find in an epic or a novel, passages in which we seem to hear the voice of the author commenting upon his own characters. This is as true of the works of Ibsen or Beckett as it is of Shakespeare and is one of the reasons why so much dramatic criticism is more primitive than that of the novel or the epic, primitive in the sense that it relies on perceptions that remain intuitive and on assumptions that are seldom made explicit. Perhaps it is also the reason why so many of the major achievements of literary criticism from Aristotle's to T. S. Eliot's consist of essays upon the drama, writing which is the most difficult form of literary criticism and is also the most noteworthy when done well.

Just as our ability to comprehend "melody" from a series of horizontally and vertically presented notes of music includes and is preceded by our ability to hear sounds and, more importantly, to detect patterns in them, so our response to that illusion of a "person" created by the words in a drama includes and must be preceded by our ability to hear and see in another human being those verbal and other behavioral activities which will enable us to form some theoretical construct which we vaguely term a "kind" of person, or more simply, Artaxerxes or Bumby. To discover unreal persons, however, persons presented in a drama, we as critics require a somewhat different form of perception than we attempt to use with real human beings. We require some protocol, some "theory of characterization" that enables us to perceive the "persons" who speak to us in a drama as illusion-products of the author's artistic constructions, a protocol somewhat analogous to but infinitely more elusive than one which might enable us to respond to Modigliani's *Portrait of Mme. Haydn* as a superb and sophisticated blending of color and line rather than as a "real" woman who moves us. In this book I shall attempt to make as explicit as possible my own sense of this protocol, this theory of characterization, that the tragedies of William Shakespeare seem to require us to hold.

Clearly, Modigliani and Shakespeare would not be important in our culture if they had not been able to deceive us in magnificent ways. I take it that the whole point of our valuing Hamlet over, say, the Heironymo in Thomas Kyd's *Spanish Tragedy* of the 1580s is that Hamlet does indeed seem real to us and is therefore important to us as a person. The Mona Lisa, Oedipus, Tom Jones: the number of these "persons" we have come to know have enriched our comprehension, our sympathies, and our lives to the point that we could assert that they have just as surely existed in our culture on earth as the billions of humans who have lived and died to leave fossilized bones or forlorn masonry as the only trace of their own passing. But it is important that we do not simply accept an Achilles as automatically as we accept the result of human sexual reproduction. These persons were made, not begotten (except in the spiritual sense), and if they have meant something to us—these beautiful, and in the best sense, artificial beings created by humans who have died and decayed—we will not only want to know that in some profound and racial sense they have existed, but we will also wish to reaffirm the essential dignity of the human spirit through our knowledge that these timeless "persons" are indeed human creations. It is the purpose of this book to remind us of art, to honor Shakespeare's identity with the most important Attic sense of the poet as "maker." We are interested in how Shakespeare may have made his dazzling persons, not with the admittedly wonderful fact that he made them at all.

If the criticism of drama is difficult for the reasons we have suggested, it becomes even more so when all that remains from the times of a vanished art are the words. The texts of Renaissance plays, as we are all too aware, have seldom retained even so crucial a dimension of the visual medium they represent as designated physical gestures for the actors.[1] We might, of course,

---

[1] The various and intriguing exceptions are sufficiently known but insufficiently studied. George Wilkins' novel, *The Painfull Adventures of Pericles, Prince of Tyre; being the true history of the play of Pericles as presented*

argue that the nature of any one character can nevertheless be gathered from the printed speeches which we have. These convey his statements of principles, his enunciated reactions to situations, his opinions of those around him or the opinions of others who comment on him, but this kind of evidence can never be definitive without some awareness of the accompanying physical minutiae. Facial expressions and other telling physical gestures will often modify or contradict the literal evidence, and what remains for the critic is some such last resort as an appeal to the "necessary implications of language" or the "surrounding dramatic situation." But our analysis of sixteenth- and seventeenth-century linguistic structures has not arrived at that point where each and every utterance, with the assemblage of its components, can be indisputably construed to convey authorially intended meanings.[2] If the "accurate" interpretation of a line in drama must be derived from an accurate interpretation of the "surrounding dramatic situation," logic will remind us that such "situations" are themselves inevitably composed of the printed words and unreported physical gestures which have already established themselves as doubtful principles of any certainty.

If an investigation of "character" in drama is so hampered from the beginning by the historic, mimetic, and even physical complications offered by the particular medium in question, can one not at least make an argument for the existence of certain indisputable "facts" which might serve as the point of departure? When Macduff enters with the severed head of Macbeth in his hands (assuming the accuracy of the stage directions), or when Brutus, in the absence of stage directions, nevertheless has

---

by J. Gower (London, 1608), is a good example of such a source. It has been discussed most recently by F. D. Hoeniger in his New Arden *Pericles.* The use of "bad" and "doubtful" quartos as indications of the purely visual aspects of the medium, though never thoroughly studied in this respect, has been sufficiently emphasized by W. W. Greg in *The Editorial Problem in Shakespeare* (Oxford, 1954), 76; and in his Malone Society publication, *Two Elizabethan Stage Abridgements* (Oxford, 1923).

[2] See E. J. Dobson, *English Pronunciation 1500–1700* (Oxford, 1957), as qualified by R. C. Alston, "Bibliography and Historical Linguistics," *Library,* XXI (1966), 181–91.

spoken of running on his sword, speaks words to the effect that he is killing himself, and is then pronounced dead by Strato, there is "fact." An audience, we conclude, was to understand that Macbeth was dead and that Brutus consciously performed an act which would lead to his own death. In the latter case, as in the case of Othello strangling Desdemona, we could even go so far as to state that such facts demonstrate something "interior," something about the exertion of a will in Brutus and Othello. Yet such "facts" have limited epistemological utility as departure points for any theory of characterization. The "fact" or "deed" has no intrinsic relevance to anything else, no specific relation to some structure other than our mere understanding that the "fact" has been presented within the confines of the play. It only becomes significant to the whole when, for example, a critical act relates the "deed" to some compilation of elements in the play which has been hypothesized as an ideational entity from the very first. When a "characterization" is the hypothesis in question, one usually relates the "deed" to the "character" by the grammar of antecedence:[3] "Brutus" is related to the "fact" of his death through the concept of "motivation" wherein his suicide is relevant to some interpretative version of his characterization. But we will agree that connections between a "deed" and that which produced it can be tenuous in the ascription, that "facts" in a play are not necessarily definitive even for the analysis of motivation. For the individual deed serves not to define one but merely to limit the number of possible linkages with the concept of a character. The fact that Brutus killed himself, for example, limits the range of possibilities to where we can state that his characterization was not the picturing of a person determined to go on living under all circumstances. However, his suicide does not, as an indisputable event in the play, tell us his motives for killing himself. We arrive at these

[3] The term "grammar" is used throughout this work in the sense indicated by Ludwig Wittgenstein, *Philosophical Investigations*, trans. G. E. M. Anscombe (New York, 1953), secs. 244–57, where he uses "die Grammatik" (p. 92ᵉ). Kenneth Burke's definition is roughly similar, at least in implication: see A *Grammar of Motives* (New York, 1952), 465–66.

by a hypothesis which will cause us to link the death with a particular concept of what constitutes the Roman's "characterization." Interpretation may seem obvious here, but Lear's death may suggest the difficulties inherent in the use of fact as a way to character.

The problem of selecting those relationships between indisputable fact and hypothesized character returns us, then, to our prior dilemma. If a collocation of such linkages (which we most often term "motivation") is to be garnered so that their particular combination in principle or subordinated relationships serves to precipitate a theory about one particular character, the consolidation is itself from the words of speeches, from physical gestures, and from deeds; and these are elements subject to the procedural difficulties to which we have already alluded.

With these considerations in mind, the problem of evolving a procedure aimed at recapturing what can be ascertained about a dramatist's conscious intents for specific characterizations inevitably becomes intertwined in other conditions. The principles of certainty available to us in the examination of Renaissance dramatic media are meaningless as such, for they can only be interrelated by means of hypotheses which combine elements into some form we will choose to term a "characterization." But if the hypothesis seeks to recover artistic assumptions about general "characterization," it cannot be derived from only one play. It is true that assumptions about methods of characterization are most rigorously tested within the total art structure of a given, individual drama, but if the hypothesis would evade the imputations both of implausibility and anachronism, it must derive from wider samplings. Reminding ourselves, then, that inquiry into the formally enunciated philosophies of a particular historical period is a related but essentially different discipline from the analysis of an art object created in that period, we confine ourselves to the formulation of hypotheses having to do with the proposition of "character" as a theoretical entity in the first place.

One such hypothesis is that "motivation" in life may appear kaleidoscopic and, at our present stage of psychological knowledge, often resistant to analysis, but that drama itself tends to some kind of ordering of these elements. Unless we are bardolaters, we can assume that what one finds in Shakespeare's plays are not randomly gathered human traits but patterns of activity. Furthermore, such patterns will adhere to those general principles which the poet, himself a fallible human being, rightly or wrongly assumed as governing human activity. And because, in the construction of those materials which create character, the dramatist was also governed by "artificial considerations" limited to the possibilities of his medium, he needed to make his audience abstract a character from the conglomeration of words in the play by the recognition of some conceptual entity. An audience will always refuse the proposition that the people on stage are engaged in activity which is purely random. In fact, the music of experimenters such as Stockhausen suggests the dangerous alternative: if randomness is deliberately created (a paradox in itself), the spectators will nevertheless attempt to organize that randomness into wholes, themselves creating their own forms from the formlessness.

Therefore, a reasonable procedure for analyzing Shakespeare's characterizations would be to suggest those principles of human behavior which, by their own system of interrelating logic, would have given the impression of "entity" to the speaking parts which are the fabric of Shakespearean tragedy. We could then continue by observing how such principles might have been qualified by dramatic selection, and finally we could test the results by extended reference to specific characters in specific plays.

To find the principles of human behavior from which Shakespeare might have made his selections for structuring a character, we must brave the notorious dangers of historicism and consider the assumptions of the period in which Shakespeare lived. The dangers of doing so are like the harmful activities of Al Capone, as real as they are notorious, but the realities are not identical with the notoriety. Mr. Capone was, after all, eventually defeated by conscientious accountants.

There is a certain well-deserved notoriety about restrictive readings of Shakespeare which utilize various Renaissance guides to conduct or psychology as chapbooks for the tragedies. In such cases, proponents of methods which deal not with *kulturge- schichten* but with artistic "necessities" within the dramas them- selves may rightly question the critical validity of tabulating given concepts in the history of ideas without a consequent submission to other disciplines. If Lily B. Campbell argued, for instance, that in *King Lear* the old king's wrath is to be under- stood as deriving from the condition of his senility, she had the support of Renaissance handbooks, it is true; but her interpre- tation of character itself had to be accepted as merely implicit, allowed as an axiom within the larger argument that all Renais- sance men, and thus Shakespeare's heroes, could in specific ways be understood as "slaves of passion." But to be acceptable her arguments about Lear would have required additional support from a thorough analysis of her assumptions about the "necessi- ties" imposed not only by contemporary ideas, but also by "form." Otherwise, is it not as if *King Lear* illustrates Renais- sance theories of old age, as Miss Campbell carefully studied them, rather than that theories of old age necessarily illuminate our understanding of the play, *King Lear?* At the investigatory point where she ended, we only know that the king is old and becomes angry, and consequently, that *King Lear,* as a historical document, may show that in the Renaissance old men and anger were regarded as compatible.

Nevertheless, we will agree that suppositions about "character" in any period of history ultimately have been shaped by con- temporary theories, not only of personality but of existence in general, the question of human motivation being an obvious aspect. But insofar as personality theory is itself a specific con- sideration, we sense the immediate relevance of historical con- siderations. Sugar-Boy, in Robert Penn Warren's novel, carries a gun, drives a car recklessly, and continually pops lumps of sugar into his mouth, sucking them so hard that his cheeks become hollow. In our period of history we react to this portrait, with some justification, by recourse to such concepts as "compen- sation," "insecurity," and "sucking instinct." But the implica- tions of this rather obvious point are not always readily subscribed to: that different theories of personality in different historical periods can, in far-reaching ways, determine how one defines not only the assumptions but also the "technique and theory of characterization" for any given era. If Sugar-Boy had existed on the Renaissance stage, for instance, with similar traits and historically equivalent paraphernalia (a horse instead of an automobile, for example), the manner in which one would "interpret" his character might differ. Certainly there are choices. As historians we would refuse to attribute to the Renaissance author the intention of operating according to a conscious knowledge of modern psychodynamics. But might it not also be rather risky to make the sweeping claim that our hypothetical author had not even the remotest notion of conveying something at least vaguely akin to Warren's intentions? If we would take Spenser's Medina as our bride, we might even prefer to hedge. The Elizabethan character may suck sugar because the playwright unconsciously had some sense of a sucking instinct and consequently endowed his figure with the trait simply because it "felt right." The example is extreme, but it may operate as an epitome of our dilemma, if we recall the number of "natural reactions" by which we explain the acts of Shakespearean characters while we simultaneously tend toward chapbook Procrusteanism in other cases. The crucial question is when to invoke which body of knowledge, and in what respects.

Answers could of course be legion and would not necessarily arise from the handbooks only. Rather, once having performed the proper adjustment to another era, we must then reckon with those complex possibilities most often adumbrated by criticism which values and analyzes the work of art for what it suggests (even if anachronistically) to the individual reader or viewer. Such criticism constantly turns up matters which rigidly historical scholars ignore, at the risk of losing possible routes to a different kind of information which may not necessarily be anachronistic. Hamlet and Oedipus; Iago and homosexuality. One need not espouse either of these lines, but to the responsible critic, such "modern" reactions may suggest an important corollary to historical method. Psychodynamics, since Freud, has attained the status of a science, of a body of truth about human beings. If we even partially accept this claim as truth, elements in this science, however different in nomenclature or even conceptual description, must necessarily be taken as applicable retroactively. It is naïve, for instance, to consider that in Shakespeare's time it was the *objective* universe which was Copernican. The poet and his contemporaries may have assumed that it was, but if space is indeed definable according to the closed-surface definitions initiated by the Michelson-Morley experiments, then this definition in theory applied in Shakespeare's day. By the same token, if some of the tendencies in human personality have indeed been isolated and defined by post-Freudian theory and experiments, then presumably these tendencies were not only extant in Shakespeare's day but may even have been recognized in some way. It is not that similar conclusions may then have been drawn but that perceptions could have arrived at similar approximations which were stated differently and perhaps led to different conclusions. Is it not possible, merely for the sake of argument, to suggest that Shakespeare became interested in the curious relationship between sons and mothers even though he had no Freudian organization of concepts with which to analyze and enunciate what his mind grasped?

But Freud is perhaps a misleading reference, for it is not a question here of arguing that mother-son relationships were necessarily defining factors in Shakespeare's world or that Freud's own rather restrictive theory might adequately account for the general complexities of human personality. It is perhaps more accurate to suggest that many of the elements in human personality which post-Freudian research of the last sixty years has more clearly defined for us need not have escaped certain Renaissance observers, no matter what conclusions they might then have drawn. Bishop Hall is illustrative:

It was a wittic and true speech of that obscure Heraclitus, That all men awaking are in one common world, but when we sleepe, each man goes into a severall world by himselfe; which though it be but a world of fancies, yet is the true image of that little world which is in every mans heart. For the imaginations of our sleepe, shew us what our disposition is awaking. And as many in their dreames reveale those their secrets to others, which they would never have done awake; so all may and doe disclose to themselves in their sleepe those secret inclinations, which after much searching, they could not have found out waking.[4]

If Hall is suggestive on the role of dreams, Charron is equally instructive on the problem of guilt, and at the same time, on symbolic displacement.

Those sacrifices that in former times have been used thorowout the world . . . not only of beasts, but also of living men, yea of inno-cents, were they not shamefull marks of humane infirmitie and miserie? First, because they were signes and symboles of his condem-nation and malediction (for they were as publike protestations, that he had deserved death, and to be sacrificed as those beasts were) without which there had never been any bloodie offerings or propitia-torie and expiatorie sacrifices.

Montaigne is interesting on what we might term "unconscious urging" when he speaks of the limitations of the Stoic concept of "virtue":

Witnesse *Cato* the younger; when I see him die, tearing and mangling his entrails; I cannot simply content my selfe to beleeve, that at that time, he had his soule wholy exempted from all trouble, or free from vexation: I cannot imagine, he did onely maintaine himselfe in this march or course, which the rules of the Stoike sect had ordained unto him, setled, without some alteration or motion, and impassibilitie. There was, in my conceit, in this mans vertue overmuch cheerefulnesse, and youthfulnesse to stay there. I verily

---

[4] Joseph Hall, *The Works* (London, 1625), sig. F^v. Plutarch, quoting Zeno, points out the same principle. "If a man dreame that he seeketh to have carnall company with his owne mother" and other unlawfull matters are proof of the fact that this tyrant, "the imaginative & sensual part of the soule," is "Let loose at such a time which by day the law either by feare or shame doth represse & keepe downe." See Plutarch, *The Philosophie, commonlie called, the Morals*, trans. Philemon Holland (London, 1603), sigs. Y2–Y2^v.

beleeve, he felt a kind of pleasure and sensualitie in so noble an action, and that therein he more pleased himselfe, than in any other, he ever performed in his life. Sic abiit è vita, ut causam moriendi nactum se esse gauderet (Cic. *Tusc.* Qu.i.). So departed he this life, that he rejoyced to have found an occasion of death. I doe so constantly beleeve it, that I make a doubt, whether he would have had the occasion of so noble an exploit taken from him. . . . In which action me thinks I read a kinde of unspeakable joy in his minde, and a motion of extaordinarie pleasure, joyned to a manlike voluptuousnesse, at which time it beheld the worthinesse, and considered the generositie and haughtinesse of his enterprise.[5]

We are sometime impeded by an overly sophisticated sense of cultural relativity: to aver that Renaissance men did not think precisely in our terms is not necessarily to conclude that they did not think at all. Clearly, the authors of the foregoing passages were moving close to what one might term "psychological problems," even though these common facts were assessed from different viewpoints and from cultural orientations which may not prevail today. Therefore, though we need not argue, on the one hand, that the modern psychiatric view of, say, the homosexual was likely to be represented in Elizabethan stage characterizations, do we then, on the other hand, need to conclude that when we witness instant repentance in some Renaissance play, such "instant conversion" was an article of rigorous and universal assumption as a fact of human nature? May we not simply be dealing with what, even for Elizabethans, was a bad play?[6]

[5] For Pierre Charron, see *Of Wisdome, three Bookes,* trans. S. Lennard (London, 1612 [?]; SR, July 17, 1606), sig. Kᵛ. Montaigne is most conveniently cited from *The Essayes,* trans. John Florio and ed. Desmond MacCarthy (London, 1928). The immediate reference is to II. xi. 111.

[6] Instant repentances in such plays as AYL and TGV may be opposed to the problem presented by Barnardine in *Measure* or by the kneeling Claudius in *Hamlet,* despite Madeleine Doran's contentions about the willingness of an Elizabethan audience to accept sudden emotional *volte face*: see her *Endeavors of Art* (Madison, 1954), 236. Helen C. White, *The Tudor Books of Private Devotion* (Madison, 1951), 225, briefly alluded to the Protestant emphasis on penitence in such a work as Richard Day's *Booke of Christian Prayers.* Indeed, the 1590 edition (STC 6431) is quite

If we accept the possibility that "psychological" materials were everywhere at hand in the Renaissance, we may then be able to accept the proposition of an art of characterization which was subtle not merely in spite of its Renaissance background but perhaps because of it.

---

useful in demonstrating the emphasis on "true" repentance and thus reminding us that "instant repentance" may, at best, have been a dramatic effort in calculated unreality. For "true repentance" (see Day, sigs. X3–Y) involved, among other things, a recollection of Christ's anguish in the Garden when He "sweat water like to blood" (sig. X4) and His anguish on the cross. More comprehensive would be the material written on the matter in *The Second Tome of Homilies* (London, 1563), where a three-part sermon constitutes what the "Book of Homilies" presented on this particular subject. Here we are reminded that English Protestant orthodoxy segmented repentance into four parts: "contrition of hart," "an unfaigned confession," "fayth," and "amendement of lyfe" (sigs. 2K7–2L3).

The historical problem is to the general point, too, for confession had, we recall, been a sacrament, and the Protestant effort had to maintain certain general principles underlying sacraments while abolishing the ceremonies accompanying them. The concomitant dialectic friction between outward forms and inward sincerity would thus tend to organize Protestant definitions of repentance according to principles which might thus emphasize problems of psychological awareness. The homily itself, for instance, condemned auricular confession (sig. 2K8ᵛ) and supported various forms of public or private self-confession. In any event, repentance continued to have a form, one which was well enough known for Robert Greene to use it for his own *Repentance of R. Greene* (London, 1592). He begins with contrition, proceeds with confession, and reaches the third stage wherein one must be bold enough to embrace "fayth." Greene tells us that he did with "teares confesse and acknowledge" that although he was a most miserable sinner, "The anguish that Christ suffered on the Crosse was able to purge and cleanse me" (sig. B4ᵛ). From a dramatist who is thought to have set the tone of romantic comedy (of what we may, after Heilman, term "farce" in its formalistic eschewing of realistic psychological consequences), this familiarity with "real" psychology, as it were, is not without significance for those who would infer psychological theory from particular incidents in otherwise undefined genres of drama. Early theories about repentance may be reviewed in R. C. Mortimer, *The Origins of Private Penance* (Oxford, 1939); and in John T. McNeill and Helena M. Gammer, *Medieval Handbooks of Penance* (New York, 1938), especially 414–16. Some biblical *loci* are Isa. 58 : 6 and 2 Cor. 7 : 11. The latter is subjected to some exegesis by John Calvin, *Institutes of the Christian Religion*, ed. John T. McNeill and trans. F. L. Battles (Philadelphia, 1960), III. iii. 15. Calvin's own views are summarized in iii. 16–iv. 19, where he not only condemns auricular confession but also examines the psychological problems which might be presented by Catholic modes of repentance.

Centuries of the confessional box, for instance, and as many centuries of hortatory workaday preaching which examined the nature of "sin" (not always in its theological implications, but as it might operate and be recognized in the daily lives of middle-class parishioners) forced some practical familiarity with what moved men. Arthur Dent's *Sermon of Repentance* is illustrative. Going through twenty-one editions between 1583 and 1638, this conventional tract is forced by its nature to analyze and, in effect, to define an emotional experience which had to be something more than a vague sense of guiltiness or the sudden burst of instant and profound regret. In fact, we know there were set steps which defined true repentance, and it is interesting to observe Dent's description of one of them, which he calls "Clearing of our selves":

For this is to be noted in the godly man, that when he hath committed any sin, and his conscience telleth him of it, by and by he feeles lead within him, and is all heavy, and cannot sleepe quietly, till hee hath gotten into some corner where hee may mourne and lament to the full, and confesse and lay open himselfe unto God, and so cleere himselfe through Jesus Christ, his conscience bearing him witnesse that his sin is forgiven. Whereas contrariwise the ungodly man, when his conscience accuseth him of sin, he dispatcheth away all such thoughts, and treadeth them under foot: and by and by calleth for a paire of cards or tables, and some merry companion to drive away time, and to put out all such thoughts out of his head: and so indeed hee increaseth them more and more, and causeth them to rankle inwardly.[7]

Although Dent was not an extremely perceptive man, it is interesting to note that, as if forced to by his role, he had to cope with what we might today call "repression," for the mere analysis or determination of "true repentance" drew attention to this mental phenomenon.

That Shakespeare was close to such teachings and to the subtleties implied by them is clear enough in the interesting

[7] Arthur Dent, A *Sermon of Repentance* (London, 1611), sig. B4.

vignette of the reluctant second murderer in *Richard III*. He refers to his conscience and says to the first murderer, who accuses him of becoming fainthearted, "Nay, I prythee stay a little: I hope this passionate humor of mine, will change, / It was wont to hold me but while one tels twenty" (953–55).[8] Then, when Murderer 1 reminds his companion of the coming reward, Murderer 2 decides that his conscience is now at rest.

1. What if it come to thee againe?
2. Ile not meddle with it, it makes a man a Coward: a man cannot steale, but it accuseth him; a man cannot Sweare, but it Checkes him; A man cannot lye with his Neighbours Wife, but it detects him. 'Tis a blushing shamefac'd spirit, that mutinies in a mans bosome: It filles a man full of Obstacles. It made me once restore a Pursse of Gold that (by chance) I found: It beggars any man that keepes it: It is turn'd out of Townes and Cities for a dangerous thing, and every man that means to live well, endevours to trust to himselfe and live without it. [967–78]

Significant here is the paradox of the purse being returned by a character who does not strike one as overly scrupulous.

The mental problems and the abnormalities, too, were not necessarily locked from sight. Shakespeare, in an interesting sociological moment, sketches one such situation in the character of Barnardine, the inmate in *Measure for Measure*. He has been a prisoner for nine years, we are told, and seems completely unaffected by the sentence of death under which he labors.

Duke. He wants advice.
Pro. He wil hear none: he hath evermore had the liberty of the prison: give him leave to escape hence, hee would not. Drunke many times a day, if not many daies entirely drunke. We have verie

---

[8] References to Shakespeare are to the First Folio as edited by Charlton Hinman in collotype facsimile for W. W. Norton (New York, 1968), and to the through line numbering. In many cases, the quartos are obviously more authoritative than F, but Hinman is now a universal old-spelling reference. Occasional act-scene-line references, however, are more convenient. In these cases, reference is to the *Complete Works*, ed. G. L. Kittredge (Boston, 1936). Quotations silently normalize *i-j*, *u-v*, *i-y* and tildes.

oft awak'd him, as if to carrie him to execution, and shew'd him a seeming warrant for it, it hath not moved him at all. [2012–18]

There were others, on the streets, for everyone to see. "Madmen" were perhaps very much food for thought to the reflective, if only because the rhetoric of madness, as artificial as it was to become (at least from the clinical point of view) would force some thinking about the problem of free association. As Bacon put it, more trust should be given "to Countenances and Deedes, then to wordes: and in wordes, rather to suddaine passages, and surprised wordes: then to set and purposed wordes."[9] It is instructive to work through the revenge plays of the early nineties, as well as to observe the variously contrived visits to madhouses in later drama, noting how the rhetoric of madness occasionally could be used to formulate something rather close to the stream of consciousness which principles of associative thinking have contributed to later literature.[10]

Indeed, it is possible to isolate at least two kinds of structural organization in such rhetoric, which was, after all, an interesting opportunity (just as drunkenness might be) to present character in more subtly self-expository terms than the strictly traditional "*Ad Herrenium*" techniques might have allowed. Marlowe, in *1 Tamburlaine*, toys with the matter in his presentation of Zabina, who has been living with her emperor-husband in a wheeled cage as Tamburlaine's captive. Bajazet has not been able to endure the treatment and has dashed his head against the bars, and we recall that Zabina, seeing him, is given the following well-known lines (V. ii. 242ff.):

What do mine eyes behold, my husband dead?
His Skul al riven in twain, his braines dasht out?
The braines of *Bajazeth*, my Lord and Soveraigne?
O *Bajazeth*, my husband and my Lord,

[9] Francis Bacon, *The Advancement of Learning* (London, 1605), sig. 3B2.

[10] For suggestions as to how Shakespeare might have differed from his contemporaries in his view of the mad, see Winfred Overholser, "Shakespeare's Psychiatry—And After," *SQ*, X (1959), 335–52.

O *Bajazet*, O Turk, O Emperor, give him his liquor? Not I, bring
milk and fire, and my blood I bring him againe, teare me in peeces,
give me the sworde with a ball of wildefire upon it. Downe with
him, downe with him. Goe to my child, away, away, away. Ah, save
that Infant, save him, save him. I, even I speake to her, the Sun was
downe. Streamers white, Red, Blacke, here, here, here. Fling the
meat in his face. *Tamburlaine, Tamburlaine*, Let the souldiers be
buried. Hel, death, *Tamburlain*, Hell, make ready my Coch, my
chaire, my jewels, I come, I come, I come.
                    She runs against the Cage and braines her selfe.[11]

The allusion to Tamburlaine's sequence of white, red, and black
banners is not the least interesting touch in this passage where
the water Zabina had brought to quench her husband's thirst
seems to prompt her discursion into a nursing image of sorts.
Marlowe is attempting to pack references to all aspects of her
fallen position into a paradoxical discourse which we may call
"madness" if we observe that the rationale behind this madness
is an ordered and perceptive one dominated by a fairly strict
principle of association in which elements in Zabina's stage life
have been reviewed.

Preoccupation was another form of madness, at least of literary madness: we recall it in the many visits to madhouses where
the attendant describes the history of each inmate. But again,
what might interest us is how the rather elementary mechanics
of neurotic preoccupation were sometimes fitted into the modes
of free association which the writers themselves might have observed in very different kinds of cases. At least this is so in *1
Honest Whore*, where we are asked to contemplate the man
gone mad with jealousy. Obsession in thought transmits itself to
a free sense of obsessive but associative language, revealing in the
author an awareness of the revelatory quality of words not necessarily in syntactical order. "Stream of consciousness" again is a
provocative parallel (xv. 310ff.):

[11] References to Marlowe are to *The Complete Plays*, ed. C. F. Tucker
Brooke (Oxford, 1925).

all these are whoremongers, and lay with my wife. Whore, whore, whore, whore, whore . . . Gaffer shoe-maker, you pulled on my wife's pumps and then crept into her pantofles. Lie there, lie there.— This was her tailor. You cut out her loose-bodied gown and put in a yard more than I allowed her. Lie there by the shoemaker.—O master doctor, are you there. You gave me a purgation and then crept into my wife's chamber to feel her pulses and you said, and she said, and she said, and her maid said, that they went pitapat, pitapat, pitapat. Doctor, I'll put you anon into my wife's urinal. Heigh, come aloft jack. This was her schoolmaster and taught her to play upon the virginals and still his jacks lept up up. You pricked her out nothing but bawdy lessons, but I'll prick you all, fiddler— doctor—tailor—shoemaker—shoemaker—fiddler—doctor—tailor. So, lie with my wife again now.

Duke. How will you do now sirrah. You ha killed him.[12]

In these respects, Shakespeare is similarly speculative, as we might anticipate. We can even speak of his awareness of what is required in repentance as he presents the Duke-Friar shriving Julietta, just as we can readily turn to the myriad implications of his major creations, but balder expositions argue for the poet's awareness of some of the subtleties that interest the modern mind. We have, for instance, one officer's specific conjectures regarding Coriolanus' hostility to the people.

If he did not care whether he had their love, or no, hee waved in-differently, 'twixt doing them neyther good, nor harme: but hee seekes their hate with greater devotion, then they can render it him; and leaves nothing undone, that may fully discover him their opposite. Now to seeme to affect the mallice and displeasure of the People, is as bad, as that which he dislikes, to flatter them for their love. [1219–26]

When we adduce other elements from this very interesting and presumably late play, it is tempting to continue our speculation,

[12] References to Dekker are to *The Dramatic Works*, ed. Fredson Bowers (Cambridge, 1953–61).

for we have the remark by a member of the mob that Coriolanus fights not from patriotism but to please his mother, we have his son described as crushing a butterfly, we have the warrior's almost oafish modesty regarding his own exploits, and we have his visit to the town in which Aufidius lives. Exile leads Coriolanus here to offer either his throat or his service to his great enemy, either the destruction of himself or his use in destroying Rome. He offers his "self," too, we learn, since he cannot bring himself to destroy his mother and wife and returns instead to Corioli with "forebodings" of his own destruction. But not to wander into specific criticism here, we can as easily turn to *Julius Caesar*, where Brutus is subjected to a curiously contemporary "test." Cassius, writing the note which is to be thrown in at Brutus' window, not only helps himself but us, for he cannot witness Brutus' reaction to the following note: *"Brutus thou sleep'st; awake, and see thy selfe: / Shall Rome, &c. speake, strike, redresse."* Brutus responds to this test solely for the benefit of the audience.

> *Shall Rome, &c.* Thus must I piece it out:
> Shall Rome stand under one mans awe? What Rome?
> My Ancestors did from the streetes of Rome
> The *Tarquin* drive, when he was call'd a King. [665–73]

But this is not, after all, the only possible way to "fill in" the "blank" left by "etc."

It is not a question here of preparing ourselves for a neo-Freudian foray into the jungles of Renaissance personality theory. It is better to argue for a mean. If one respects the historical, there is no concomitant necessity to exclude from our notions about "character" in the Renaissance a psychological subtlety of the kind which we like to think of as very modern. Nor, in any approach to the problem of character in Shakespeare's plays, is there any equally pressing reason to eschew historicity. If Shakespeare indeed wanted to depict a jealous man, and assuming that he was interested in the "imitation" of human beings, we must allow that he may have looked beyond the standard moralistic portraits of envy-as-sin to what we would call the "personality problem."

Even granted the level of psychological sophistication adumbrated by the foregoing examples, we find food for thought in the whole matter of how "character depiction" might have been understood by a Renaissance poet since he would indeed be operating in the artistic and ideological idiom of his own time. Even if *Hamlet* does strike us as "Freudian," Shakespeare nevertheless had not read Freud; and while Shakespeare may have observed traits that modern psychology generally accepts as extant in human nature, the structure of ideas by which he sought to account for such phenomena would have been quite importantly different. Thus while the preceding examples may and should alert us, they of course cannot be definitive. We may even show ourselves as being too much within our own age in the very attempt to isolate statements which might not have been grouped together by Shakespeare's contemporaries. In any event, it seems wise to evade dualisms. It is neither necessary to subordinate the problem of Shakespearean characterization to an educated and learned interest in the ideology of the plays nor to reject historicity for a critical approach informed by the subtleties of modern personality depiction, for, we will agree, these are not the only possible positions.

2
The Motions of Men

As a way of beginning our inquiry into Renaissance concepts of character, let us glance at Shakespeare's probable context by asking ourselves whether Renaissance notions about human beings reduced to a few general assumptions the fundamental traits that all men had in common, for clearly this would be the point of departure for any artist. Since any age will generalize about human nature, however, it seems wiser to direct our query not to what some people said that human nature was but simply to the way in which they talked about these matters. Again, we are not interested in particular terminology but in the structure of thought that any given collocation of terms might suggest, since specific vocabulary might change from writer to writer. (Today, for instance, one speaker may intend by "paranoid" what another intends by "inferiority complex.") To find repositories of such interests, could we begin where T. W. Baldwin suggests that the schoolchild began, in the area of formal rhetoric? Although this subject, a favorite in the Renaissance curriculum, would not have been needed to teach a thinking man or boy, who could just as easily observe the personalities of his contemporaries, rhetoric might have offered a general vocabulary according to which he could organize those phenomena which he did observe. Rhetorical manuals suggested how to depict people; in doing so, they are likely to have made and imparted assumptions about human nature.

Intimations from classical rhetoric are sparse, however, and though not as confused as is sometimes claimed, the rhetorical handbooks were nevertheless oriented toward a particular mode. If the tradition of Aristotle's *Poetics* and, ancillary to it, the influence of Horace's *Ars Poetica* defined one pole, the quasi-empirical tradition of Roman rhetoric constituted another. The various Continental argumentations regarding Aristotle's observations on character assumed a preoccupation with moral criteria, with the kinds of persons who should be allowed to appear in a poetic work. It was not common to find a statement such as Guarini's observation that the end of a poet "is then not to imitate the good, but to imitate well, whether he imitate good or bad moral character; and if he imitates what is good poorly, he will not be a good poet, but he may be called a good poet if he imitates well what is bad."[1] Roman rhetoric, on the other hand, was essentially oriented toward the art of persuasion in the law courts, and even though the social milieu was long gone, the connotation remained.

Such terms in rhetoric as *mimesis* and *characterismus* might tempt us; but the latter, at best, led to the Theophrastan character, while the former, when described at all, was constantly assumed to serve the distinctive purposes of formal rhetoric. As Richard Sherry put it, "Mimisis" is that device "whereby we counterfayte not onelye what one sayde, but his gesture also," for the purpose of a more compelling argument. Thus when it is a question of such terms as *sermocinatio, prosographia, prosopopeia, ethopoeia,* and *pathopoeia,* we may have in hand potentially interesting distinctions. But the bent was, importantly, toward the presentation of exemplary types for the purpose of more effective persuasion. A Richard Sherry might differ from a Henry Peacham even if they both followed Erasmus's *De Copia,* while retaining similar emphases. With Sherry, for instance, *prosographia* might be the description of a feigned person; the rendered example has to do with endowing dumb or inanimate objects with speech for the purpose of persuasion ("If Rome could speak, it would say," etc.). Henry Peacham, however, noting this same category, calls it *prosopopeia.*

In general, despite the confused forest of relevant terms, the categories which the rhetoricians traditionally understood when it came to what we might call "impersonation" were bound by the tradition of Latin letters. When writing a formal history, for instance, it was conventional to invent speeches for statesmen, ambassadors, and even messengers. We can therefore under-

[1] Quoted by Bernard Weinberg, *A History of Literary Criticism in the Italian Renaissance* (Chicago, 1961), I, 29–30, from Guarini, *In difesa del Pastor Fido* (Florence, 1593), 66.

stand how any given speech would have to be "appropriate" to the situation. One recalls Thucydides and the oration of Pericles. If literary art was also a matter of continually rewriting well-known classical stories, it is also understandable that Sherry, speaking of *pathopoeia* as an "expression of vehemente affections and perturbations," could write of its two categories as he does. The first, "Imagination," is the category in which extreme "passions of the mynde is described and styred up," and "Exaumples of these bee everye where in Tragedies." In the second, "Commiseration," grief is stirred up as in the "perorations of Cicero" or "in Poetes, in their complaints." And Puttenham could suggest a similar evasion when speaking of *prosographia* as the device of making dead men air their hypothetical views, while explaining *prosopopeia* in the following terms:

No prettier examples can be given you thereof, than in the Romant of the rose translated out of French by *Chaucer*, describing the persons of avarice, envie, old age, and many others, whereby much moralitie is taught.

Similarly, when Rainolde describes *ethopoeia*, he gives as one example Achilles' determination to fight after Patrocolus is killed, observing that "the determinacion of hym sheweth the maner. The frende slaine, the affection," as if emotion is simply *topos*. Yet Sherry, too, even if *ethopoeia* is for him one of the six branches of *prosopopeia* and is to be described as "a large settyng out of maners," specifies in a similar manner: "So Terence setteth out boasting Thraso, Plautus a craking souldyoure. And thys facyon properlie belongeth to Commoedies, and Dialogues."[2]

   [2] For these allusions, see George Puttenham, *The Art of English Poesie* (London, 1589), sigs. 2D2–2D2ᵛ; Richard Rainolde, *The Foundacion of Rhetorike* (London, 1563), sig. N; and Richard Sherry, *A Treatise of the Figures of Grammer and Rhetorike* (London, 1555), sigs. F5–F5ᵛ. The foregoing discussion should be compared to Doran, chapter 9 ("Character"). Despite her differing approach, Doran is useful in calling attention to Castelvetro's impatience with rhetorical theory as applied to concepts of character (see p. 224 and n. 17).

The whole development of the purely Theophrastan character is ultimately implied by such classificatory trends, and as Boyce has observed, "one gathers that the habit of seeing men as types must have been as firmly established in the English mind as pedagogical persistence could make it."[3] It is the latter part of his sentence which may also suggest the limits of rhetorical classification, for if there was the pedagogical effort logically realized in the "character," there was also Elizabethan drama which did go beyond the *senex, adulescens, meretrix* purview. When dramatic presentation began to go beyond its strictly rhetorical ramifications in a *Fulgens and Lucrece* on the one hand, or a *Ralph Roister Doister* on the other, classical rhetoric was no longer an adequate description unless it was a question, as in early Jonson, simply of presenting "types."

Perhaps rhetorical attention to the language of emotions itself might be a promising alternative in our search for some theoretical basis for dramatic characterization. If most remarks in the handbooks of rhetoric dealt with how to present a specific and hypothetical emotion as generalized in a person of specific social status, there were also remarks about general ways of "saying things." But even here we look in vain for seeds of the art of "revelatory speaking." For the intent of such instruction as existed is clear in Rainolde and Puttenham. The latter can promisingly allude to "figures Auricular working by disorder," and he can, for instance, mention "parenthesis" as a way "to peece or graffe in the middest of your tale an unnecessary parcell of speach, which neverthelesse may be thence without any detriment to the rest" (sig. I4ᵛ). Rainolde can describe *Apoplanesis* as useful "when the cause of the Orator is weake, and not able to abide the uttermost trial," for one then tries to lead the minds of the hearers away from "the question in hand, which maketh against him." We might argue that here are our theoretical bases for the art of depicting psychologically uncon-

---

[3] Benjamin Boyce, *The Theophrastan Character in England to 1642* (Cambridge, Mass., 1942), 49. Chapters 1 through 3 are generally illustrative, for although Boyce is depicting a specific genre, his own findings tend to emphasize the paucity of theory relevant to our concerns.

scious self-interruptions or mental evasion, but any specific appli-
cations would ultimately be irrelevant to our central problem.
For rhetoric, we agree, had a specific purpose, and all its devices
of speaking were directed to the ends of oratory, which were
ultimately the besting of an opponent in argument. All devices
of language and modes of personification were accordingly, and
by definition, premeditated modes of persuasion. As such, our
awareness of them may clarify some speeches by Cassius, say,
and Iago, in their efforts to seduce minds. We will assume in an
Elizabethan audience of former schoolboys something less than
naïveté when such manipulation was depicted on stage, but none
of this knowledge, at least in theory, reveals in the Elizabethans
the acquisition of any formally learned technique by which one
might make a character speak so as to reveal himself in an unknowing way. If *pathos* and *ethos* were major Aristotelian divisions of "persuasion," and if *ethos* comprehended the art of
convincing an audience of the speaker's probity, we may then
admire Menenius with the mob, but we are not offered an authorial means for analysis. In fact, for *ethos* to have been successfully realized, it would sometimes have had to deceive even
the audience. It is of course obvious that the shape of an intellect as imagined on stage might be determined by how he utilized rhetorical ways to persuasion, as in the case of Polonius.
But then, are we not already speaking of techniques which have
gone beyond rhetorical theory as such by using elements of this
theory as one of the ways to structure "character"?[4]

If we agree to the existence of such limitations in rhetorical
theory, and if we observe that such theory necessarily utilized
basic but, for us, uninformative assumptions as to the manner
in which human nature might operate, we are justified in shift-

---

[4] For expositions of *ethos* and *pathos* as they were understood in the
Renaissance, see Sister Miriam Joseph, *Shakespeare's Use of the Arts of
Language* (New York, 1947), chap. 9. For a different view of the matters
discussed above and for citations of other relevant scholarship, see C. O.
MacDonald, "Decorum, Ethos, and Pathos in the Heroes of Elizabethan
Tragedy," *JEGP*, LXI (1962), 330–48; and more generally, *The Rhetoric
of Tragedy* (Amherst, 1966).

ing our ground. We learn from rhetoric that one will be sorry
if someone dies or that one will be angry if insulted, and the
like, but these necessarily archetypal situations offer little insight
into those complexities with which we associate the manner and
mode of Shakespearean characterization. It seems plausible,
then, to glance at treatises which sought to discuss and analyze
the impulses of men. If rhetoric assumed that human reactions
did indeed exist, there was, after all, some psychological speculation as to causes. The resulting discussion, after being circu-
lated in print, might at least have formed the basis for jargonis-
tic thinking similar to that with which we are familiar today.

When the question of "Elizabethan psychology" is taken in
hand, we find that the answers have not only tended to be traditional but various. We hear much of the "humors," for instance, and it is true that sixteenth- and seventeenth-century
physicians might indeed have spoken in terms of "black bile,"
the "mother," or "sanguine" propensities. That a writer might
have shaped character in such terms, however, offers us not sim-
plification but aesthetic and ideological complexities. For to depict according to the humors would lead to results equivalent
to those produced by allegory or, again, by the concept of the
Theophrastan character. Ultimately, the theory of "complexions," when not used strictly for medical purposes, was perhaps
only the Renaissance shrug of the shoulder at the basic differences among men. Why does one man seek riches, another,
power, and a third, love? Humor theory could in part account
for such inclinations. As La Primaudaye put it, "That which be-
falleth the inclinations, is procured also unto them by the humors and qualities of the body, which have a certain agreement
with the affections." Therefore, it could be asserted that all
"temperatures" and "complexions" are "seed and provocations,
either to vertues or to vices, according to that correspondence,
which is between the bodie & the soule, and the temperature of
the one with the affections of the other." The matter could also
enter doctrine, as we gather from the bent of a sermon preached
at Paul's Cross in 1607.

The divell doth subtilly pry, and judicially looke into the natures and complexions of men, and according to the predominant and overruling humor in man, he applieth his temptation unto this or that sinne: (for in every man there is some one humour that is most inclinable to some sin).[5]

Methodologically speaking, it is then only a step, is it not, to speculation on prelapsarian conditions in respect to these humors? And we do indeed find that all the bodily humors existed in perfect balance before the Fall, an equilibrium which may even have accounted for Adam's earthly immortality. This balance, we gather, was confused after the Fall; and all men, now imperfect, suffer from individual imbalances which could account for different "inclinations" in persons or, more clearly, for the great variety of psychological predispositions.[6]

It is well to remember, however, that humor theory cannot be an adequate description of Elizabethan or Jacobean concepts of the psychological process because the "humors" system answers only one kind of question about character: why do men differ in the goals they pursue? This is very much like asking, is it not, why one person reacts "aggressively" to a traumatic childhood while another reacts "regressively"? And if we ponder its utility for the problem of dramatic characterization, we may also observe that the theory of humors could become so complex in its mixtures and percentages that any physical clues—pale skin, sanguine face, etc.—would no longer serve as accurate guides, probably not even for the Elizabethans themselves. Burton could write an *Anatomy of Melancholy*, but it is not by mere coincidence that such a work ultimately had to become a compendium of all that was thought not only about "complexions" but about the whole matter of psychology, considerations moving far beyond questions that had to do with the purely physical bases for emotion. Actually, when it moved outside the realm of purely

[5] G. B., *The Narrow Way* (London, 1607), sigs. F3–F3ᵛ; cf. Pierre de La Primaudaye, *The French Academie* (London, 1618), sig. 2Q5.
[6] See Robert Farley, *Lychnocausia* (London, 1638), emblem 10; and Henry Cuffe, *The Differences of the Ages of Mans Life* (London, 1607), sig. F6ff.

medical therapy, the theory of humors never attempted to account for the cause of humor imbalance as it affected human personality. The gifts of God or Nature—skills, talents, the proportioning of humors in the body—were to be taken as axiomatic, for the humors were, if we wish, efficient causes in the Aristotelian sense. A man with a sanguine temperament might have done nothing to make himself "sanguine" except to be born, but he might, by virtue of his inherently sanguine orientation, be led to behavior which it was his soul's responsibility to judge and control. His penchant to various kinds of activity and his values might not be analyzable as to cause, but these impulses could at least be described, and in terms of "humors."

If all this was simply to say, in modern parlance, that certain types of people had different "chains of genes" in their makeups, we may proceed to the consequent point by observing what the purely mimetic areas of characterization might be in such a conceptual context. We are often misled by Jonson's theory of the humors, not necessarily by what Jonson said but by the form in which this dramatist most frequently operated. The distinction is clear enough if we compare the poet's effort to the modern cinema cartoon. Given the fact that a humor is an axiomatic predisposition, cartoon comedy has to deal with what the eighteenth century termed the "Ruling Passion": the mouse's obsession with cheese as opposed to the cat's obsession with sleep. Cartoon characters are, in a sense "humor" characters because a certain concept of comedy derives structure from juxtaposing mutually exclusive obsessions.

Sejanus is instructive here, for in this tragedy humors already give way, as they do in the major Jonsonian comedies, to other emphases. Humor theory, in the end, was not useful in the kind of tragedy which sought to analyze the deviations of an imagined character from some ethical norm since, by definition, there was no "cause" for humors and since "innate" bases for more complex activity were not definitive of anything but themselves. Therefore, to expect, a priori, a Renaissance dramatist to have possessed a detailed theory of the humors as a guide to examining character might be as implausible as the presentation of the percentage figures of a metabolism test to suggest that the hero of a modern play is hyperthyroid and thus extremely nervous. We think of another cinema cartoon in which the cat visits a doctor to discover that since his high blood pressure makes him angry, he must cease and desist from his irascible pursuit of the mouse who gives him high blood pressure. Gland imbalance or vitamin deficiency might indeed determine reactions in life, but these are different principles of certainty. The question of why a character acts as he does can presumably have several sets of answers, one from the mechanistic areas of biology or neurology—areas which produced many tomes in the Renaissance, too—and another from sociological theory which holds that a man might be "unpleasantly aggressive" not because he suffers from an undiagnosed physical disorder but because of some factor explained by a system of logic which describes the bases and consequences of human behavior according to some formulation of ultimate cause.

Early in the Elizabethan period, this general point was made by a character whose relevance may be sharpened if we think of his future role as a character in one of Shakespeare's earliest plays. In the 1559 edition of the *Mirrour for Magistrates*, King Henry VI, true to his traditionally contemplative nature, regales the reader with a series of observations. They suggest that even before Shakespeare was born, there was some sophistication about the problems of human character—and in a work which has so often been taken by scholars, rightly or wrongly, as one of the ideological foundations of Elizabethan tragic theory.[7]

---

[7] The *locus classicus* is, of course, Willard Farnham, *The Medieval Heritage of Elizabethan Tragedy* (Berkeley, 1936). L. B. Campbell's editions of the *Mirrour*, by their care and opulence, have lent implicit support to this view. The quotation which follows above is from her larger volume, *The Mirror for Magistrates* (Cambridge, 1938), 213–14. The sentiments voiced may be those of the well-known William Baldwin, whose *Treatise of Morall Phylosophie* was reprinted so often between 1547 and 1610. If the selection is, on the other hand, by George Ferrers (see Campbell on the problem, 24ff.), then clearly more than one person held the views uttered by Henry VI, who might otherwise seem a characteristic spokesman for Baldwin's opinions on such matters.

Alas what should we count the cause of wretches cares,
The starres do stirrc them up, Astronomy declares:
Or humours saith the leache, the double true divines,
To the will of god, or ill of man, the doubtfull cause assignes.

Such doltish heades as dreame that all thinges drive by haps,
Count lack of former care for cause of afterclaps.
Attributing to man a power from God bereft,
Abusing us, and robbing him, through their most wicked theft.

But god, doth gide the world, and every hap by skyll.
Our wit and willing power are paysed by his will:
What wit most wisely wardes, and wil most deadly urkes,
Though al our power would presse it downe, doth dash our warest
    wurkes.

Than destiney, our sinne, Gods wil, or cls his wreake,
Do wurke our wretched woes, for humours be to weake:
Except we take them so, as they provoke to sinne,
For through our lust by humours fed, al vicious dedes beginne.

So sinne and they be one, both wurking like effect,
And cause the wrath of God to wreake the soule infect.
Thus wrath and wreake divine, mans sinnes and humours ill,
Concur in one, though in a sort, ech doth a course fulfill.

If likewise such as say the welken fortune warkes,
Take Fortune for our fate, and sterres thereof the markes,
Then destiny with fate, and Gods wil al be one:
But if they meane it otherwise, skath causers skies be none.

Thus of our heavy happes, chiefe causes be but twayne,
Whereon the rest depende, and underput remayne.
The chiefe the wil divine, called destiny and fate,
The other sinne, through humours holpe, which god doth highly
    hate,

The first appointeth paine for good mens exercise,
The second doth deserve due punishment for vice:
This witnesseth the wrath, and that the love of God,
The good for love, the bad for sinne, God beateth with his rod.

The area covered by what were termed "humors" is finally most similar to that area of interest both to modern psychodynamics and to the post-Freudian novel. An excessively "choleric" disposition, while not ultimately explainable, today remains a typical subject of causative investigation. Psychiatry seeks the "reasons" for such "complexions," and similar reasons are realized, as it were, in one explanation for Sutpen's "humor" in *Absalom, Absalom!* His obsession with his plantation is a trait partially "explained" by detailed reference to environment and conditioning, to his childhood in the West Virginia shack.

But the concept of humors, we all realize, hardly embraced the gamut of formal Elizabethan psychological enquiry. There was the body of writings to which L. B. Campbell and Ruth Anderson have so usefully called our attention but which they have emphasized in a manner requiring some qualification. Tradition offered, it is true, such terminology as the "will," the "reason," and the "passions," but these words operated as counters in an argument whose basic assumptions have too often been ignored. When it treated the "will," such argumentation emphasized the basic distinction between pre- and postlapsarian states. In the former case, the will naturally gravitated toward God. This kind of statement is crucial to our understanding of even this limited system of formal psychology, for all subsequent language in the system assumes that in the fallen world the corrupted "natural will" gravitated not toward God but toward the "earthly self." And if such dichotomies as "reason versus will" tried to account in sometimes very careful ways for the processes of decision in the mind, the basic proposition was always that men could not depend for guidance on their own postlapsarian modes of wishing. Accordingly, Elizabethan psychology described the theoretical functions of the mind in the same terms as, but in contexts slightly different from, those posited by Campbell and Anderson.[8]

According to this general dialectic, when the body's senses or

[8] See Ruth L. Anderson, "Elizabethan Psychology and Shakespeare's Plays," *University of Iowa Humanistic Studies*, III (1917); and L. B. Campbell, *Shakespeare's Tragic Heroes* (San Marino, 1930).

the mind's wishings—both aspects of the "will"—yearn for some object presented by "fantasy," "imagination," or "opinion," there is danger because senses and desires both tend to be fallible. Therefore, the "will" must refer itself to the "reason" which, in its role as counselor, determines whether the "will" is urging toward what is truly beneficial. Yet even a judge must evolve his decision from laws, and this is especially true when an appellant such as the will has a tendency toward things "illegal." Therefore, the crucial point is the nature of the law to which this judge, the reason, will refer itself. One is the law of the love of God; the other is the law of the love of one's earthly self. Reason's decision might be arrived at with difficulty because of the great power of the love of self—the acknowledged strength of the corrupted affections and senses. But in optimal circumstances, the judge would decide in terms of the correct law and would perhaps find that the will's "motion" was indeed "legal." In such a case, reason and will would agree in a correct action. Most often, however, the will would be so strong and corrupt, the reason so weak, that this judge could be forced to cite the other law, the law of the love of self. And in this instance, reason would then be in the position of permitting the will to indulge itself, to act as if reason had shown the way: a corrupt reason directs the corrupt will in a corrupt action. At other times, the will might be so strong that it would not bother to appeal to the reason at all, and a "passionate" act would result, agonized repentance being the presumable consequence if the reason were a correct, if weak, judge.[9]

---

[9] Shakespeare's plays adhere, in general, to the dualities we have suggested above, but although the term "affections" is to be found throughout his writings (see the various concordances to the plays and poems), "blood" is often operationally synonymous. We conclude this, for example, from the countess speaking of Helena's love-sickness: "If ever we are natures, these are ours, this thorne / Doth to our Rose of youth rightlie belong / Our blood to us, this to our blood is borne, / It is the show, and seale of natures truth, / Where loves strong passion is imprest in youth" (AWW, 452–56). Cf. Ado, II. iii. 169–71; and MV, I. ii. 20–21. It is difficult, of course, to speculate on what "blood" ultimately implied, for this liquid not only carried the humors but also the "animal" and "vital" spirits ("animal" being of such vague definition that it suggests everything from physical

Whether there is profit for the critic in all this is something
else again. In modern terms, we tend to contrast "impulse" with
"mature reflection," but if our familiarity with this set leads us
to label Jim's leap from the *Patna* as "impulsive," such dichotomies alone do not enable us to follow Conrad's presentation
of the psychological events leading to Jim's death. The specific
terminology of Renaissance psychological jargon may share with
rhetoric and the theory of humors a begging of similar questions.
If we acquiesce in the ultimate relevance, say, of *pathos* or humor imbalance or an inversion of the reason/will relationship,
our analysis of character is merely a process of labeling. The
question of Hamlet might be answered by reference to his
"melancholy," to his passion's tendency to dominate his reason
(and vice versa), or to Shakespeare's use of *prosographia* as he
learned it in school; but we all know that such descriptions are,
in critical practice, waived for somewhat more sophisticated efforts at character analysis. It would seem that if we adhere to
the ways offered through formal Renaissance theories of physi-

---

energy to the highest effort of the imagination). For a review of these
matters, see P. Cruttwell, "Physiology and Psychology in Shakespeare's
Age," *JHI*, XII (1951), 75–89. The term "will" is predictably dual in
Shakespeare. It is a positive element in *Ham.*, I. iii. 15ff.: "And now no
soyle nor cautell doth besmirch / The vertue of his will" (Q2. F: "feare").
It is a neutral element in II. i. 103ff., where "Love . . . leads the will to
desperate Undertakings." In *Tim.*, V. iv. 4, the word implies evil will. Thus,
understandably, the will can "dote" or be "benummed" as in *Tro.*, II. ii.
55–170. As concerns the "reason," clearly it can pander the will or be the
bawd to lust's abuse. A useful and illustrative exchange in *WT* indicates as
much about the relativities here as does Hector's better-known speech in
Tro. II. ii. 163ff. In *WT*, 2332–39 (IV. iv. 491–96) Florizel's impassioned
insistence on loving the commoner Perdita is worded as follows: "From my
succession wipe me (Father) I / Am heyre to my affection. *Cam.* Be ad-
vis'd. *Flo.* I am: and by my fancie, if my Reason / Will thereto be
obedient: I have reason: / If not, my sences, better pleas'd with madnesse,
/ Do bid it welcome. *Cam.* This is desperate (sir.)." Shakespeare's usages
are sometimes misleading because "will," "affection," and even "blood" are
abbreviated forms implying *corrupt* will, *corrupt* affections, and *corrupt*
blood. "Affections" are most often used with this implication, but certain
instances show the ambivalent nature of the term. *Oth.*, I. iii. 111ff. dis-
cusses the hero's subduing and poisoning "affections," while Malcolm
(*Mac.*, IV. iii. 76ff.) feigningly speaks of "my most *ill-compos'd* Affection"
(italics mine).

ology, rhetoric, or faculty psychology, we cannot ultimately ask what we take to be the relevant questions about "character" in Shakespearean drama.

However, bases for subtler questions about character did exist. They derive, in fact, from those same handbooks cited by Anderson, whose bibliography to her own monograph we have used for previous and differing observations.[10] And we find such a basis if we ask whether mankind was assumed to share some fundamental trait, whether there was some reductio analogous in its

[10] A general examination of most of the Elizabethan writers cited by Anderson will support our summary about the assumptions of faculty psychology. The "judge" metaphor which we have adduced may, in fact, be found in Charron (cf. sig. E2 to sig. F4ᵛ). It is necessary, however, to take issue with Anderson's work because of her statement prefacing the second edition (New York, 1966). In her brief observations which introduce what is actually a reissue, she remarks that despite certain changes she would have liked to make, "the exposition of Elizabethan faculty psychology I have made is sound; it remains the most comprehensive treatment of the subject that exists" (p. 1). There may be much to the latter part of this claim, but it may be argued that, in general, Mrs. Anderson and a number of other writers on faculty psychology tend to allude only to the second halves of Elizabethan psychological treatises, the usual "religious" first parts being subordinated to the purely mechanistic discussions. But general documentation concerning the relationship of the "will," the "reason," and the "affections" to a more comprehensive system of thought is to be found not only in the very treatises adduced in *Elizabethan Psychology and Shakespeare's Plays*. To allude to both groups, we may consult John Norden, *The Labyrinth of Mans Life* (London, 1614), sigs. H3ᵛ–K2; Marcellus Palingenius, *The Zodiake of Life*, trans. Barnabie Googe (London, 1588), sigs. D3–D4, H5ᵛ, I6ᵛ–I8ᵛ, P5–P6, and N2ᵛff.; John Davies of Hereford, *Microcosmos* (Oxford, 1603), sigs. M3ᵛ–2G; Henry Crosse, *Vertues Common-wealth* (London, 1603), sigs. B–C3ᵛ; La Primaudaye, II, chaps. 26, 28, 33, 34, 36, 39, 41, 43, and 48; William Perkins, *Two Treatises*, "Of the Combat of the Flesh and Spirit" (London, 1597); Bacon, *Advancement*, sigs. 2R2ᵛ and 3E3ᵛff.; Charron, I, chaps. 13 and 14 and chaps. 3 through 5; Sir John Davies, *Nosce Teipsum* (London, 1602), sigs. F2–H2ᵛ; Phineas Fletcher, "The Purple Island," cantos VI–VII, in Giles and Phineas Fletcher, *Poetical Works*, ed. F. S. Boas (Cambridge, 1909); Thomas Wright, *The Passions of the Mind* (London, 1604), I, chap. 3, II, chap. 1, and VI, sigs. O–S2ᵛ; Fulke Greville, "Of Humane Learning," in *Poems and Dramas*, ed. Geoffrey Bullough (New York, 1945), I; Richard Hooker, *Of the Lawes of Ecclesiastical Politie* (London, 1597), I, v–viii.

ubiquity to the heredity/environment duality as a basis for modern theorizing about personality. Bacon, Spenser, La Primaudaye, and John Davies of Hereford did assume such a common trait: the possession of those fundamental urgings termed "affections." "There are appetites," observed La Primaudaye, "of another kinde, which are bred without any touch at all, and follow the thought and imagination of a man." These are properly called "affections," he avers, and enlarging on the subject, he notes that:

by the affections we meane properly those motions of the heart, which follow knowledge, and either seeke after or reject, that which is offered unto them: so that according to the order of nature, knowledge goeth before these motions.

Affections are, ultimately, "that naturall power in the soule which openeth itself towards *Good* and withdraweth itself from evil"; and they have always existed, not for the oppression but for the benefit of man. They could be understood as yearnings, perhaps, and they were implanted in man's mind by God as "pricks and bridles" to keep the spirit from being "lulled asleep" or "oppressed" with that "heaviness of body" so to be guarded against in many Renaissance transcendentalist recensions. Accordingly, Erasmus can present Folly as asserting

I take it for all readie granted, that all the affections of man, pertaine unto Folie. In as much as philosophers put this distinction betwene a wyseman, and a foole, that *the one is ledde by reason, the other by sensualitie,* and therefore dooe the Stoikes seclude all affections from a wyseman, as so many diseases of the mynde. But that not withstanding, these affections are not onely sette in steede of pilotts to suche as woulde recover the porte of wysedome, but also in any acte of vertue, are lyke certaine pricks, or incitations provokyng a man to dooe well.[11]

[11] D. Erasmus, *The Praise of Folie*, trans. Thomas Chaloner (London, 1549), sig. E4ᵛ; and La Primaudaye, sigs. 2P3, 2Q4ᵛ, and 2R[3ᵛ]. The "affections" are also discussed by Richard Barckley, *A Discourse of the Felicitie of Man* (London, 1598), sigs. 2Qᵛ–2Q5ᵛ; Wright, sigs. B7–Cᵛ;

If, ideally, the "affections" existed for man's benefit, reality was shaped by the corruption of man so that, one gathers, these implanted yearnings or thrusts seldom functioned as had been intended. "Although our nature doth of it selfe alwaies tend to that which is *Good*," observed La Primaudaye, "nevertheless wee differ much, nay we are clean contrary to GOD, when we come to the election of *Good*, because of the bad judgement we have, by reason of the darkenesse of ignorance wherwith our mindes are blinded" (sig. 2R2ᵛ). It is as if the affections are raw emotion and that this basic thrust had originally tended to the (spiritual) survival of mankind. In modern phraseology, we will, of course, be reminded of talk about man's "instincts," "atavisms," or perhaps even "drives." We also speak of "subconscious" urgings which power the personality, wrongly or rightly, to successful or disastrous behavior; and the Renaissance concept of the affections seems, in some respects, to have been equivalent. Even if the speaker remained quasi-Thomistic, alluding to "concupiscence," the effect itself, if not the epistemological details, was similar in its assumption as to a basic impulse in man. Preaching on the text of 5 Galatians, Benjamin Carier, one of the chaplains to the prince, could observe in a sermon at Richmond in 1606:

Davies, *Microcosmos*, sigs. G4ᵛ and Y4ᵛ; Norden, sig. K3; Palingenius, sigs. D2ᵛ–D3; Hooker, sigs. I5 and G–Gᵛ; Davies, *Nosce*, sig. I; W. Jewel, *The Golden Cabinet of True Treasure* (London, 1612), sig. K2; and Augustine, *The Citie of God*, trans. John Healey (London, 1610), XIV. Augustine is quite relevant to this general context. Barckley had read the Augustinian La Primaudaye as well as Augustine himself (see sigs. 2A8 and 2B8); and Wright (sig. B7), Charron (sig. C4ᵛ), and Montaigne (II, 138) all support arguments for Augustine's relevance here. This relevance is also supported by Thomas Burt's Whitsunday sermon of 1605, *The Glorie of the Godlie Graine* (London, 1607), sig. C; and by R. Wakeman's *Christian Practice* (Oxford, 1605), sigs. C5ᵛ–C6. See also Herschel Baker, *The Image of Man* (New York, 1961), 312–22. For the importance of the commentaries of L. Vives in Healey's translation, see Barroll, "Some Versions of Plato in the English Renaissance," *Shak. S.*, II (1966), 229. The popularity of the Augustinian La Primaudaye is discussed by Madalene Shindler, "The Vogue and Impact of Pierre de La Primaudaye," *DA*, XXI (1960), 192.

Concupiscence in it selfe, as it is a facultie of the soule, and a gift of GOD, is no sinne, but may be made a helper unto Vertue, if it be will looked unto, although I confesse Concupiscence is commonly taken in the evill part for originall sinne: but if shee be kept at home, and set a worke, in sweeping of the house, and lighting the candle, shee may in the end prove a chast virgin, fit to meete the bride-groome at his comming.[12]

If there was indeed something called the "affections," and if they were thought to be the basis of human impulse, the term had an important ideological synonym. In many kinds of discussion, reference to the word "love" operated in just the manner often reserved for the affections themselves. We observe the equation from Frevile's easy talk in Marston's *Dutch Courtesan*, for as argument is being used to hearten the lovelorn Malheureuse, "love" and "affection" are identified in a tone of almost careless cliché:

> Hell and the prodigies of angrie Jove
> are not so fearfull to a thinking minde
> as a man without affection, why frend,
> Philosophie & nature are all one,
> love is the center in which all lines close
> the common bonde of being.[13]

If such synonymity was indeed operative, it is obvious that psychology characteristically faded into the larger premises of ide-

---

[12] Benjamin Carier (or Charier), *A Sermon Preached before the Prince at Richmond* (London, 1606[?]), sig. C. Cf. B. Castiglione, *The Courtyer*, trans. Thomas Hoby (London, 1577), sig. S7; *Pathomachia: or, the battell of affections* (London, 1630), *pass.*; Montaigne, II, 283; Barckley, sig. 2P7; Charron, sig. E6ᵛ; Wright, sig. B7ᵛ; Davies, *Microcosmos*, sig. G4ᵛ; Norden, sigs. I3ᵛ–I4; Hooker, sigs. G2 and I7; Palingenius, sig. L2; and Fulke Greville, I, 52ff. This documentation is in support not of the ubiquity of Christian thought in the period but of one specific line of reasoning within the general *ethos*, the doctrine of the perverted impulse, so to speak. Probably having its roots in Plato's *Protagoras* (sec. 357ff.), the doctrine appears as a central point in Augustine, who influenced Aquinas to support the view in disagreement with Aristotle (*Summa Contra Gentiles*, III. i. 1–6). [A. M. T. S.] Boethius, *Five Books*, trans. I. T. (London, 1609), Books 3 and 4, espoused the same view, although Calvin disagreed.

[13] Citations from Marston's dramas are to *Plays*, ed. H. Harvey Wood (Edinburgh, 1934–38). The immediate citation is to II. i. on p. 84.

ology, for to speak of "love" is to allude to a concept with a well-known role in Renaissance philosophy. Affection then merges into the vast tradition of Thomistic, Augustinian, and Neo-Platonic thought, with their bases in Plato and Aristotle. The synonymity of affection with love will also remind us that to claim all Renaissance men possessed a theory of the affections is to explain nothing. In order to comprehend subordinate vocabularies or, if we will, the verbal systems in which the term "affections" really moved, and to understand thereby some Elizabethan approaches to the problem of character, we need to recall the various premises about love as a concept in itself.

The most useful method of coping with "love" is not necessarily or initially a formal exploration of the influence of Ficino and of other Neo-Platonists, despite the obvious importance of such a line of thought. One perhaps views the epiphanies of Stephen Daedalus as related to theories of Plotinian immanences, the Kierkegaardian attitudes of Meursault as related to the Neo-Augustinianism of his creator, or the "acts" of Lafcadio as functions of a Lucretian bent. But in our analysis, do we not, at our peril, ignore childhood's learning, as in Gide's early exposure to the kinds of Protestantism so restlessly immanent throughout *La Porte Etroite*? The most pertinent point of departure in the study of character depiction may be the most elementary level— for us, the point at which the boy, the future Renaissance dramatist, would himself have been formally initiated into the first thinking on such subjects. The Renaissance child began with the catechisms. It is important at once to qualify their role, for catechetical treatises in themselves could hardly serve as a guide to every convolution in the personality organizations of Shakespeare's own creations. Rather, the value of the catechisms lies in their implicit suggestions as to the ideal, for these concepts of personality "perfection" allow us to infer elementary structures of imperfection, the youthful foundations upon which the dramatist, in his maturity, would form his own sophistications, his sense of the "complex character."

Most Renaissance catechisms, even the shortest, included the Creed, the Lord's Prayer, and the Ten Commandments; but these last were always presented with commentary in the form of generally stereotyped interpretations of each law as well as of the Commandments as a whole. It is these interpretations which suggest how a web of theory soon began to be spun upon the loom of "love," which itself would appear in other contexts, operating in synonymity with the concept "affection." We may advert, for instance, to the very popular catechism of Alexander Nowell which, merely during the span of time when Shakespeare was between six and eleven, appeared in six Latin editions and five editions of an English translation by Thomas Norton, the coauthor of *Gorboduc.* In Norton's translation, the catechizer, speaking to the scholar in the usual dialogue form, indicates for us the role of the Commandments in the use of the term "love."

"Hetherto thou hast shortly and playnly opened the law of the ten commaundementes," observes the instructor, "but can not all these things that thou hast severally and particularly declared, be in a few wordes gathered as it were into one summe?" "Why not," the student is supposed to respond blithely, after which he proceeds to quote Matthew on the point that all the law and the prophets are comprehended in the principle of "love" for God and "love" for one's neighbor. And between them, student and catechizer agree that "Charitie or love" is "one of the principall partes of Religion" and "the soule of all other lawes." Indeed, we gather, to hold oneself within the compass of this rule is to be able, ultimately, to dispense with any other kind of laws such as men "do dayly devise to hold men in from doying wrong one to an other, & to mainteine civile societie." And thus if love (and its various synonyms) was introduced so early as the complex terminological basis of a Christian and basically Pauline doctrine, Berowne's joking may adumbrate consequent verbal conventions. "Charity it selfe fulfills the Law," he argues in *Love's Labour's Lost*, concluding with humorous triumph, "And who can sever love from Charity." His comically outrageous derivation—that "love" as God's law justifies their pursuit of the young ladies on the most Christian grounds—can only take its humor from an audience's familiarity with the most elementary tenets of a system of thought within which most of the playgoers were probably raised.[14] This system is ultimately describable as "Renaissance Christianity," if we like, but for the sake of philosophical clarity, we would use another term. Let us speak of "transcendentalism" rather than of "Christianity," stipulating that the former term will also embrace those idiosyncratic manipulations whereby different writers of the period thought in the specific vocabularies of Anglicanism, Puritanism, Renaissance Humanism, Neo-Scholasticism, Neo-Platonism, Neo-Stoicism, and the like.[15]

The tenets of this kind of thought are observable as early as the "little Catechisme appoynted in the *booke of Common Prayer*" which, Nowell suggested on his title page, should ordinarily precede study of his more advanced volume. This "little Catechisme" introduced the child to a manner of organizing his thinking into that configuration describable as "transcendentalism." We thus encounter with interest an initial maneuver which served to stress the interaction between the Ten Commandments and the New Testament. This reconciliation had, of course, always been implicit (but perhaps not so emphatically explicit) in Patristic writings; and any student of Pauline and Augustinian recension structures will not be surprised to find the "little Catechisme" beginning just as the more advanced manuals. The Ten Commandments are presented, and then, in the traditional reconciliation of "Old Law" with "New Law,"

---

[14] For Nowell, see A. Nowell, *A Catechism, or First Instruction of Christian Religion* (London, 1571), sig. F2ff. Cf. the more popular treatises and handbooks of religion: Gervase Babington, *Exposition of the Commandements* (London, 1596), sig. G4ᵛ (four editions between 1583 and 1596); John Dod and Robert Cleaver, *A Plaine and Familiar Exposition of the Ten Commaundements* (London, 1606), sig. 2D2ᵛ (nineteen editions between 1604 and 1635); John Bradford, *Godly Meditations* (London, 1607), sig. Eff. (seven editions between 1567 and 1607); and William Perkins, *A Golden Chaine* (London, 1597), sig. Dᵛff. (nineteen editions in English between 1591 and 1635). Cf. also Otto Vaenius, *Emblemata Divini Amoris* (Antwerp, 1615), sig. Q3ᵛ.

[15] "Transcendentalism" is hereafter used to indicate that mode of thought which assumes the existence of an agency governing man from a supernatural plane of existence which is unavailable to the human senses.

allusion is made to Christ's comment on the Law in Matthew 22:38–39: "Love the Lord thy God with all thine hart, with all thy soule and with all thy minde," and "love thy neighbor as thy selfe." But an interesting and important consequence of such interaction, as transmitted in the elementary Renaissance catechism, was the development of this casual dualism into a system which maintained, but was also something other than, say, Christ's new dispensation of mercy through his own submission to *lex talionis*. In short, the consolidation by Elizabethan and Jacobean catechisms of "all the law and the prophets" of Matthew 22:38–39 into two commandments used Christ's summation of the Law not as a replacement for the Ten Commandments but as a way of formally dividing them into two groups. That this bifurcation did not exist solely for the sake of mnemonic symmetries is suggested by the resultant systems. If the "little Catechisme" stated that the love of God summed up the "first Table" of the Law and that "Love thy neighbor as thy selfe" summed up the "second Table," we observe that the division was not arithmetical. The first Table comprehended only the first four commandments and, summarizing Christ's first injunction, was said to teach the proper love of God. The second Table included in itself the last six of the Ten Commandments and summarized Christ's second injunction, to love one's neighbor. Such a grouping was considered proper for, in the words of Babington, this love of neighbor is "the verie grounds of all civill societie, from whence all mens lawes proceede, if they be just" (sig. G4ᵛ).

This integration of the Ten Commandments with Matthew into "Tables" of the Law is extremely important for understanding the concept "love" to which the Elizabethan or Jacobean adult—the playgoer—had been exposed in early childhood, because the direction of the resultant dualism is toward what would seem to be a quite different vocabulary. Division is in terms of "obedience" and "order." As the commentators explained matters, each Table had a "first" and therefore primary commandment. Table One (Commandments I through IV) obviously contained the First Commandment, which enjoined love and obedience toward God and forbade the substitution of any object of veneration above the Supreme Being of the universe. Table Two (Commandments V through X) obviously began with the Fifth Commandment. And if Table Two comprised the laws dealing with the love of man, we may ponder the interesting fact that the Fifth Commandment itself deals with honoring one's parents. It is at this point that we can observe how those traditional complexities, inherent in the dialectics of "love" from the time of Plato, had been obtruded in simplified form upon the formation of the child's own idea system. By almost unanimous interpretation, the "first commandment" of Table Two was construed in the catechisms as enjoining respect not only for parents but for all superiors— all properly constituted authority. The matter is most illustratively summed up by the popular Dod:

Hitherto the duties of pietie to God, out of the first table, have beene handled. Now follow the Commaundements of the second table, concerning the duties of righteousnesse towards our neighbour. This [the fifth] is the first Commaundement of the second table, upon which all the rest doe depend. As in the first table, the keeping of all the Commaundements following, dependeth on the keeping of the first: so heare, if this first commandement were well observed; both of superiours, inferiours, and equalls, there could be no disorder against any of the commandements following. For, all disorders in the other, doe flow from hence: that either superiours are negligent in performing their duties of governing, or else inferiours are proud and stubborne, and refuse to obey their superiours, or equalles bee envious or ambitious betweene themselves.[16]

We are thus led to contemplate the seeming paradox that each of the "Tables" of "love" had as its first and primary commandment the precept of obedience. To possess love of God was to obey God; to possess love of neighbor was to obey the last six of the Ten Commandments as they might be interpreted by the prevailing laws of societal structure. But, paradox or not, the

[16] Sig. O7. Cf. Babington, sigs. H2 and H4ᵛ; Bradford, sig. F9ff.; Nowell, sigs. Eᵛ–E2; Perkins, *Golden Chaine*, sigs. Fᵛ–F2ᵛ; and Hooker, sig. G4ᵛ.

effect of these childhood catechisms was to establish a frame of reference about love which absorbed its loose synonym, the affections, into systems implicitly structured in the grammar of submission. The characteristically skeptical Francis Bacon is himself illustrative:

All other affections though they raise the minde, yet they doe it by distorting, and uncomlinesse of extasies or excesses; but onely Love doth exalt the mind, and neverthelesse, at the same instant doth settle and *Compose* it. So in all other excellencyes though they advance nature yet they are subject to Excesse. Onely Charity admitteth no Excesse. [*Advancement,* sigs. 2Y4–2Y4ᵛ]

The question of human affections—of emotions—would then seem to have been answered in words resembling the modern parlance of "self-control," but the difference between Renaissance and modern, more than adumbrated in these respects by childhood catechisms, achieves its predictable realization in Montaigne's "Apologie of Raymond Sebond" (II. 186) where, specifically, "self"-control is not a maximal consideration:

The first law that ever God gave unto man, was a Law of pure obedience. It was a bare and simple commandement whereof man should enquire and know no further: forasmuch, as *to obey is the proper dutie of a reasonable soule, acknowledging a heavenly and superiour benefactor.* From obeying and yeelding unto him proceed all other vertues; even as all sinnes derive from selfe-overweening.[17]

Modern theories of "self-control," or more accurately, the psychodynamics of personality integration, could be said to operate in philosophical independence from, say, modern astronomical efforts to account for the discernible universe. But if the "order-

---

[17] For various statements about this law imposed by love, cf. Nowell, sigs. B4–B6; Dod, sigs. B2ᵛ–B3; and Edmund Spenser's "Hymne of Heavenly Love" and *Faerie Queene,* I. x. 25–44, where Redcrosse must discipline himself before he is ready for Charissa. Cf. also William Perkins, *The Idolatrie of the Last Times* (Cambridge, 1601), sig. G7ᵛ; William Cowper, *A Conduit of Comfort* (London, 1606), sig. F2ᵛ (a sermon preached at St. James); and La Primaudaye, I, chap. 50.

ing" of an expanding universe seems today to require a philosophical framework *other* than that utilized by present-day psychodynamics, we will agree that a great many Renaissance tractarians required no such dichotomy, at least in their vocabulary of "order." Rather, if we return to the "magistrate" imagery suggested by the "faculty psychology" of the period, it would seem that the function of the rational intellect was not only to discover "emotional balance," if we will, through an imperative vaguely termed "love," but to verify this psychological imperative from observations of the physical universe. As students of the period are aware, these observations were derived not from an epistemology different from but *similar* to that invoked for the study of the human personality. Accordingly, the principle of obedience as the way to that emotional security describable as "love" could be verified through an insistence on analyzing the physical universe not in terms of, say, a "table of elements" but as a particular cultural approach used when coping with the phenomenon of self-awareness. Hence the "observable universe" need not necessarily have been organized by the atoms of Lucretius but by "commandments": two different kinds of investigation, as Bacon knew, were being referred to only one methodology. The kind of language which had always been generated from this modus operandi persisted, as we might gather from part of a sermon by the former satirist Thomas Bastard, even in 1615.

Wee see the nature of the light is to reconcile contrarieties, by influence and immission of beames: for what were this world, but a Chaos of discord, consisting of contrarieties, still resisting, fighting, destroying each other? This strife, this discord the light of the Sunne doth take away, and binde and reconcile things hot and cold, and moyst and dry, in a *band or knot of love and concord:* so that of that these natures of contrary qualities, set and tuned together, is made that excellent Musicke and harmonie of the life of all things under heaven: when these jarre and fall out of tune, then death ensueth. Thus then wee see that were it not for this materiall Sunne, nothing under heaven could live, but all things would dye and perish. For, as *Damascene* saith . . . Composition is the beginning of discord, discord of distance, distance of dissolution. Thus was our spirituall state contrary to God, at discord with ourselves and contrary to one another. Thus we are all dead in our sins.[18]

If we speak of Renaissance concepts of "order," therefore, we see only a part of the Elizabethan "world picture." The root notion was "love," as taught from early childhood, and this complex term not only permeated what has been called Elizabethan "faculty psychology," but it inhered in those analogies that reasoned from the structure of the cosmos to the ideal balances in society and in the mind of man. John Davies of Hereford might speak of man's "judgement" in his *Microcosmos*, but his magistrate imagery had the judgment appealing to a specific kind of law. When judgment has deemed a thing "good," he observed, she tenders it to the will, which embraces that thing with a "joyful moode" because it fulfills "hir *Soules* desire." And when that joy remains, "Its called *Love*, which doth the wil incline / To *simple good*, or good scarce toucht with ill" (sigs. Y4ᵛ–2A4ᵛ). Even in 1621 a somewhat more representative version of attitudes toward "order" was still available in the poetizing of "R. A.":

> As in the Frame and Microcosme of Man,
> The Soules great power all other motions sway
> And the whole Frame which of the Chaos came,
> To the prime Mover alwayes doth obay;
> So do all spirituall heav'nly Vertues ay,
> Depend upon this gracious Queene of Love,
> And e'en as Man and the whole World decay,
> When Soule departs and Spheres doe cease to move,
> Ev'n so all Vertues die not quickened by Love.[19]

There would then be no inconsistency if some commentators saw (or seem to have seen) reality as a web of obediences, as a

[18] Thomas Bastard, *Five Sermons* (London, 1615), sig. G3. A better-known work is his *Chrestoleros. Seven Bookes of Epigrames* (London, 1598).

[19] *The Song of Songs which was Salomons. Metaphrased by R. A.* (London, 1621), sig. D3ᵛ.

pattern of what some modern commentators term "order," while other Renaissance writers saw the cosmos as organized by "love," for in philosophical reality, sixteenth century epistemology rendered the terms mutually dependent. Neither concept was definable except as qualified by the other, despite the observations of Ulysses to the assembled Greeks. Thus while the sermon on "Charitie" in the Book of Homilies might establish one aspect of "love" as the maintenance of that order in the state which was a reflection of God's ideal order, the "Homily on Obedience" could explain submission to the order of the state as love for God who had enjoined such obedience to prevent that "Babilonicall confusion" which confounds the relationships possible within society.[20]

Whether this matter of "obedience" conflicted with the freedom of the will—whether "love" in one sense allowed certain modern connotations of "self-determination"—was, of course, a hoary argument. The usual key, as we will recall from even minimal readings in Renaissance writings, was the concept of "Christian liberty," the line of argument which suggested that the human will was only describable as "free" when it urged itself toward "the natural End of Man." William Covell reviewed the matter in 1603, writing in defense of Hooker's *Lawes of Ecclesiasticall Politie* that:

there is a three-fold freedome, from necessity, from sinne, from misery: the first of nature, the second of grace, the third of glory. In the first, from the bondage of coaction, the will is free in it owne nature, and hath power over it selfe. In the second, the will is not

[20] Ludovico Vives, annotating Augustine's discussion of the order of the universe (XII. 5), accordingly observes that "every thing keeping harmonious agreement both with it selfe and others, without corrupting discorde . . . made some ancient writers affirme, *that the world consisted all upon love*" (sig. 2O). One such "ancient writer" would presumably be Aristotle in his *Metaphysics*, 1072b3. For the "Homily on Charity," see *Certaine Sermons appointed by the Queens Majestie* (London, 1595), sigs. F2ʳ–F4. Cf. also, for example, Edmund Spenser's introduction to Book V of *FQ*, with his "Hymne of Heavenly Love." Finally, cf. Palingenius, sig. D2. For charity as harmony, see Thomas Churchyard, *A Musicall Consort of Heavenly Harmonie* (London, 1595).

free, but freed, from the bondage of sin. And in the third, it is freed from the servitude of corruption.

In the context of this language system, Covell can then contend that the "freedom" by which the will of man is termed "free" is only the first freedom, the freedom from any theory of "necessity." Quoting Aristotle, Covell observes that this essential freedom is a double one, the distinctions emerging as follows. First, there are things that men can will—walking, speaking, sitting, and the like. But there are also those things which men, although not necessarily constrained to do so, always tend to "will," as when they desire to be "happy." It is at this point, Covell maintains (with tradition behind him), that human beings go astray, for desiring to be happy or yearning after "good," they are deceived by "the inferiour appetite of the flesh," an appetite which makes those things seem good which really are not. Thus, although willing good "by nature," men ultimately "will" just the opposite of "good." By misusing his liberty, man has lost his "free will," not "in respect of the naturall libertie from coaction, but in respect of the libertie which is from sinne." True freedom of the will, Covell concludes, lies in delivering oneself from the bondage of vain desires. This freedom is attained by rediscovering the divine in oneself, and this discovery can only be attained by disciplining the will to the law of God, through which the will attains freedom or "Christian liberty."[21] We have returned

21 William Covell, A *Just and Temperate Defence of the Five Books of Ecclesiastical Policie written by M. Richard Hooker* (London, 1603), article 5, "Of Freewill." Covell refers his reader to Clement of Alexandria, Boethius, Damascenus, Aristotle's *Ethics*, Seneca's *De Beneficiis*, and St. Augustine. For the paradox of freedom in bondage, see especially Joshua Sylvester's "Little Bartas," in *Workes* (London, 1620), sigs. R7–R7ᵛ; Saluste du Bartas, *Devine Weekes*, trans. Joshua Sylvester (London, 1605), sigs. Y3ᵛ–Y4; G. Cinthio, A *Discourse of Civill Life*, trans. Lodovick Bryskett (London, 1606), sigs. Y3–Z3ᵛ; Thomas Elyot, *Of the Knowledge which maketh a Wise Man* (London, 1534), sigs. H3–I; J. L. Vives, *An Introduction to Wisdome* (London, 1544), sig. E8ᵛ; Palingenius, sigs. I7–I8ᵛ; Philippe de Mornay, *The True Knowledge of a Mans owne Selfe*, trans. Anthony Munday (London, 1602), sig. A8ᵛ; and William Wrednot, *Palladis Pallatium* (London, 1604), sig. C3ff., with references here to Cicero, Gregory, and Aulus Gellius. See also the chorus of the third act in Sir

to the paradox of the Ten Commandments in which obedience was the primary law of each of the "Tables" of "love."

In the context of our general discussion, such a return emphasizes those complexities inherent in Renaissance approaches to the problem of human personality. If emotion was analyzed as a series of impulses called the "affections," and if these in turn were vaguely summarized in "love," such a summation obviously served to join "affections" not with an analytical process but with a value system already established. We must gather that man's emotions existed not so that Homo sapiens might "survive" in some Pleistocene crisis but so that he could realize "love," his basic drive. And if this drive was toward a transcendental rendezvous defined by society as the "Good," the "Beautiful," or "God," then personality theory in the Renaissance was asserting a concept of optimum emotion, one to be arrived at, as in other societies and other philosophies, by obedience to certain cultural tenets. If "love" made one "free," such emotional "freedom" was to be gained through emotional control, through "obedience." Although this is to state matters in a somewhat elementary fashion, we have perhaps established a vocabulary which will enable us to follow with some insight the admittedly domestic argument in the *Comedy of Errors* between the unmarried Luciana and her shrewish sister who insists on her own freedom of action.

> *Luc.* Oh, know he is the bridle of your will.
> *Adr.* There's none but asses will be bridled so.
> *Luc.* Why, headstrong liberty is lasht with woe.
> There's nothing situate under heavens eye,
> But hath his bound in earth, in sea, in skie.

William Alexander's *Julius Caesar*; F. Lewes, *The Sinner's Gyde*, trans. Francis Meres (London, 1598), sigs. O3ff.; Thomas Adams, *The Mysticall Bedlam* (London, 1615), sig. H; J. Osorio, *of Civill and Christian Nobilitie*, trans. W. Blandie (London, 1576), sig. T4ᵛ; Davies, *Nosce*, sig. L4ᵛ; Davies, *Microcosmos*, sig. H2; and Richard Braithwaite, *Times Curtaine Drawn* (London, 1621) (see the section entitled "Bound, yet free"). *Contra*, see Charles Trinkaus, "The Problem of Free Will in the Renaissance and the Reformation," *JHI*, X (1949), 51–62.

The beasts, the fishes, and the winged fowles
Are their males subjects, and at their controules:
Man more divine, the Master of all these,
Lord of the wide world, and wilde watry seas,
Indued with intellectuall sence and soules,
Of more preheminence then fish and fowles,
Are masters to their females, and their Lords:
Then let your will attend on their accords.
Adri. This servitude makes you to keepe unwed.
Luci. Not this, but troubles of the marriage bed.
Adr. But were you wedded, you wold bear some sway.
Luc. Ere I learne love, Ile practise to obey. [278–303]

Luciana's reasoning is perhaps Aristotelian, but it seems clear that to an audience her final response would have meant something more than conveniently clever repartee.

The concepts implied by "love" would in themselves have had limited value in any of the systems upon which fictional characterizations could have been built, for the emotional condition of "perfect love" arrived at by perfect obedience—whether through processes of Florentine or French Neo-Platonism, Neo-Scholasticism, or Anglo-Catholicism—was essentially a statement of negatives. One attained an order of emotion which was "not of earth" and was not bound by human understanding, human impulse, human desires, or human fears. And since no one could attain this perfection, any concerns about strictly human personality must inevitably be expressed as an investigation of shortcomings. The study of how men really behave, the characterization of human beings, develops as a study of departures from the desirable. Transcendentalist analyses of human motivations emerge from descriptions of "sin."

However bemused we become in the face of this curious but unavoidable fact—that to study theories of personality in transcendentalistic societies is to study their teleologies of nonconformity—we need not become lost in the inevitably evaluative matrices within which discourse about the human mind was

available. Rather, if our purpose is to study material available
to the Renaissance playwright, the reminder of modern parallels
may be useful. While Freud's and Jung's theories of motivation
were undoubtedly influenced by the philosophical commitments
of the nineteenth century, present-day novelists and playwrights
use Freudian and Jungian material as the stuff of their character
constructions without necessarily subscribing to nineteenth-century ethics. For the Renaissance playwright, the mechanics of
human personality might have been labeled in discourses as
"evil" or "sin," but at least a description was thereby available.
One could hardly present on stage a figure with a sign around
his neck reading "Evil," even in the moralities. There were the
practical problems of human depiction, and whatever moral
evaluations the artists themselves might ultimately feel, the per-
vasiveness of transcendentalist argumentation offered a means of
organizing their observations. The role of intuition in the artist,
as a concept, is not hereby denied its own play; rather, a modi-
fication from the opposite direction might suggest that nineteenth-century theories of artistic creativity sometimes under-
estimate the molding force of a culture on "intuition" itself,
even when these Victorian and Georgian theories appear in the
form of twentieth-century "poetics."

Waiving philosophical precision of vocabulary as not to the
immediate purpose here, it is worth risking a review of perhaps
familiar material in Anglo-Catholic terminology. Specifically, let
us recall the elements of transcendentalist approaches to the
actual human condition, whatever might ultimately be hoped
for mankind. Man's affections, in the prelapsarian state, were
"naturally" oriented toward God, but after the Fall, human
affections became permanently "corrupted." Thus while unfallen
man "loved" God, after the Fall he repeated Adam's original
sin by tending not to love God and trying to elevate himself
over the Creator. Yet there was, we gather, enough of the divine
nature remaining in postlapsarian man so that he was still
capable of following certain dictates of his transcendentally
oriented nature, of loving God whether he knew it or not. And

long ago, Augustine had adapted the classical truism that men are never satisfied and had organized a system within this context. Men are never satisfied, he observed, because they have continued to desire Absolute Being and cannot ever be content with less. Men's strivings after goals are all, as it were, subconscious strivings after that Absoluteness of Being realized only in God. Their emotions reflect their transcendental aspirations, and even if they do not know "God," they nevertheless strive for an undefined Supremacy of Being without understanding why. Later, the proposition would be refined somewhat in the words of Lady Philosophy as she put it to Boethius in the ever-popular *De Consolatione:*

The good seeke to obtaine the chiefest good, which is equally proposed to badde and good, by the natural function of vertues, but the evill endevour to obtaine the same by divers concupiscences, which are not the natural function of obtaining goodnesse.[22]

[22] The currency of Boethius in this period is attested to variously. Vives referred to him in his edition of Augustine (sig. N3). Thomas Chaloner, who translated *Moriae Encomium*, also rendered Boethius into English in 1563, as did George Colville in 1556, while Phineas Fletcher translated the meters. See G. and P. Fletcher, II, 243–45 and 333–39. Boethius' most famous translator was probably Queen Elizabeth, who rendered the whole *De Consolatione*. See *Queen Elizabeth's Englishings*, ed. Caroline Pemberton, *EETS, OS* CXIII (London, 1889). Boethius possibly did not very often circulate as an individual title because a translation was so easily accessible in the fourteen-odd editions and issues between 1532 and 1602 of Chaucer's complete works. See, for example, the 1598 edition, sig. 2Q6ᵛff. The relevance of Boethius may also be inferred from the remarks of I. T., the 1609 translator whose work we here have quoted. He dedicated the translation to Sir Thomas Sackville's widow and mentioned that the poet (whose hand we may recall in *Gorboduc* and the *Mirror*) had planned a translation of Boethius himself. The remark seems plausible when the Boethean argumentation of Jack Straw's tragedy in the *Mirror* is recalled. For other translators and for the significance of Boethius generally, see W. E. Houghton, Jr., "English Translations of Boethius's *De Consolatione Philosophiae*," Ph.D. diss., Yale University, 1931; and H. R. Patch, *The Tradition of Boethius* (New York, 1935), 73–86 and 111 n. (for Lipsius on Boethius). The relevance of Boethius to early Neo-Platonic strains of thought is discussed by Patch in "Fate in Boethius and the Neo-Platonists," *Speculum,* IV (1929), 62–72; and "Necessity in Boethius and the Neo-Platonists," *Speculum,* X (1935), 393–404. These latter discussions are also relevant to the previous footnote.

This way of thinking about human personality was, in a sense, as old as Platonism. We therefore find the view shared by Augustine, who held it in common with later thinkers oriented to philosophical systems which, in other respects, differed somewhat among each other—Aquinas, Pico, Ficino, Calvin, Charron, Erasmus, and Hooker, for example.[23] And there was general agreement, too, on the usual corollary to the view expounded by Lady Philosophy. Persons who ignored the "natural" ends of their beings might, if one liked, be termed "sinful," but to be more accurate, one could view them as "sick" or simply as "weak." In one instance, if certain personalities forsook virtue and followed vice from their own lack of awareness, they might be regarded as subject to the sickness inherent in any blind ignorance: they lacked the power to attain what all men ultimately desired. In another instance, if they knew what "good" should indeed be followed but were driven by their corrupted affections to seek the wrong tokens of this "good," they then showed that they were weak, too weak to resist vice. Finally, in ontological terms all such "weak" or "sick" men could be regarded as "nonexistent," for, as Aquinas put it, "they which leave the common end of all things which are, leave also being." Accordingly, such men could be said to have become "nothing"; and if the usual synonym for this state was "naught," or "naughty,"[24] it is significant that the term would pass into the *koine* maintaining the variable but related senses that emerge in the vocabularies of both Portia and Ophelia.

Existential subtleties aside, the underlying concept, the notion

[23] Augustine, sig. 3Tff.; Aquinas, *Contra Gentiles*, III, 1–25; Hooker, sig. F6; Pico della Mirandola, *De Ente et Uno*, trans. V. M. Hamm (Milwaukee, 1943), chap. 8; M. Ficino, *Commentary on Plato's Symposium*, ed. Sears Jayne, University of Missouri Studies, XIX (1944), chaps. 4–6; Calvin, II. ii. 12–17; Charron, sig. E6ᵛ; Erasmus, sig. S4ff. Cf. La Primaudaye, sig. 3F2; Davies, *Microcosmos*, sig. Zᵛ; and Barckley, sig. 2P4.

[24] On this subject, Aquinas is instructive in his agreement with Augustine: see *De Lib. Arb.*, chap. 3; and *Contra Gentiles*, III. i. 7. Cf. G. Bruno, *D'gli Heroici Furori*, ed. L. G. Nelson (New York, 1958), 245; Pico, 31; Davies, *Microcosmos*, sig. H4ᵛ; and Sir Philip Sidney, *The Countess of Pembroke's Arcadia*, ed. Albert Feuillerat (Cambridge, 1912), 88. The basis presumably lies in Aristotle, *Metaphysics*, III. ii. 8.

of, as it were, "subconscious desire" as an explanation for the various urgings of human emotionalisms away from the culturally imposed optima for the composition of personality, is to be found everywhere in the contexts of Shakespeare's lifetime. La Primaudaye, for instance, presented a familiar elaboration of the argument.

For who ever saw an ambitious man satisfied with honours, or a covetous wretch with riches? And from whence commeth this that they are so insatiable, but only because the spirit that God hath given them, is of so noble a race and of snch [sic] an excellent nature, that how much soever it be fallen from his first nature and nobility, yet it can never content it selfe with any thing, that is of another nature more base & vile then it owne. . . . it hath ever-more a secret sense of it owne nature and dignity, which keepeth it from being contented with any thing whatsoever. [sig. 3F2]

It is interesting to note that this urge, these affections, even when directed wrongly, could themselves be described in terms of "love." The age-old rationale for this manner of speaking is reiterated in a sermon delivered at Cambridge on July 7, 1607, by Martin Fotherby, chaplain to King James.

Our God and Creator who is perfect love himself hath made us his creatures of such a loving nature that (as Plutarch well observeth) we needs must always be loving of some thing: so that if our love be diverted from the world, it needs must be converted unto God.[25]

Joseph Hall elaborates somewhat more scholastically:

As love keeps the whole Law, so love is the only breaker of it; being the ground as of all obedience, so of all sin; for, whereas sin has been commonly accounted to have two roots, Love and Fear, it is plain that fear hath his origin from love; for no man fears to lose ought, but what he loves. [sig. F2]

[25] Martin Fotherby, *Four Sermons* (London, 1608), sig. A3ᵛ.

William Baldwin, seldom one for the subtler paradoxes, as we might observe from some of his work in the *Mirrour for Magistrates*, established the same distinction for the child in his little *Treatise of Morall Philosophie*, which was used in most secondary schooling. In the chapter on "Love and charitie" the author, as usual, quotes from all the classical philosophers on the subject and then, as usual, sums up the matter in a bit of doggerel:

> In this life, of love there are two kindes,
> That draweth men to joy and paine,
> On filthie love some set their mindes,
> And godly love some men retaine.[26]

If "filthie love" does not strike us as sufficiently analytical, we may observe that the most common Elizabethan term for that emotion which Hall regarded as the first "breaker" of the law was "self-love." When, in our study of Renaissance psychology, we refer to texts such as Thomas Wright's *Passions of the Mind*, we may not often enough recall that book 1, chapter 3 of this treatise (which went through five editions between 1601 and 1628) is entitled *"Of Selfe-love"* and that most of the standard psychological handbooks of the period began their discussions of human nature not with the problem of humors or of the judging capacity but with Wright's early emphasis. Even Shakespeare's familiarity with the cliché that self-love was the root of all emotional troubles can be observed readily enough in Parolles' jesting reference to "selfe-love, which is the most inhibited sinne in the Cannon."[27] And if the poet's sonnets are at all indicative in their

[26] William Baldwin, *A Treatise of Moral Philosophy* (London, 1591), sig. P7ʳ. Cf. George Gascoigne, *Droomme of Doomesday* (London, 1576), sig. T2; Otto Vaenius, *Emblemata Divina Amoris*, sig. O3ʳ; Charron, I. xix.; and Wright, chap. 3. More traditional *loci* are Plato's *Symposium*, secs. 185–88; Aquinas, *Summa Theologica*, Q, 26, 1–4; Augustine, sig. 2Y6ʳ; Calvin, *Institution of Christian Religion*, trans. Thomas Norton (London, 1599), sigs. Pʳ–P2; and M. Luther, *A Proper Treatyse of Good Workes* (London, 1535) sigs. C2ʳ–C6.

[27] *AWW*, I. i. 158. The biblical *locus* was 2 Tim., III. x. 1, from which Augustine derived his section on the subject in *De Civitate*. Random refer-

tendency to weave conceits out of various widely accepted and contemporary notions, Sonnet 62 is illustrative.

> Sinne of selfe-love possesseth al mine eye,
> And all my soule, and al my every part;
> And for this sinne there is no remedie,
> It is so grounded inward in my heart.
> Me thinkes no face so gratious is as mine,
> No shape so true, no truth of such account,
> And for my selfe mine owne worth do define,
> As I all other in all worths surmount. [1609 ed.]

Even if the poet goes on to "correct" himself by stating that he should love instead the person to whom the sonnet has been written, the playing is to the point here, for the sonnet does not urge that Shakespeare's primary concern was self-love: it demonstrates his familiarity with the language of a salient idea system in the Renaissance.

As a term, self-love, the *amor sui* of patristic writings, was inherently subject to the ambivalences characteristic of transcendentalist ontologies since, under certain circumstances, love of self could represent an approved mode of thought. The distinctions here were ancient, and Joseph Hall followed tradition when he observed that "there be three things that I may love without exception. God, my neighbor, my soul" (sig. F2). And if the last element in the series tends to blur distinctions, La Primaudaye's

---

ence to the subject as a Renaissance commonplace might include Spenser, *FQ*, I. iv. 10; Ben Jonson, "The Fountain of Self-Love" (e.g., IV. i), in *Ben Jonson*, ed. C. H. Herford and Percy Simpson (Oxford, 1932), IV, 99 (all future references to Jonson are to this edition); and James Cleland, *The Institution of a Young Noble Man* (London, 1607), sig. 2H. To the various expositions on the matter, cf. Thomas à Kempis, *Of the Imitation of Christ*, trans. T. Rogers (London, 1587), pass. The *Imitation* went through four translations and at least twenty-eight editions between 1503 and 1605. Antonio de Guevara's *Familiar Epistles*, trans. E. Hellows (London, 1584), sig. N4, is indicative if we recall Guevara's great popularity in his recension of the "Golden Book of Marcus Aurelius." An excellent statement on the subject can be found in Haly Heron, *The Kayes of Counsaile* (London, 1579), chap. 5.

recension clarifies what was taken to be the proper orientation of personality here. A man "loves" his "soul" only by loving himself:

as the gift of God, as also his life and being which God hath given him, and that blessed estate for the enjoying of which he hath his being, and that *Good* wherein it consisteth, and whereby he may attaine unto it, and shoulde love no other thing, not otherwise.[28]

Ludovico Vives had offered a more extended analysis of the complementary negation in this dialectic regarding self-love in his *Introduction to Wisedome*, which had not only entered its fifth English edition in the year of Shakespeare's birth but would also appear in Latin after the poet's death, during the year in which the First Folio was published. Vives begins with the now-familiar affirmative and then proceeds to define the negative.

He loveth him selfe, that with all his endevour and fervent prayer, desireth of god, that he vouchsafe to garnishe the minde, the moste excellente parte of man, with her trewe and naturalle ornamentes, that is to wite, with Religion and Godlinesse.

He loveth not him selfe, whiche setteth his minde upon riches, honoures, and worldly pleasures, or any other bodely thinge: for so moche as the most preciouse parte of man is the minde.

Nother loveth he him selfe, whiche for lacke of knowledge of his owne misery, deceiveth him selfe, or suffereth other to deceive him: beinge gladde as having those giftes, whereof in verie dede he hathe none at all.

Such love in a man is not to be counted the love of him selfe,

---

[28] Sig. 2R^v. Cf. Perkins, *Golden Chain*, sigs. D3–D4; Dod and Cleaver, sigs. E5–E7; Babington, sigs. B6–B6^v; Davies, *Microcosmos*, sig. O3; Charron, III, 5; and Simon Robson, *The Choice of Change* (London, 1585), sig. C3 (this work went through three editions between 1585 and 1598). A biblical *locus* is 1 John 4:7f. as opposed to 1 John 2:15. Although Aristotle and Plato in their own ways suggested the distinction between proper and improper love of self, Augustine's concept of *quies* formalizes the duality involved. One of the better discussions which relates this line of thought to classical philosophy is still Anders Nygren's 1938 study, *Agape and Eros*, trans. P. S. Watson (Philadelphia, 1953), especially 482–503 and chaps. 1 and 2 pass.

but a blinde, beastly, and inordinate love of the body, hurtful both
to him selfe, and to other. The whiche love Socrates complained, to
be the originall beginning of all mischeves. For in dede this taketh
away frendeshippe betwene man and man, whereby arise all miserie,
all mischeves amonges men, he that overmoch loveth him self after
this maner, he loveth no man, and no man him. [sigs. L5–L5ᵛ]

From this we gather that "self-love is justifiable when we love
our selves for god only," as John Davies of Hereford put it; but
if such negations merely adumbrate the areas of emotional confusion, areas into which the human personality was assumed to
wander when not conforming to societal theory, further clarifi-
cations and specifications were available in the oldest traditions.
To recall the rather harsh words of John Downame, the specific
concerns of the "wrong" kind of self-love could be referred to
three heads: "to wit, voluptuousness, whose object are unlawfull
and immoderate pleasures; covetousness, whose object are riches;
and ambition, whose object are honours and preferments." St.
John had, as we know, offered the original version of this triad:
"lust of the flesh," "lust of the eyes," and "pride of life." As
headings, these are reasonable enough when we consider that the
gesture of defining "wrong" self-love had to be an effort to reason
out, in a transcendentalist framework, the possible results of
directing one's affections away from a sense of the reality of
Absolute Being to cognitional immediacies.

This triadic substructure of the concept "self-love" was ubiq-
uitous on all levels of Renaissance writing and serves warning
to the student of characterization that subjects other than lechery or the urge to murder might have been theoretically regarded
as human problems in Shakespeare's cultural context. If we
speak, for instance, of "Renaissance self-inflation" or of a "natural
Renaissance sense of pride" as if these traits were regarded as
desirable norms, we must reckon with the fact that even a Montaigne adheres to what we have argued as the theoretical consen-
sus in his casual remark that "custome hath made a mans speech
of himselfe vicious. And obstinately forbids it in hatred of boast-

ing."[29] While historical investigation sometimes tends to be simplistic, the use of modern senses as to what constitutes taboo behavior can be an equally constricting measure of what was possible in Renaissance theory, the elementary sum of which may be aptly epitomized in the words of a dramatist of the period. In 1602, Anthony Munday, the hard-working playwright and hack, presented a translation of Mornay, a philosopher in great favor with the Sidneys. (Sir Philip's translation of one tractate went through four editions between 1587 and 1617, and Lady Pembroke's rendering of another of Mornay's works called for an equal number of editions between 1592 and 1607.) Munday translated Mornay's primarily anatomical *True Knowledge of a Man's Owne Selfe,* and the dramatist's own preface may offer, in its almost casual assumptions, an appropriate compendium of the basic approaches to general problems of human motivation in Renaissance thought.

By the judgement of the best and learnedest Philosophers, as also by some apparent proofe in our owne selves, wee finde, that our affection or desire after any thing, is a quality proper and peculiar to the soule: for from it onely are our affections derived, and thereby are we led to the prosecution of whatsoever we can most covet. Now, all our longings and desirous appetites, are not evermore for the best, albeit in our fraile judgements it may carry a wel seeming likelihoode: but too often we finde by wofull experience, that we have no greater enemies then our owne affections, nor fall into heavier daungers, then those we are led to by our owne wilfulle follies.

To runne into particularities of our severall appetencies, as some after honour, others after riches, others after temporarie glory or applause, and others vaine and frivolous pleasures: would require a larger discourse then this whereto I am limitted, and I should follow the olde track of custome, which almost is handled in every tractate. [sigs. A7–A7ᵛ]

[29] For Montaigne, see II. vi. 59; for John Downame, see *The Second Part of the Christian Warfare* (London, 1611), sigs. M8ᵛ–N. For the tripartition into kinds of self-love, see, for example, Charron, I, 19–23; La Primaudaye, sigs. 4G5–4G7; and G. B., *Narrow Way,* sig. Dᵛ.

Our primary concern here should not be judged as moralistic, despite the foregoing tonalities. But if we agree that any Renaissance dramatist was undertaking, among his many creative tasks, the construction of "persons" engaged in some aesthetically ordered activity on a stage, the question of ethical systems will inch into relevance at that point where the character does something besides sleep on the stage. To depict a statically happy man as one sketched activity for the character would have been quite simple or insanely difficult; to depict a man with "problems" was perhaps easier and at least was more usual. In either instance, however, our subsequent understanding of the dramatist's way with "character" would depend on our awareness of what he defined as the presence or absence of "problems." And in this matrix, the local cultural desiderata for human activity—the matter of "ethics"—would to a large extent define "problem" in the first place. We must nevertheless subordinate purely ethical considerations when they might tend to distort any line of discourse directed toward the exploration of character construction in itself. Hence we need not extend ourselves so unwisely as to argue, for instance, that characters in Renaissance drama were simply and merely depicted either as the essence of perfect "love" or as suffering from (1) "pride of life," (2) "lust of the eyes," or (3) "lust of the flesh." Such a tangent would be as reductive as contentions that the mixture and proportions of the four humors or that an "excess" and "defect" of Aristotelianly defined "passions" might account solely for any playwright's method of characterization. Let us, rather, summarize our contentions thus far by suggesting only that there were ways of talking about "personality," that there were certain assumptions abroad. There were orientations, derived from teachings in early childhood, in the light of which those *loci* which are often taken as statements of norms for Shakespearean attitudes might resume a more plausible status as speeches of self-revelation by the character who talks rather than as enunciation of authorial character theory. The statements of a Vives or an Anthony Munday, for instance, may be at odds with the views of one character whom we know well, but is it not possible that the precepts of this great preacher, Iago,

may deviate somewhat from his author's own comprehension of
what his culture understood about love?

I have look'd upon the world for foure times seven yeares, and
since I could distinguish betwixte a Benefit, and an Injurie: I never
found man that knew how to love himselfe. Ere I would say, I would
drowne my selfe for the love of a Gynney Hen, I would change my
Humanity with a Baboone. [664–69]

Iago's dialectic sounds somewhat familiar, yet not completely.

But we have Reason to coole our raging Motions, our carnall Stings,
or unbitted Lusts: whereof I take this, that you call Love, to be a
Sect, or Scyen.
Rod. It cannot be.
Iago. It is merely a Lust of the blood, and a permission of the will.
Come, be a man: drowne thy selfe? Drown Cats, and blind Puppies.
I have profest me thy Friend, and I confesse me knit to thy deserving,
with Cables of perdurable toughnesse. I could never better steed
thee then now. Put Money in thy purse. [682–92]

It is Iago's argument, we gather, that while sensuality, which he
defines as "love," may be immoral, a singleness of purpose in
making money is not. If his contentions seem to ignore the most
elementary contexts of the culture within which *Othello* was
produced, and if many critics view Iago as ultimately an "un-
sympathetic" figure in the play, there may be a more significant
connection between these facts than between Iago's speech and
Shakespeare's understanding of what traditionally had been argued about the bases of human personality in general.

The same comparison may be applied, too, to a more sweeping
and complex speech which appears only in Q2 *Hamlet* (1604/
1605) and which is used much more often than Iago's speeches
to derive observations about Shakespearean character theory.
Hamlet, waiting for the ghost to appear, has answered Horatio's
question about the ordnance and trumpets rather oddly. Claudius, we remember, had told the prince that there would be such
celebration to emphasize the designation of Hamlet as heir to

the throne, but when Horatio hears the noise, the prince tells him that it simply represents another of Claudius' drunken moods. Enlarging on drunkenness as the Danish vice, he expands on the matter by applying a moral.

> So oft it chaunces in particuler men,
> That for some vicious mole of nature in them
> As in their birth wherein they are not guilty,
> (Since nature cannot choose his origin)
> By their ore-grow'th of some complexion
> Oft breaking downe the pales and forts of reason,
> Or by some habit, that too much ore-leavens
> The forme of plausive manners, that these men
> Carrying I say the stamp of one defect
> Being Natures livery, or Fortunes starre,
> His vertues els be they as pure as grace,
> As infinite as man may undergoe,
> Shall in the generall censure take corruption
> From that particuler fault: the dram of eale
> Doth all the noble substance of a doubt
> To his owne scandle. [1604/1605Q; sigs. D–Dᵛ]

Throughout the play and by the circumstances of the plot, Hamlet is quite concerned about Heaven and Hell, expending a great number of observations on specifically Christian doctrine. It is therefore interesting that his discourse here has offered him two openings for speculation on the origins of "some vicious mole of nature" in men and that, in both cases, he has not adduced transcendentalist answers. Drawing on a theory of humors by his reference to the term "complexion" and reverting to a Gloucesterian fatalism in an allusion to "Fortunes starre" (less analytical than Rosalind's specification that "Fortune reignes in gifts of the world, not in the / lineaments of Nature") Hamlet astonishingly does not even mention the concept of original sin, which did indeed define men as "guilty" in their births. Surely the tense considerations which follow, the question of his father being in Hell, would offer a not-inappropriate context for such an allusion. And if the prince later suspects the ghost of being the Devil, it is interesting to speculate on the possibly unknowing pun which takes shape when we recall just this series of observations, for not long after, Hamlet will, in his own words, be dealing with an "olde Mole" that can "work it'h [sic] earth."

But this is not to seek an interpretation of the play: we are considering the validity of Hamlet's speech as *locus* for Shakespeare's own theory of human personality. We ask whether, if he had written according to Hamlet's prescriptions here, the dramatist might not have penned *Every Man in his Humour*. This is, of course, surmise which must give way to the more serious issue. Hamlet's speech has often served as the basis for a quasi-Aristotelian approach, according to which each of Shakespeare's tragic characters is to be understood as organized in terms of "one defect," of the "tragic flaw." And if our ready assent to such a view will not be qualified through the inconsistency of the prince's speech with the verbalized concepts which are the fabric of conversations throughout the play, we can at least admit, with equal justification, other speeches, other plays. If we wish to draw the poet's theory of personality quite literally from the theories in his characters' speeches, there is, for instance, much to contemplate concerning Shakespeare's awareness of "things hereditary" in the playful conversation between Polixines and Hermione as she tries to persuade him to prolong his visit. Sentimentally recalling his childhood friendship with Leontes, Polixenes observes:

> We were as twin'd Lambs, that did frisk i'th'Sun,
> And bleat the one at th'other: what we chang'd,
> Was Innocence, for Innocence: we knew not
> The Doctrine of ill-doing, nor dream'd
> That any did: Had we pursu'd that life,
> And our weake Spirits ne're been higher rear'd
> With stronger blood, we should have answer'd Heaven
> Boldly, not guilty; the Imposition clear'd,
> Hereditarie ours.
> *Her.* By this we gather
> You have tript since.
> *Pol.* O my most sacred Lady,
> Temptations have since then been borne to's: for

In those unfledg'd dayes, was my Wife a Girle;
Your precious selfe had then not cross'd the eyes
Of my young Play-fellow.
Her. Grace to boot:
Of this make no conclusion, least you say
Your Queene and I are Devils. [*Winter's Tale,* 130–48]

This harmless play of ideas can have no point unless the poet assumed that his audience was familiar with the concept of original sin, for Hermione develops the theme with her riposte that Polixines' metaphorical logic will give the two wives Satan's traditional function in Eden.

The truth is that no one speech by one character in any one play need necessarily be accepted as the paradigm of Shakespeare's theories or beliefs regarding human motivation, for were this so, then analysis would reduce itself to the question of the critic's choice of the play, character, and speech which he himself happened to prefer. Are we not equally free, if we espouse this manner of seeking out the dramatist's notion of the general sources of human problems, to revert to Ulysses on "degree"? And to those who do indeed espouse the Greek's presentation on the subject, may one not adduce Lorenzo's observations to Jessica who, as Shylock's daughter, we would probably not imagine as thoroughly schooled in transcendentalist amalgams? Like Ulysses, Lorenzo speaks of planets, but his conclusions differ. In a context which will later present Portia comparing candlelight to a good deed which shines in "a naughty world," Lorenzo explains to Jessica:

There's not the smallest orbe which thou beholdst
But in his motion like an Angell sings,
Still quiring to the young eyed Cherubins;
Such harmonie is in immortall soules,
But whilst this muddy vesture of decay
Doth grosly close in it, we cannot heare it. [2472–77]

In a play written earlier than Q2 *Hamlet,* it is Rosalind who speaks as suggestively as any character on the grounds of human emotion. Her response to Touchstone provokes consideration because she is speaking in a play whose textures include an old man, Adam, hostile brothers, and a Forest of Arden with Eden-like qualities that are reinforced by a serpent whose presence can tempt Orlando to a fratricide-by-omission. But it is Touchstone's joking which may strike those cultural chords familiar from our previous discussions and presumably not unheard by Rosalind.

wee that are true Lovers, runne into strange capers; but as all is mortall in nature, so is all nature in love, mortall in folly.
Ros. Thou speak'st wiser than thou art ware of.

[*As You Like It*, 835–38]

Hamlet's theory of a puzzling "defect," whatever Shakespeare's own attitude, is rather more naïve, it would seem, or at least is less comprehensive than the views of other characters who, we may assume, have equal right to speak.[30] And if we have previously adduced something about the common thought regarding human troubles in the Renaissance, let us confine ourselves at this point to the observation that, in Shakespeare's time, a certain language was used in connection with the problem of personality. Orientation toward or away from the transcendental, both concepts expressed by the term "love," appears to have been the analytic point of departure, the basis for consequent distinctions. A vignette of Julietta in *Measure for Measure* may not necessarily indicate Shakespeare's views, but it will again illustrate the

---

[30] The duke, preparing Claudio for death in MM, speaks to Hamlet's other concern, that of "complexion." Both this problem and that of "Fortunes starre"—the problem of planetary influence as conceived by Shakespeare's contemporaries—are placed in perspective by consulting D. C. Allen, *The Star-crossed Renaissance: The Quarrel about Astrology and its Influence in England* (Durham, 1941). Hamlet's musings on the puzzling defect are also usefully commented upon by the number of references to Adam in Shakespeare's work. The reader need merely scan the concordances under such heads as "corruption," "taint," "frailty," "Adam," and "Eve." Falstaff's play on the concept (1H4, 2171–74) is also appropriate: "Thou know'st in the state of Innocency, *Adam* fell: and what should poore *Jacke Falstaffe* do in the dayes of Villany? Thou seest, I have more flesh then another man, and therefore more frailty."

point in hand. For Duke Vincentio, in his role as therapist/
confessor, is intimating that Julietta's sense of guilt about her
pregnancy is not in itself sufficient. She must, we gather, make
sure that her affections reach back to their "anthropological
roots" in their instinctive attraction to the transcendental and
consequent hate for its antithesis.

> *Du.* Ile teach you how you shal araign your conscience
> And try your penitence, if it be sound,
> Or hollowly put on.
> *Jul.* Ile gladly learne.
> *Duk.* Love you the man that wrong'd you?
> *Jul.* Yes, as I love the woman that wrong'd him.
> *Duk.* So then it seemes your most offence full act
> Was mutually committed.
> *Jul.* Mutually.
> *Duk.* Then was your sin of heavier kinde then his.
> *Jul.* I doe confesse it, and repent it (Father).
> *Duk.* 'Tis meet so (daughter) but least you do repent
> As that the sin hath brought you to this shame,
> Which sorrow is alwaies toward our selves, not heaven,
> Showing we would not spare heaven, as we love it,
> But as we stand in feare.
> *Jul.* I doe repent me, as it is an evill,
> And take the shame with joy.
> *Duke.* There rest. [975–93]

3
Man and His Reflection

Julietta's and Vincentio's language, with which chapter 2 concludes, is not necessarily the usual transcendentalist grammar surrounding the concept of "love." The problem of studying the poet's work is not thereby simplified, for transcendentalist approaches to the phenomenon of human personality offer their own inherent complexities in any application to theories of fictionalized characters. For if we are at all concerned with, say, mental process, the mere matter of "describing" a man—without, that is, the glorifying adjectives sarcastically alluded to by a Hamlet—becomes a conceptual problem. After all, what were the theoretical possibilities? Within the system, a "correct" aspiration of personality involved subscription to some particular set of philosophic terms favored by one or another Renaissance school of thought: Platonism, Neo-Platonism, Neo-Stoicism, Aristotelianism, or Thomistic/Augustinian Anglicanism, to name a few. By their definitions, a man's character could only be saved, attain Beauty, climb Castiglione's quasi-Climacian and quasi-Aristotelian "stayre of love," advance in "virtue," or see "Reality" by certain socially evolved systems of psychological desiderata. On the other hand, if the personality, through the very fact of its humanity, indeed aspired but did not aspire to the approved transcendentalist goals, then the prevailing philosophical systems available in the early education of any potential playwright tended to reject such human effort, to describe it as a cultivation merely of one's earthliness, as the promulgation of that posited aspect of man's nature which, in the traditional language of one of the most popular Platonic treatises of the time, was simply to be dismissed as "bestial."

Too unluckie were the nature of man, if our soul (in the which this so fervent coveting may lightly arise) should bee driven to nourish it with that onely, which is common to her with beasts, and could not turne it to the other noble parte, which is proper to her. [Castiglione, sig. X5]

To aspire to Truth, or to live like a beast? Such an evaluative dichotomy was hardly promising as the basis for any innovations of character structuring in drama, and it is fortunate that this elementary distinction was sophisticated by the Renaissance mind. The resulting developments more clearly showed the nature of the possibilities as well as the limitations inherent in this theoretical impasse posed by transcendentalist assertions. One approach to the ancient concept of self-love, for instance, offered some room for maneuvering.

To love our selves is to cherish that Image which is given us by the true *Prometheus*; but Selfe-love is an advancing of that Image, above the same in other Men, whereas equall things should retaine equall honour, and so it becomes an hatefull Bough, or rather an accursed Root of the Tree of Pride. [*Pathomachia*, sigs. E2ʳ–E3]

This reference to "image"—whether or not we specifically associate the term with Platonism—suggests a way of thinking about characterization with greater flexibility than would otherwise be possible within the philosophical orders to which we have been attending. In fact, the contexts surrounding "image" shed some light on ways of looking at mental process. Thomas Lodge, the dramatist, uses the term "image" in his translation of Seneca's complete works. In "Epistle LVIII," where Seneca explains Plato's doctrine of ideas, it is significant that Lodge uses the correct form, εἶδος, from Aristotle, which Seneca did *not* employ in drawing a distinction between idea and imitation.

I have a will to make thy picture. Thou art the patterne of my picture, of which my mind gathereth some habit, which he will delineate in his worke. So that face which teacheth and instructeth me, and from which I derive my imitation, is *Idea*. Nature then, the mother of all things, hath an infinity of these patternes, as of men, of fishes, of trees, on which is drawne and exprest all that which she ought to do. The fourth place is given to an Image. But it behooueth thee to be very carefull in understanding what this Image is, and that thou lay the blame on *Plato* and not on me, as touching the difficultie of things. Yet is there nothing that is subtil, which is not accompanied with difficultie. Not long since I used the comparison of the Image which a Painter made. He when in colours he would paint *Vergil* to the life, beheld him. *Virgils* face was the *Idea*, and the patterne of his intended worke; but that which the Painter hath drawne from that visage, and that which he hath painted on his table is εἶδος, that is to say, an Image. Asketh thou me what difference there is? The one is the patterne, the other the figure, drawne from the patterne, and put upon the worke: the one is that which the Painter imitateth, and the other is that which he maketh.

Since it is Lodge, no doubt influenced by intervening traditions, who has added the extra definition to Seneca's text (which confined itself to the Latinized term *idos*), the function of "image" in such discourse becomes not only clear but also suggestive.[1] To incorporate this sense of "image," as did the author of the "Prometheus" quotation, into the language of personality theory was to elaborate the simplistic dichotomy of God/Beast into the more complex dualities of Platonistic argumentations.

To this effect, a Francis Bacon might be viewed developing the concept of εἶδος when he wrote that "by aspiring to a similitude of God in goodnesse or love, neyther Man nor Angell ever transgressed or shall transgresse. For unto that imitation we are called" (sig. 2Y4ᵛ). If we prefer to take a jaundiced view of Bacon's pietisms, we might make passing reference to a *locus* which no doubt will have already occurred to the student of the Renaissance familiar with the enormous popularity of *The Imitation of Christ*. Organized around the traditional concept of "imitation," of human personality as an "image," that little book presented material to which *The Courtier* offered perhaps only a more sophisticated descant:

---

[1] For further discussion on this point, see Barroll, "Some Versions of Plato in the English Renaissance," 229–30. The immediate citation is to L. A. Seneca, *The Workes*, trans. Thomas Lodge (London, 1614), sigs. 2A–2Aᵛ.

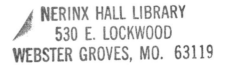

Accepte our soules, that be offred unto thee for a sacrifice. Burne
them in the lively flame that wasteth al grosse filthinesse, that after
they be cleane sundred from the body, they may be coupled with
an everlasting and most sweete bonde to heavenly beauty. And we
severed from oure selves, may be changed like right lovers into the
beloved. [sigs. Y2–Y2ᵛ]

"Be changed like right lovers into the beloved": is not all human
character required through this gesture of thought to become, in
effect, identical with something more than human, with some
theoretical entity? Regardless of the variety of dicta presented by
any given transcendentalist mode of thought or the tenets according to which such "entity" was defined, did they not hold in
common this offering, this concept? The measure of a man's
existence, whatever the ancillary ethical terms of individual systems, was the degree of human conformity to the dimensions of
one hypothetical "personality."

The relevance of the foregoing implication to the theoretical
bases for some evolutions of complex character depiction in English Renaissance tragedy will permit some obvious, though perhaps curious, inferences. If a man's "self" was to be thought of as
nonexistent through evading its imitation of, its "identification"
with God, Being, Essence, or Beauty, then it was as if a human
mind—and we still speak in terms of the possibilities for a
theory of dramatic character—could never be considered as inherently possessing that identity which one might today describe
as, say, "the inmost self." Rather, any human's claim to his own
"identity" was conditional upon his merging in some manner
with a hyper-personality. A man could only truly have a "self"
by his attainment of that essentially Proclean "oneness" with
Transcendental Being. Lacking this enosis, one had no "self," no
"identity," and though the concept was more obviously verbalis-
tic than some other kinds of personality theory, this possibly unconscious assumption was nevertheless as basic a premise of
Renaissance transcendentalism as is the quasi-mystical sense of
union implicit in twentieth-century dialectics wherein man, if he

understands his own "subconscious" desires and relates "positively" with his "environment," emerges as a psychologically "whole" person.

During Shakespeare's lifetime, and in writings which were to be sufficiently seminal to influence a Spenser and a Hooker to term Truth "Una" or "oneness," this conflict and paradox in the problem of human identity was present even in the most sophisticated statements. "For we are not one and integrated," observed Pico, "if we do not link together with a bond of virtue our senses, which incline to earth, and our reason, which tends to heavenly things." If we try to maintain such a perilous balance, then "We will be performing a juggling trick to those who see us, and among whom we live. The image will not conform to its exemplar."[2] And, as one might perhaps expect, Isabella becomes sententious on just this topic in her peroration to Angelo:

> But man, proud man,
> Drest in a little briefe authoritie,
> Most ignorant of what he's most assur'd,
> (His glassie Essence) like an angry Ape
> Plaies such phantastique tricks before high heaven,
> As makes the Angels weepe. [*Measure for Measure*, 874–79]

Whether or not the contexts of the drama render Isabella's words as insight, reemphasis, or cliché, the poet's familiarity with the concept of supreme Person, as suggested by such writers as Bacon and Pico, seems itself sufficiently clear. That imitation to which a man is called, Isabella implies, is too often debased by the actions of humanity. Through an ignorance that his affinity to God is reflected only by the state of his transcendentalist integration, man too often becomes "most assur'd" of another kind of self. His "imitation" becomes only an "aping," an animalistic

---

[2] Ficino, *De Ente*, 33. Relevant allusions to this concept may also be found in Thomas à Kempis, sigs. H6ᵛ–H7 and pass. Cf. John Robinson, *Observations Divine and Morall* (London, 1625), sig. L4; and Barnabe Barnes, *The Divels Charter* (London, 1607), sigs. L4ᵛ–M.

copying consisting of "phantastique" mortal "tricks," as with Pico; and the erring personality does not imitate in the most serious sense but merely parodies.[3]

Considered in its totality, the structure of thought implied by the theory of human affections and its summation in the terminology of love presented existential problems. The transcendentalist codes implicit in concepts of love warred with the problem of a purely human self-differentiation. The desideratum for the human personality was a purely verbal process of achieving a progressively stronger and widening dualism (as between "body" and "soul" or "heavenly" and "earthly" selves); and by this logic, any thought system not oriented toward Supreme Being was, by definition, "apart." Self-differentiation merely isolated man from that Supreme Unity which he was not supposed to be able to attain by himself in the first place. If he aspired solely to what we might now regard as the conditions of his own identity, a man was not "whole": he was isolated, alone, "nothing." To avoid this state of nullity, it was necessary to embrace, rather, the kind of outlook suggested by Thomas à Kempis when he quoted from St. Luke. Thus one might say:

For loving my selfe inordinatelie I cast awaie my selfe: but after once I sought and loved thee sincerelie, I both found thee, and my selfe, and by that love also I brought my selfe the more to nothing. [STC 23973; sig. H7ʳ]

And in effect, this is what Cardinal Wolsey does say in Shakespeare's *Henry VIII*:

Cromwel, I charge thee, fling away Ambition,
By that sinne fell the Angels: how can man then
(The Image of his Maker) hope to win by it?

[3] Indeed, the figure of the ape in Isabella's speech refers to traditional contexts which described man as attempting to "ape" God or ideally acting redeemed man in a travesty of true imitation. For a review of the "mirror-gazing ape," see H. W. Janson, *Apes and Ape Lore in the Middle Ages and the Renaissance* (London, 1952), chap. 7, especially 214–16ff.

Love thy selfe last, cherish those hearts that hate thee;
Corruption wins not more than Honesty. [2354–58]

The general implication of Renaissance transcendentalism for
the matter of character creation in drama was this inevitable
conclusion: human personality was not, in itself, an objectively
recognizable entity. Divorced from participation in a concept of
suprahumanity and its attendant value systems, the human party
to this divine contract was nothing. The proposition which accordingly faced the dramatist was that all facets of a purely
human personality were equivalent, finally, to mere aberration.

Nevertheless, it would have been clear enough to any active
observer of the human scene that mere mortal personality, whatever the ontological penalty, in fact did refuse to "aspire" in
accordance with those premises of conduct and attitude offered
as psychological optima. As a result, renderings by a subtle-
minded poet or "maker" of mimetic personalities might still
have been affected by his transcendentalist training. If the human refusal to "aspire" could be described as a misdirection of
the tendency to love, as an inability or unwillingness to redis-
cover a "natural" drive toward the transcendental, or as a vain
attempt to satisfy an innate yearning for Absolute Being through
the achievement of a purely "earthly" *enosis*, such descriptions
offered, even in their negations, no easy simplifications through
doctrine but rather a language complicated by paradox.

Within this general framework, to be specific, we can regard
any Renaissance theory of personality as a product of the tensions
inherent in that duality whereby transcendentalist thought
tended to contrast the concept of a hypothetical "personality"
(containing within itself all of the elements of "Ultimate
Truth") with "human nature." And if an impulse toward
Higher Being—the Plotinian homesickness, if we will—was taken
to be an element universal in this human nature, then the paradoxical proposition of simultaneous urges toward Absolute Being
and "things human" might suggest one shape for the concept of
stage character. As a study of the kinds and degrees of human

self-awareness within the brackets of such a dichotomy, "character invention" might seek to describe, for instance, how a given person was reconciling these disparate impulses, how an individual was translating his aspirations for infinity into the logic of his own time-bound consciousness. And as a corollary to the terms of such an imaginative inquiry, some attention would be given to the implications of such a translation both in the depiction of self-awareness in the character and in the consequences for the mimetic "society" surrounding him.

Even so, the dramatist's problem was still a difficult one since the task was, in effect, the problem of depicting negatives. The premises of transcendentalism tend to militate against the efficacy of human ability to relate to any concepts external to the "self." Theory might hold that man was instinctively striving for Supreme Entity, but the implicit injunction to visualize, to comprehend, and thus to understand such an intangible was, in effect, contradictory. The "correct" answers to the cognitional dilemma of man on earth, even if these answers varied according to the modulations of individual subsystems, had in common the inherent premise that one "visualized" correctly by not visualizing at all. Idea, Essence, Being, or God were by definition incomprehensible to the human mind; hence, any detailed analysis of the nature of that hypothetical "personality" which was to be imitated by man would be merely human and thus had to be fallible, "For our knowledge being but in part, it is not possible (saith Saint Austin) that our love can be perfect."[4]

Logically, the simpler way was to emphasize the "wrong" gestures of the human mind, the incorrect visualizations of the ultimately indefinable "right" way, for Beauty was indescribable, God could not be "seen," and so forth. As Thomas Lodge put it, "the eie of the soule (by which as *Plato* witnesseth, we behold the essence [sic] of God) is a great blessing of the Holy ghost." Through a neatly balanced antithesis Charron encapsulates the underlying premise. From a contemporary translation we gather

---

[4] Covell, sig. G4. The reference to Augustine is to the last chapter of *De Spiritu et Littera.*

that "God hath all good things in essence, all evill in understanding; man quite contrarie possesseth his good things by fantasie, his evill in essence."[5] God's essence is goodness, so to speak, but He totally understands evil.

The remark is importantly relevant, for it is finally a formulation such as this, such a particular use of the term "fantasie," which illustrates one way for a Renaissance dramatist to move not despite but by way of a transcendentalist orientation toward some of the problems posed by the phenomenon of human psychology. Operating as the common denominator of such scattered itemizations as the seven deadly sins or the triads of St. John (all of which, when construed *literatim*, presented only a series of superficial value statements), this theory of "fantasie," of, as it were, a negative human imagination, led to questions which might have relevance and use for the dramatist concerned with the construction of artificial "people" for a stage. Accordingly, some of the remarks generated by this way of observing the human mind or some of the theorists' musings which adopt these directions may be instructive. We observe Thomas Wright, for example, posing as one of the "Problemes concerning the substance of our Soules" the question of "How a corporall imagination" can "concurre to a spirituall conceit" (sig. V6ʳ–V7). It was a problem which Wright did not attempt to cope with, for he seems to have realized, with La Primaudaye, that "wee thinke, discourse, and judge of God according to our owne qualities and conditions: for we can never wholly separate our selves, from our selves" (sig. 4E4).

What follows in such a dialectic is, of course, the usual transcendentalist description of man as more easily convinced by those entities more readily conceptualized and most convinced by elements most easily and even literally seen. A Charron will accordingly observe:

Men are willing to use studie and indevour, rather for those things that have their effects and fruits glorious, outward, and sensible,

[5] Charron, sig. I6ʳ. For Thomas Lodge, see *Wits Miserie* (London, 1596), sig. G4.

such as ambition, avarice, passion, have than for wisedome whose effects are sweet, darke, inward, and lesse visible.

Wright implicitly concurs when he speaks of the "passions of the mind," for one of his four general reasons why men are more inclined to "vice" than to "virtue" lies in his concept of the negative human imagination, what he terms man's propensity for "present delectation." Specifically, if

that wee hope is future, that pleasure worldlings perceive, is present, sensible delectation feedeth the corporal substance of senses, and therefore we easily perceive it, but vertue affecteth the soule, not after so palpable and grosse manner, and therefore they despise it.[6]

In his ceaseless and instinctive striving for Absolute Being, man, in other and familiar words, stumbles over glamorous objects which he mistakes for this Being, and he rests with them. Such "transitory shows" have the advantage of comprehensibility; in any event they convey the illusion of attainment even if Truth does continue to be invisible and elusive.

Q. Why is *Man* more carefull of the body then the soule?
A. Because his minde stayeth wholely in things subject to sight: and because of the soule is invisible, it is the least of his care to furnish her with that which shee desireth.

The trend of such remarks will, of course, remind us of the familiar metaphor:

As they that have ill eyes, will mistake one man for another, specially when they somewhat resemble one another, though otherwise the difference between them be palpable; and so salute a stranger for a friend: so our pur-blinde hearts, deceived with that shadow of resemblance, which Vice sometimes carrieth of Vertue, doe oftentimes imbrace and receive grosse vices, in stead of glorious vertues.[7]

[6] Charron, sig. P6ʳ; and Wright, sig. Z7ʳ. Cf. N. A., *The Dignitie of Man* (London, 1616), sigs. F2–F2ᵛ.

[7] Daniel Dyke, *The Mystery of Self-Deceiving* (London, 1634), sig. N4ᵛ. For the question-answer statement immediately preceding Dyke's, see N. A., *Dignitie*, sig. B2.

Although these modes of speaking approach the human mind primarily through evaluation, their bent is highly suggestive in that their emphasis on correct "aspiration" reiterates a significant problem: man's conceptual relationship to orders of phenomena. Discourse may be in terms of such dichotomies as vice and virtue or body and soul, but the venerable metaphors emerging from such imperatives, those dualities of shadow versus substance or glittering shows versus naked truth, reveal one continuing transcendentalist insistence on the necessity of determining whether that which is perceived and desired by the mind or senses is "real" or "illusory." In effect, one important question about the human mind, though the query itself may have stemmed from certain characteristic value assumptions, had to do with how and whether the mind differentiated between symbol and sign. This being so, we must accordingly indicate, for the purposes of what will follow, how we define these terms. We here intend the term "sign" to mean any sensorially apprehensible "part" from which some whole can be inferred, no matter how such a "whole" might have been constituted in the first place. For example, the presence of a fox, in this case the defined "whole," may produce paw prints in the ground which therefore operate as "sign." From this sign we can infer that whole which is both the fox and his presence. We define "symbol" as any sensorially apprehensible entity which, by agreement, by custom, or by a purely personal series of associations, only serves as a representation of some conceptual structure. A cube, if it is so agreed, might accordingly operate as a "symbol" for God, for sloth, or for an ax handle, either as long as it is understood by all parties that such a representation-equation is in force or as long as such an item effects a *representation* for the individual, as in the case of what Othello's handkerchief comes to represent to him.[8]

---

[8] We should bear in mind that we are not here concerned with the psychology of private symbolism as it might exist, say, in Freudian dream theory. Rather, we follow, for example, Augustine's distinction between "natural" and conventional signs. The former class is suggested by the smoke which indicates the presence of a fire, while the latter are those "which living beings mutually exchange for the purpose of showing, as well as they can, the feelings of their minds, or their perceptions, or their

In order to clarify, through these terms, some of the directions possible for conceptions of fictive characterization which might have been derivable from the general dialectic under discussion, we note the crucial fact that transcendentalism did not really admit to the existence of signs. No sign, by definition, could ever indicate true reality, that "Reality" which was God or Being. If the transcendental optimum for human cognition was an ability to regard mortal life and the rest of the apprehensible universe as "shadow," a "glittering pageant," or a "waking dream," we deal rather with an insistence that those elements available to the senses and to the human reason—phenomena— be understood as signs not of the Real but of the un-Real. In its references to a lack of "faith" or to "worldly blindness," the transcendentalist approach to the concept of original sin finally characterizes itself by its assumption of an inborn and hereditary decay of human *perception* to a cognitive dependence on the process of mistakenly accepting phenomena as signs of reality. And although such acceptance might gain the intellectual favor of a Francis Bacon, the transcendentalist view *contra* was illustrated by the persistence of that ancient paradox phrased by St. John: "Faith is the substance of things to be hoped for, the evidence of things that appear not." In commenting on these words, Thomas Aquinas not only enunciates for us some of the ramifications to be derived from the paradox within the mode of thought which is our concern here, but he also indicates the breadth of traditional attention to the subject.

Accordingly, if anyone would reduce the foregoing words to the form of a definition, he may say that *faith is a habit of the mind, whereby eternal life is begun in us, making the intellect assent to what is non-apparent.* In this way faith is distinguished from all other things pertaining to the intellect. For when we describe it as *evidence*, we distinguish it from opinion, suspicion and doubt, which do not make the intellect adhere to anything firmly; when we go on to say, *of*

---

thoughts" (*De Doctrina*, II, 1–2, as translated in *Nicene and Post-Nicene Fathers of the Christian Church*, ed. Philip Schaff [Buffalo, 1887], II, 535–36).

things that appear not, we distinguish it from science and understanding, the object of which is something apparent. . . . Whatever
other definitions are given of faith are explanations of this one given
by the Apostle. For when Augustine says that *faith is a virtue
whereby we believe what we do not see (Tract.* XL, super *Ioann.,*
VIII, 32) . . . these all amount to the same as the Apostle's words.[9]

By such tokens, it is clear that any mental process which lacks
this transcendentalist faith might, in effect, define itself as a
tendency to confuse sign with symbol. If they lacked "faith,"
men would inevitably conclude that their minds were the measure of all things (of all "reality"), and this was as much as to
claim for their own materially oriented reasoning processes an
ability to infer all existence merely from phenomena. Phenomena,
in other words, would operate for and be accepted by such men
as signs of reality. But in the transcendental view, all phenomena
were illusory. They could have no value as signs of a Being
which by definition was apprehensible neither through the senses
nor through the intellect. Hence, any pursuit by "fallen man" of
phenomena as if they were indeed signs would simply emerge as
the pursuit of whatever might strike the materialist perception
as plausibly a sign. From the transcendental viewpoint, was this
not as much as to say that phenomena had the effect merely of
representing signs of Being to the material mind, that phenomena
operate as *symbols?* It is one thing for a group of hunters simply
to decide that all stones in the snow could stand for, could
symbolize a paw print; it is something else again to search for
stones as a means of hunting the fox, to take the stones under
the tree as signs that the fox has stood there. Elements in such
a comparison can also be taken to have applied to the problem
of human perception in its hunt for transcendental Being. Transitory existence contained a multiplicity of phenomena. Since the
number of symbols therefore could be legion, the problems of
human endeavor theoretically could be formulated in terms of
the manner in which a man's thinking could relate to the con-

[9] See Aquinas, *Summa Theologica,* XV, Q.4, a.1, as translated in *Basic
Writings,* ed. Anton C. Pegis (New York, 1945), II, 1094ff.

figuration of phenomena that precipitated his inevitable illusions of a "reality" based upon the symbolizing process. If, to find the fox, hunter A seeks stones while hunter B seeks blackberries, it is then not so much a question of who is "right" as why each believes as he does, why each clings to his own kind of "illusion."

The ultimate significance of such distinctions for any theory of character in Renaissance dramaturgy will, however, reside in their relevance to the general proposition of human identity. By such terms, human "confusion" could be construed as man's tendency, when perceiving his own consciousness, to believe that this perception of his "self" was the perception of sign. But if "cogito ergo sum" was indeed to define a future ontology, transcendentalism, conversely, would have argued that a Cartesian theory of being was ultimately an exhibition of human bias. Man's sense of self was not, after all, a sign of his "real" existence; it was a sign of his potential for identity with the hypothetical "personality," with Absolute Being which was the only Reality. To mistake an illusory earth-self for something "real" was unknowingly to employ one's sense of consciousness as a symbol for one's identity.[10] And from this viewpoint, fallen man's psychic activity on earth could be construed as a grasping for symbols in the apprehensible world to support the purely symbolic value which he attached to his own mere awareness.

If we consider how this dialectic might have shaped efforts at fictional characterizations for the stage, the Renaissance depiction of a "mind" could be conceived of, in its blueprint stage, as the imagining of what orders of phenomena might convey to some fictive individual his sense of unity with Being, the unconscious goal of all men. Transcendental theory, in other words, could have encouraged an author to consider what particular formulation and consequent manipulation of purely personal

---

[10] The relevance of this line of thought is also illustrated for the Renaissance mind in the old theory of the "king's two bodies." In this theory of kingship "self," as it were, could only be translated through the paradox of representing as a physical duality the king's simultaneously transcendental and nontranscendental role. See E. H. Kantorowicz, *The King's Two Bodies* (Princeton, 1957).

symbols might serve to differentiate a specific man from the total of human beings on earth, all of whom "aspire." And given the fact that "by nature" all men approached aspiration sensorially, the vagaries observed in human personality might have appeared formulable as various kinds of failure to distinguish between sign and symbol. The mechanics of Renaissance stage characterization—that process of character structuring which implies, or from which we can at least infer character analysis—might, finally, have been tantamount to the structuring of hypothetical and individualized perception theories.

How far any individual dramatist might have proceeded in these terms must, of course, be established through the examination of individual plays. We would not expect the conditions of drama necessarily to lend themselves to lengthy exposition on such a subject. But if we allude to theory alone, one playwright did offer a statement which indicates his sense of the human condition as a problem in perception. Although the elements of Cyril Tourneur's attitude may be found in his tragedies, the tortuous verse of his long poem, *The Transformed Metamorphosis*, offers a more extended commentary.

> What dreadfull sight (O) do mine eyes behold?
> See, frosty age, that should direct aright,
> The grassie braine (that is in vice so bold)
> With heedie doctrine and celestiall light;
> Hath bin conversing with hells taper, night,
> Whose divelish charmes, like *Circes* sorcerie,
> Have metamorphosde *Eos* Eonie.
>
> *Apolloe's* herauld, that was wont to cheare,
> Night-wounded soules with bright celest'all raies:
> Faire *Phosphorus* (whose looke was wont to feare
> Infernall hagges, that haunt frequented wayes,
> To drawe the soule to hell that wandring strayes[)];
> Is metamorphosde to a torch of hell:
> And makes his mansi'on-house blacke horrors cell.
>
> Whose deepe foundation's raisde from *Phlegeton*,
> The fi'rie river of blacke *Orcus* hall:

Whence pillers rise, which do themselves upon
Quadrangle wise, uphold *Erebus* wall:
Worldes trustlesse trust, soules unmistrusted fall.
Birds, vines and floures, and ev'ry sundry fruite
Do compasse it, for best that place they sute.

For since the spirit the bodies prisner,
Of heav'nly substance wholy is compact:
And since the flesh the soules imprisoner,
Of excrementall earth is wholy fact:
Since this with that it selfe cannot contract,
Needes must the soule (the earthly prison doubled:
For all earths pleasures slime) be smothered.

From out the lake a bridge ascends thereto,
Whereon in female shape a serpent stands,
Who eyes her eye, or views her blew vain'd brow,
With sence-bereaving gloses she inchaunts,
And when she sees a worldling blind that haunts
The pleasure that doth seeme there to be found:
She soothes with Leucrocutanized sound.

Thence leades an entrie to a shining hal,
Bedeckt with flowers of the fairest hew,
The Thrush, the Lark, and nights-joy nightingale,
There minurize their pleasing laies anew,
This welcome to the bitter bed of rue;
This little roome, will scarce two wights containe,
T'enioy their joy, and there in pleasure raigne.

But next therto adjoines a spacious roome,
More fairely farre adorned then the other;
(O woe to him at sin-awhaping doome,
That to these shadowes hath his mind giv'n over.
For (O) he never shall his soule recover:
If this sweet sinne still feedes him with her smacke:
And his repentant hand him hales not backe.[11]

---

[11] See Tourneur, *The Works*, ed. Allardyce Nicoll (London, 1930), 61–
62. One assumes that "grassie" in the third line refers to the usual concept
"all flesh is grass"; but see Nicoll, 1, 157 n. "Leucrocutanized" Nicoll derives from Pliny's *Leucrocuta* a beast which could utter human sounds. The

To apply such a theory of human perception to the practice of a specific characterization was simply to follow the corollaries. If man, looking into himself, perceived not Being but merely an illusion of his own existential validity, if he relied upon mere symbols rather than faith, and if he was attempting to achieve some sensorial equivalent of unity with Being, the dimensions of his earthly awareness were convincing enough. With a yen for wealth, riches might well seem the *Summum Bonum* with which one might unite one's self, for here was a "being" which could at least be perceived. Or instead of wishing to elevate one's personality in order to become as much as possible like Christ and so, in *Imitatio* theory, to become Christ—to reside in Him—one might attempt some purely apprehensible version of elevation. One might wish to become a king.[12]

---

derivation is logical since the emphasis in these lines is on humanity's ability to deceive itself by its very humanity.

[12] See footnote 10 in this chapter.

4
The Shakespearean Approach

M an's rage for image, this self-contradictory teleology so rich in possibilities for dramatic characterization, had been described in metaphor as old as the "glasse" of 1 Corinthians 12:12 and as "new" as Plato's myth of the cave, which was so popular in the English Renaissance.[1] Indeed, Plato's myth is especially useful, as well as pertinent, in picturing how a man might mistake his sense of selfhood through the contemplation not of his real self—of his soul or whatever equivalent element might be named in any individual subdialectic of transcendentalism—but of the shadow he saw on the wall. We may, in fact, expand upon the metaphor here by observing that, in terms of characterizations made possible by a philosophy such as we have been tracing, man's shadow might be seen as distorting him not merely because shadows have their own typically attenuated and bodiless natures but also because his shadow might be further distended by the costumes in which he preferred to dress: the robes of the rich man, the armor of the soldier, the crown and other habiliments of a king. In short, an approach to specific character construction would have been to imagine an individual who gathered his sense of what he "was" not from the degree of his conformity to the transcendental "Exemplar" but from his preference for ways of relating to what could be observed by the senses or by earthly ratiocination. Defining what he "was," for instance, in terms of what he thought he could "do," he would replace those difficult intangibles demanded by the transcendentalist theory of what constitutes true "self" with his preferences or his mere earthly expertise.

That Shakespeare may have been sensitive to the possibilities of such an approach to character construction is suggested by a

---

[1] See Erasmus, *Praise of Folie*, sig. I4; and William Baldwin's *Treatise* where the motif is explored in the section entitled "Of Parables and Semblables" (especially in reference to Hermes, Socrates, and Plato).

passing glance at Othello. "Speak of me as I am," he tells Lodo-vico at the end, and it is the immediate enactment of "I am" which may instruct us. Othello's justification of "self" is, in its final moments, a most graphically enacted recollection of stab-bing the Turk who had once traduced the state: "I tooke by th'throat the circumcised Dogge, / And smoate him, thus" (3666–67). Are we not reminded of a previous moment in the play?

> If I once stir,
> Or do but lift this Arme, the best of you
> Shall sinke in my rebuke. [1327–29]

In both cases, Othello summarizes the assertion of self into the lifting of the weaponed arm. The total characterization of the Moor is not, of course, quite so simplistically conceived, but the foregoing statements may allow us to generalize if we correlate them with Othello's frequent descriptions of himself as a man of war. Stated in one set of terms, we see portrayed on the stage a character with some personal commitment to the concept of battle, in which he believes he excels by virtue of his strong right arm. But matters are carried further than this because of the consequent equation depicted in the hero's mind. In transcen-dentalist metaphor, is it not as if the shadow which Othello sees on the wall of the cave is filled out with the shadow of armor, that "existence" itself tends to become interwoven with soldier-ship? To phrase the matter in other terms, the whole question of Othello's identity seems formulated not according to the as-sumption of "self" as an imitation of hypothetical "personality" (an imitation only incidentally engaged in earthly war as, per-haps, with Henry V) but according to the concept of "self as warrior." From the transcendentalist viewpoint, at least, it is as if Othello's propensities are depicted in the play as having led him to change the "grammar" of his self-definition. His imperfect perception does not suggest to him, say, that "I try to remember I am part of that hypothetical 'personality' which my worldly blindness does not allow me completely to imitate, but I am only partially successful for, on earth, my orientation is to meaning-less, sublunary activity, especially in the direction of armed com-bat, in which I have a certain skill." Rather, Othello's cognition is portrayed as having led him, in effect, to the statement "I am a Warrior," as if "Warrior" were not merely a societal role on earth but actually an order of Being.[2] It is the tangible of soldier-ship which operates in his perception as some sensible version or transliteration of intangible and transcendental Being for which there is no sign.

It would, of course, be absurd to insist that Othello should have "seen" himself in the stilted terms we have just suggested as a theoretical alternative. The hypothetical statement which our passing glance at Othello led us to formulate can be justified in its seemingly moralistic bent, however, through recalling that modern characterizations can be said to derive coherence from postulates similarly open, in careless discourse, to imputations of moralism. Those sociological and psychological theories which have been evolved to deal with a picture of the human mind as a discrete entity operating within a vast ecological complex have shaped their own axioms. But if the importance of experiences in early childhood or the truth of man's descent from anthropoid ancestors, for example, are concepts implicit in some novels of the early twentieth century, the student of character structure will not consequently assert that the narrator of *A la Recherche du Temps Perdu* therefore *should* have had more psychologically sophisticated parents or that a Kurz *should* have read his Darwin before venturing into the African bush. Lagerkvist's dwarf blandly recalls being sold by his mother. It is not then a question of our insisting that he consult a psychiatrist, there being no psychiatrists, in any event, in this twentieth-century version of a Renaissance culture. Rather, it is a question of the reader em-ploying his awareness of modern psychological cliché (the impli-cations of which are taken for granted) as one of many elements of information used by the author to contribute to our under-

----

[2] For a representative awareness of certain problems as formulable in terms of "modes of being," see Ficino, *De Ente*, pass.

standing of the character Nanno. Similarly, the interesting element in the character construction of Othello is not, for example, whether God likes him but how the hero may be depicted in action as a character in a period when transcendentalism tended to emphasize human perception as an important element in the theory of personality.

We can consider some more obviously symmetrical instances of Shakespeare's characters presenting aesthetic elements formulable in a language such as the one with which we have been concerned. These characters may cause us to ponder whether it is not the very bravura of many of Shakespeare's tragic heroes which sometimes diverts us from the fundamental issue of perception implicit in the mere variety of their assertions. Hamlet, though speaking in a passionate moment, asks:

> What is a man
> If his chiefe good and market of his time
> Be but to sleepe and feede, a beast, no more:
> Sure he that made us with such large discourse
> Looking before and after, gave us not
> That capabilitie and god-like reason
> To fust in us unusd. [1604/1605Q; sig. X3ʳ]

Although this statement can also be regarded as a *locus classicus* for "Shakespeare's" theory of human character, let us withhold opinions on such a matter if only because it is difficult to demonstrate which characters indeed do "speak for" the poet, or when they do so. Rather, let us observe that at this moment in the play, a character is in the act of glorifying reason, praising it, indeed, in much the same terms as Cicero used to exalt "letters" in Montaigne's example (alluded to on p. 104) of man's propensity for glorifying that to which he is devoted. Yet we do not necessarily need a Montaigne to cause us to wonder whether Hamlet may be praising God-like reason, for his other speeches and actions in the play seem to present him as one who regards the thinking process as his strongest suit. We may even be intended to understand, if an element in Renaissance characterization is some postulate concerning one's conception of "self," that the act of discursive thought is the criterion according to which a Hamlet is to be understood as defining his own personality. If a sense of the self, in other terms, relies for its objectification on the sense of doing something (an admittedly ironic consideration in this particular play), Hamlet's picturing process seems to involve performing the "act" of thought. The fact that Hamlet later seems to reverse this concept of "looking before and after" by enunciating faith in some sort of providence will not necessarily interpret the character or the play for us, but the very depiction of this tendency to reversal may alert us to some of the possibilities in Renaissance perception portrayal. We are observing, on the whole, a fiction, a characterization partially delineated as the effort of an individual to define the terms by which he can observe his sense of his own existence. His effort is challenged by situational devices only adumbrated by one of his consequent queries: "To be or not to be?"

If an Othello seemed willing to take his rest in an objectification of "self" somewhat different from that suggested by Hamlet's words, will not these divergences precipitate for the morally preoccupied the question of choosing between these two ideal forms of "being" as the statement of Shakespeare's own theory of man? Othello's words picture the strong right arm; Hamlet's picture a "reason" equipped with eyes, as it were, which can look before and after, a capacious entity with "large discourse." But if we are concerned with characterization, our gaze is perhaps more steadily maintained if we waive the espousal of any ethic, the search for any *locus,* and instead observe method. We will not then be surprised or dialectically inconvenienced by a more direct and symmetrically posed contradiction of Hamlet's temporary definition. Macbeth's words project a somewhat different assumption as to what man is. His wife has taunted him for a "Coward" in his vacillation about Duncan's murder, and Macbeth exclaims, "I dare do all that may become a man." "Who dares do more, is none," he persists.[3] From this we gather the

[3] The F reading, "Who dares no more, is none," whether in error or not, has little effect on the point at hand.

polarities of his own private universe wherein it is not a Hamlet's definition of man, a large discourse of reason, but a noncoward-ice, a quality of (battlefield) daring which constitutes a man and, by implication, Macbeth's objectified identity. To be queasy about asserting this military expertise on a sleeping man is no reason, he seems to imply, to be judged "Coward." His emphasis on this particular definition of his self, of his being as a man is, in fact, stressed to such an extent that the strategy of the charac-terization sometimes requires the play to present, as does *Hamlet*, opportunities for restatements of the position. The ghost of Banquo generates further insistences, does it not?

> What man dare, I dare:
> Approach thou like the rugged Russian Beare,
> The arm'd Rhinoceros, or th'Hircan Tiger,
> Take any shape but that, and my firme Nerves
> Shall never tremble. Or be alive againe,
> And dare me to the Desart with thy Sword:
> If trembling I inhabit then, protest mee
> The Baby of a Girle. Hence horrible shadow,
> Unreall mock'ry hence. Why so, being gone
> I am a man againe. [1376–85]

But Hamlet's definition of man seems to allow him to cope with ghosts, refusing as he does early in the play (and refusing rather firmly) to follow the lead of the specter one step farther. It is irrelevant to ask whose definition of man is correct, for the term, in any event, operates as the verbal externalization of dif-ferent senses of self. Macbeth knows too well for his own good when it is time for swordplay; Hamlet is not quite so sure. But he can ponder suicide at various lengths, while Macbeth shows not the least desire to take his own life, even if he may have many more plausible reasons at the end of the play. Despite his enunciations of despair, his "tomorrow and tomorrow" speeches, he will not "play the Roman Foole." While each character is shown as equally committed to what he regards as his grounds of identity, the structurings of the respective plays produce challenges to these conceptualizations, stimuli occurring in numbers sufficient to suggest some elements of artistic emphasis on the matter of self-objectification in these particular portraits. While his sense of entity revolves around a concept of God-like reason, Hamlet's proneness to accidental circumstances and casual slaughters is the reality presented by a play in which few conscious plans are ever successfully realized. And while, in Macbeth's depicted thought, "to be" is to be a man/warrior, while he is constantly presented as arguing for the reality of this manhood, the play itself surrounds him with other dimensions of the term. We observe his wife, who wishes to turn "man," to unsex herself; and we observe the "nonman," Macduff, not of woman born, who ultimately cows the "better part of man" in the hero who has picked his way through the continual irony of the term "monster" applied to the exercise of his self-styled manliness by others in the play.

The ultimate significance of these brief samples, if we admit them as not wholly impertinent to our sense of what transpires in the plays, lies in the dialectical orientation which they reveal. We observe a sensitivity to the distinctions inherent in that process whereby a fictional personality is depicted as possessing a teleology which arises from a certain set of traits, characteristics presented, in turn, as having an effect on the manner in which the figure may relate to the particular ontological mode he has chosen. When these samples also suggest that a character might be emphasized through the dimension of his abstract reasoning whose efficacy is measurable according to "objective" (transcendental) reality, we may say that from some points of view the process of Renaissance characterization must be regarded as "intellectually" conceived. The term is not worth adhering to except as illustration, however, for there is little intellectual difference between the propositions of "character as perception" before Shaftesbury and Locke and "character as perception" in the nineteenth and twentieth centuries. The terms merely differ. To depict a figure as capable of destroying himself because he is not "aware" in post-Freudian terms may be to carve from a different model, but the center of gravity does not appear too removed from the thrust of Renaissance interests. To assume that there were different planes of reality and that a human inability to perceive these differences properly could produce ratiocination that was self-destructive was merely to approach the problem of self-consciousness from a different and possibly more obviously intellectual tangent.

In terms of these distinctions, there can accordingly be a variety of general mimetic consequences, at least in the case of Shakespeare. Going beyond our previous consideration of how some characters used certain words to define their "selves," a more general overview of some Shakespearean situations will finally suggest, or at least adumbrate, valid reasons for assuming the poet's concern with the broader dimensions of a character theory shaped by transcendentalist dialectic. If problems of external perception, the relation of the mind to exterior phenomena, were a familiar issue in transcendentalist musings on the problem of human personality, elements in *Hamlet*, to eschew the more obvious examples of *Othello* or *Macbeth*, are resonant of such a concern. A ghost appears, and immediately the question arises as to what the ghost "means," what it stands for. Any critic is aware of the possibilities: the ghost may be the devil decked out in the form of Hamlet's father, or he may in fact be the spirit of the hero's parent, but this particular issue is not pertinent here. Rather, we stress that this particular dilemma is only one of a number of problems presented to the audience concerning Hamlet's relationship to the question of representation itself. This emphasis reveals itself at once when the hero appears at the coronation dressed in black. His mother asks him why his grief "seemes" so special a case to him. "Seemes Madam?" he answers, "Nay, it is: I know not Seemes." Purely customary forms of mourning indeed might seem, he points out to her, but such forms cannot denote him truly.

> These indeede Seeme,
> For they are actions that a man might play:
> But I have that Within which passes show;
> These, but the Trappings, and the suites of woe. [257–67]

It is interesting to note that although Hamlet insists on distinctions between facts and their manifestations, he is nevertheless conducted by the author through a series of representational dilemmas which he is not always allowed to meet with the most rigid logic. The ghost, for instance, may indeed be intended as Hamlet's father, but Horatio's remarks offer ambiguity.

> What art thou that usurpst this time of night,
> Together with that Faire and Warlike forme
> In which the Majestie of buried Denmarke
> Did sometimes march. [59–62]

This curiously careful distinction, which suggests that the ghost's appearance may not in itself define its nature, is reiterated in Hamlet's reaction.

> Be thou a Spirit of health, or Goblin damn'd,
> Bring with thee aires from Heaven, or blasts from Hell,
> Be thy [intents] wicked or charitable,
> Thou com'st in such a questionable shape
> That I will speake to thee. [625–29]

"Shape" and "forme" emerge into consideration in an early sequence and are maintained as continual problems for the character Hamlet, even when it is not a question of ghosts. Although, after the horrifying news, Hamlet writes, with a surprising naïveté which we may regard as madness if we wish, that "one may smile, and smile, and be a villaine," the poet does not seem to depict him as remembering this lesson. Rather, Hamlet is made to construct the "mousetrap" play as an instrument for determining the king's criminality by offering a view of his countenance, by showing whether or not Claudius "looks" guilty. The issue is joined, however, by the fact that Claudius does not appear unduly disturbed when, during the dumb show at the very beginning of the performance, he sees enacted before him the very core of his crime, the pouring of poison into a sleeping man's ear. "Have you heard the argument?" he asks Hamlet during the brief intermission, "is there no offence in't?" But Claudius does indeed call for lights (as Queen Elizabeth once did) at the point in the play where one Lucianus, described by Hamlet as "Nephew to the King," enters alone and begins speaking murderous lines. Waiving all the interpretative arguments which contemplation of this whole rich scene could produce, we must agree that Claudius has departed at only one of a number of points in the playlet which Elizabethans might have regarded as offensive to a newly married sovereign with a troublesome nephew. The king, of course, is a murderer, and the play has indeed elicited guilt; but although we see this guilt expressed in his private attempts to pray, we have seen little else. Knowing he is guilty through his own remark prior to the play, we are aware that during the dumb show he has stood his ground. And having survived what one might imagine was the stunning onslaught of seeing poison poured into the ear of a sleeping man, it is conceivable that the king consequently exercised his own tactical choice for the moment of his public exit. Certainly, those not privy to the secret have not been made suspicious. Rather, it is important to observe that Hamlet is reproved for having offended the king; and unless we conjure a conspiracy which includes Polonius, Gertrude, and Hamlet's schoolmates, it is significant that none of these characters seem puzzled by the king's displeasure.

For Hamlet, however, this sequence is incontrovertible proof not only of Claudius' guilt but also of the ghost's identity since the hero will unhesitatingly refer to the apparition as "My father" when it appears in Gertrude's bedroom. Even omitting the whole matter of the king's guilt, can we say that the issues suggested in the words first spoken by Horatio and Hamlet to the specter will necessarily be resolved by proof of the ghost's veracity, a truthfulness which anticipates that of the witches? Not one but a series of questions have been precipitated by the "sencible and true avouch" of those eyes which have seen the apparition, and the questions have various possible answers. If the ghost is telling the truth, is it therefore Hamlet's father? Or conversely, if it is lying, is the ghost therefore not Hamlet's father? And if it is indeed telling the truth, are the ghost's commands for revenge to be obeyed? If they are to be obeyed, is this so because the commands come from a ghost or because they come from Hamlet's father? And in either case, why? The prince, however, is depicted as cutting through all these questions, dismissing some standards for perception in the case of the ghost to espouse others and basing his choice on the same criterion of "seeing" which he brings to the activity surrounding the dumb show.

Such problems continue to be thrust at Hamlet, even after the dumb show, for when the opportunity presents itself (or is presented by Shakespeare), the prince refrains from killing Claudius because the king is on his knees and *appears* to be praying. But immediately following Hamlet's departure from the king's closet, two lines spoken by Claudius inform us that he has been unsuccessful in his effort to repent, that he has not attained to that holy state which his visible posture suggested. The irony is capped when Hamlet kills Polonius because his mere form behind the arras *seems* to be the king's. Rather than persist in this vein, however, we may suggest that these obvious motifs are among the more convincing examples of how a transcendentalist orientation might influence one kind of character structuring, at least in the more elementary phases. By weaving a relationship between Hamlet and the problem of representation, the poet uses the concept of perception to build one kind of aesthetic nexus which may serve as the pattern for mimetic complexities ranging from Hamlet's confrontation with the actor's Hecuba speech to the prince's interpretation of the difference which seems to exist between "to be" and "not to be."

Hamlet's famous soliloquy will remind us that the general approach to characterization which has been our concern may order a set of problems oriented not only to external but also to internal corollaries to transcendentalist emphases on perception. We have already glanced at self-definition as an aspect of this matter; here it is only a question of noting that this phase of cognition theory might also be used in characterization. Such theory could conduct a figure through the multiple possibilities of dramatic sequence which result when the hero concludes that things can be gained, effects accomplished, by an assertion of what he takes to be his self. Macbeth has only to be a man and he will gain a throne; Hamlet has only to be a reasonable man and he will set right the time which is out of joint. Perhaps so, except when dialectical confusions intrude upon the initial business of self-definition. One consequently finds structured into Shakespeare's characters a tendency to pit those abilities which are used to define the self against objects of desire which may not only be illusory in strictly transcendental terms but are also not necessarily to be gained by the particular abilities in question. The resultant confusions are, in effect, a major portion of characterization in many cases. For example, Coriolanus' frustrations are relatively amenable, per se, to analysis, but those of Hamlet or Brutus are rendered in a more complex fashion. To have a firm concept of the self is perhaps to have confidence in those talents according to which one defines the self; but Brutus and Hamlet, in a development of the initial, basic proposition, are rendered as sufficiently unsure. Their problems are intensified not only by alternate possibilities but also by the author forcing them to cope with those who suggest for them other identities. In order to realize their selves, it is hinted that they must kill a Claudius or a Caesar. Cassius is perhaps more obvious—or at least more explicit—in this vein than is Hamlet's unearthly adviser.

> *Bru.* Into what dangers, would you
> Leade me *Cassius?*
> That you would have me seeke into my selfe,
> For that which is not in me?
> *Cas.* Therefore good *Brutus*, be prepar'd to heare:
> And since you know, you cannot see your selfe
> So well as by Reflection; I your Glasse,
> Will modestly discover to your selfe
> That of your selfe, which you yet know not of. [157–65]

What Brutus finally discovers and what Cassius thinks he discovers, in both senses of the verb, are sufficiently different to furnish one of the dominant ironies of the play: Cassius himself will become the target for that sense of personal honor which Brutus, through Cassius' midwifery, has realized within himself as the conceptual means whereby murder can be effected. We finally observe a Brutus placed by the dramatist in the position of pitting an image of self—defined, created, and interpreted according to his own propensities—against the complexities of the external political realities surrounding him in a structure which he cannot quite comprehend through the mental *persona* which he adopts.

The very adherence of a Brutus to his concept and his growing insistence on the validity of his own views, even to the extent of overruling Cassius' projected tactics for the battle of Philippi, seem to be the complementary aspect of self-realization from the transcendentalist viewpoint. It is as if the stronger the subscription to one configuration of self, the more unremitting the insistence on the reality of those perceptions induced by the personal conceptual commitment. *Timon of Athens* is most obviously suggestive of the point, for if this play strikes some critics as rudimentary in artistic execution, the lineations are at least pronounced. Timon's *volte face* has comprehended two diametrically opposed perceptions of reality just as his two different senses of self have generated radically differing analyses of the objective world around him. Behind his benevolence lay the self-portrait of "benefactor to mankind" until disillusionment with what the world really is produced the internal picture of "prophet of universal corruption." If this complementary dependence of internal and external perception is here presented to an audience in rather an elementary manner, we can glance at *Lear*, to which the Greek play has often been compared. At the risk of oversimplification, we can see one side of the coin of perception in the old king's misapprehension of phenomena, which results in the exile of Cordelia and Kent. Is not the other side adumbrated by Regan's remark? Concurrently, Lear has ever but slenderly known himself. Losing what he has erected as self, his kingship, he begins to "perceive" via modes of insanity which are a frenzied and purely verbal attempt to reorder external reality so that it will conform with that alternate self (or those alternate selves) which may therefore be realized in this spinning coin, in this conceptual circle. "Down from the waist they are centaurs"; but also, "Is man no more than this?"

PART II

PYGMALION IN PLATO'S CAVE

5
The Human Image in Renaissance England

It is our purpose to proceed to the problem of character in Shakespeare's tragedies by raising questions somewhat different from those which constituted the bulk of inquiry in Part I. We are now concerned with a dialectic which will precipitate such questions as "what happens to Macbeth?" or "what constitutes the tragedy of Hamlet?" These queries differ from the ones which we have posed before because in the final analysis the study of characterization, as opposed to the study of cultural presuppositions about personality in a specific historical period, is a study of artistic process. We suppose the dramatist attempted to solve the problem of characterization not by presenting "very human" actions and reactions at random but by arranging an ordered series of behavioral phenomena related to some kind of sequence (or process) so as to convey to an audience that important fiction, the illusion of a "person."

As historical critics we often lose sight of the importance of this issue of individuation. To bring a figure upon the stage exhibiting a series of "lifelike" attitudes and "human" reactions may theoretically achieve (as for eighteenth-century criticism) "liveliness of impression," but the artistic result can only be a generalized "mankind." Individuality itself is a function of a system of process, but the distinction between the exhibition of random human traits and the presentation of characterization often becomes lost in our analyses through a defect of an otherwise necessary virtue. The scholar, observing some figure on stage in the grip of an emotion, may be led by a form of historicism to view the situation according to the restricted terms of, say, Elizabethan faculty psychology. Thus if a Renaissance character is wildly angry, he may be describable as having the "mother"; if he dies of grief because, like Enobarbus, he says that his heart has "dried up," the historian can refer to the handbooks to retrieve the lexical meaning of such a term. Having performed such translations, however, scholarly research often exhibits a tendency

to equate symptom with cause. Cassius, for example, may excuse
himself for the passion resulting from his mother. To define the
mother as a sixteenth-century term is one matter, but to aver
that the mother is all we need understand about Cassius' anger
is a gesture of the same order as attributing Willy Loman's death
to his inability to control his automobile. By the same petard,
if not for reasons strictly analogous, it is equally reductive to find
cause for the acts of a character merely in his "transcendental
blindness." Explaining rage by explaining the mother is no more
embracive of the merely symptomatic than explaining rage as
being derived from a loss of unity with Being or an inability to
conceptualize one's goal.

From an historical viewpoint, it is true that Renaissance dramatic characters may reinforce the historian's tendency to skirt
the basic problem of artistic process by themselves talking about
the "passions," and the interplay of humors or by alluding to
various dichotomies between "reason" and "will". We are also
familiar enough with the general use of terms such as "neurotic"
by characters in modern novels and plays not to mistake such
talk as the totality of an author's characterizational strategy for
the figures commented upon in this manner. This is because such
terms can apply not to one but to all members of the human race.
Passion, will, neurosis—these touches of nature may make the
whole world kin, but they do not separate, they do not individuate
for the purposes of character interplay in tragic drama.

It is obviously the dramatist, not one of the characters, who
achieves this individuation. To be aware of this process or at
least to delineate it is the task of critical analysis when it is concerned with characterization, despite the lack of any relevant
Renaissance vocabulary which might aid and orient discussion
toward the vistas of some generally accepted dramatic historiogra-
phy. The term "process," as we have indicated, can describe such
interests; and the model which we propose as the basis for Shakespeare's own possible individuation of character, for his creation
of individual processes, might show the dramatist engaged in an
effort to present a cognitive situation, a hypothetical and fictitious
perception structured according to psychological systems inherent

in the myriad possibilities of transcendentalist ontology. Such a fictitious perception would presumably involve transcendentally formulated dilemmas or problems corollary to the propositions which might inform one particular hypothesis of "person," and such involvement might be described as "individual" process, as "characterization."

Our presentation of such a model would assume Shakespeare's familiarity with some general transcendentalist differentiations in modes of perception, but we need not therefore assume that the dramatist must have systematically surveyed the theoretical totality of any formally enunciated dialectic. There is no reason for him to have had to do so. It is more plausible to assume that Shakespeare was capable of gathering structures from within a general ideational context with which he and his contemporaries were at least familiar, if only from elementary schooling. If we acquiesce in this reasoning, we can find a way to one understanding of Shakespeare's particular selectivity, his approach to the individuation of character through process, not only by pursuing the possibilities for variation emanating from the nexus of these ideational elements but more importantly, by observing whether or how these potentialities accord with gestures of characterization within the tragedies. The caveat, though apparent, must be stressed. Conclusions derived from such lines of thought will not interpret the tragedies or account for their art and structure: the best that can be hoped for when applying any kind of historicism in the attempt to recover artistic maneuver in the work of an earlier age is a narrowing of the general possibilities.

Without requiring too great a sense of the abstruse in even the average Elizabethan dramatist, we may allude to some of these ideational elements by recalling that in a transcendentalist climate of opinion, it is assumed that all men essentially wish to be united or gain identity with some superhuman hypothetical "personality." Because of "original sin," human fallibility, or other conditions taken to be inherent in mortals, men were also understood as being unable to comprehend the existence of this desire for unity in themselves. They did experience the drive, the aspiration, it is true; yet such a basic "thrusting-on" (to purloin

Edmund's phrase) seemed only to lead error-prone man to seek his fulfillment, his sense of Absolute Being, through the medium of visible and concrete objects of perception. But even in this general condition, men could differ among themselves according to the very variety of "concretions" which served as the erroneous objects of search. Or to classify differently, distinctions among men could conceivably derive from gradations, from some sort of scale in terms of which the clarity of a conceptual vision could be measured against the "perfect" transcendental perception.

In either case, it is useful to review the terms and orientation of the "perfect" vision in the realm of perception, for differings or gradations would necessarily deviate from this hypothetical norm. The perfect mind would use only transcendental modes of thought and would realize, for example, the impermanence of visible objects while seeing through them to the Truth that they "shadowed." Such a person would not be like those who, in Charron's proto-Einsteinian description, row upon the water and

thinke the heavens, the earth, yea cities themselves to moove, when they moove; we thinke to draw all with us, and there is no man amongst us that sufficiently thinks he is but one. [sig. L5ᵛ]

The ideal thinker would realize he is "but one." Aware that his own perception was not necessarily the measure of all things, he would grasp the relativity of all conceptualizations, saying with Montaigne:

Man cleane contrarie [to the Gods], *possesseth goods in imagination, and evils essentially.* We have had reason to make the powers of our imagination to be of force: For, all our felicities are but in conceipt, and as it were in a dreame. Heare but this poor and miserable creature vaunt himselfe. There is nothing (saith *Cicero*) so delightfull and pleasant as the knowledge of Letters; of Letters I say, by whose meanes the infinitie of things, the incomprehensible greatnesse of nature, the heavens, the earth, and all the Seas of this vast universe, are made knowne unto us. They have taught us Religion, moderation, stowtnesse of courage, and redeemed our soule out of darknesse. . . . Seemeth not this goodly Orator to speake of the Almighties and everliving Gods condition? And touching effects, a thousand poore seelie women in a countrie towne have lived, and live a life much more reposed, more peacable, and more constant, than ever he did. [II. 187]

An ideal mind, unlike Cicero's, would evade such a "conceipt" of earthly "felicities" and would see through these concepts to "Truth." More importantly, he would also see through his earthy sense of his own being to separate that which is dross in the self from that which has reality from taking part in Supreme Being, in hypothetical "personality." "We have no communication with being," such an ideally thinking mind might observe, again in the words of Montaigne:

for every humane nature is ever in the middle betweene being borne and dying; giving nothing of it selfe but an obscure apparence and shadow, and an uncertaine and weake opinion. And if perhaps you fix your thought to take its being; it would be even, as if one should go about to graspe the water: for, how much the more he shal close and presse that, which by its owne nature is ever gliding, so much the more he shall loose what he would hold and fasten. [II. 323]

It is important to recall that while he might think laudably according to any transcendentalist value judgments leveled at him, such a paragon would also gain epistemological approval. He would not only be able to differentiate appearance from reality, an elementary gesture in some respects, but he would also be able to think in such a way as to separate symbol situations from sign situations. Our ideal man would know that the more real an object seems to the corrupt human senses, the more illusory it might actually be, if only because humans tend to transform their own perceptions into symbols for their otherwise undefined aspirations.

But if Man is a rational Animal, how contrary is it to Reason, that in the Conveniencies, rather than the real Goods of the Body, and in external Things, which Fortune gives and takes away at her Pleasure; we had rather have the Thing itself than the Name; and in the real Goods of the Mind, we put more Value upon the Name, than the Thing itself.

So Erasmus states in his colloquy "Of Things and Words." The educated transcendentalist, however, might prefer Pico who, not writing for schoolboys, stressed the same point with different argumentation.

Since the final cause has priority over the exemplary cause, and that over the efficient (we first desire to have something to protect us from the weather, then we conceive the idea of a house, and finally we construct one by making it materially), if, . . . the good pertains to the final cause, the true to the exemplary, [and] being to the efficient, God as cause will have first of all the attribute of good, then of true, and finally of being.

Bacon, speaking of atheism, might also appeal more to the sophisticate in such matters.

It is true, that a little philosophy inclineth man's mind to atheism; but depth in philosophy bringeth men's minds about to religion. For while the mind of man looketh upon second causes scattered, it may sometimes rest in them, and go no further; but when it beholdeth the chain of them, confederate and linked together, it must needs fly to Providence and Deity.[1]

The perfectly thinking model who might understand these matters is useful for a study of characterization possibilities in Shakespearean tragedy not because such a model can or should furnish the criterion for any ethical evaluations, (hardly our present concern) but because of the principles according to which his ideality has been constructed. When we deal with any system of thought, polarities always emerge, and by definition either pole within the system will exist as some related function of its opposite. Good-evil, brilliant-stupid, black-white, fat-thin, fast-

[1] Bacon, "Of Atheism," in *Works*, ed. James Spedding *et al.* (London, 1887), XII, 132—hereafter cited as *Works*. See Pico, 33; and Erasmus, *Colloquies*, trans. N. Bailey (London, 1878), II, 134.

slow, and early-late constitute pairings which derive juxtaposi-
tional coherence from their interdependence within the same system. We may, for example, contrast a system which polarizes
fast-quick with one which polarizes fast-smooth or fast-slow. In
each case, "fast" exists with its companion in a specific ideational
construct in which neither is understandable except in terms of
the other.

The point is perhaps obvious, but it must be emphatically applied to the matter of Renaissance transcendentalist characterization if we are to extrapolate models of stage persons from the
hypothesis of the man endowed with ideal perceptions. To speak
without excessive precision for the sake of immediate illustration,
this is as much as to say that if the mind of a stage hero has been
conceived and constructed according to transcendentalist theories
of perception, then the mind of the stage villain (the opposite
pole within the system) will be conceived and constructed according to the same dialectic. Both "villain" and "hero" will accord with the laws of the particular system which polarizes so
that they may be regarded as opposites or modulates so that characterizations may occupy various intermediate positions.

An example removed from our present interests offers itself in
the cases of Heremod and Hrothgar. Within the system of *Beowulf* the willingness to give rings to the members of one's *comitatus* is an orientation suggested as one of the optima for leaders
or kings, just as a sense of loyalty to one's lord is an outlook sufficiently relevant for *comitatus* to inform the psychological tension
of the long winter described in the Finnsburgh episode. Within
such a system, however, the opposite pole cannot necessarily be
embodied by Grendel but by Heremod, whose mind is described
as turning against this loyalty concept. Heremod is not a negative
example because he sets fire to halls, eats warriors, or is cowardly
in battle, but because he ceases to give rings and turns against
his followers. By the same token, in the second part of the poem
Beowulf's *comitatus* contrasts with the old king's characteristics.
The final speaker does not condemn their fear of the dragon as
much as the desertion which the fear precipitates, an act contrasting with Beowulf's willingness to be roasted alive by dragon

fire for the sake of his people. Within this total context, therefore, it is logical that the dragon, Grendel, and his dam exist as
monsters. This is as much as to say that they are extrasystemic,
nonhuman, precisely because they have no concept, positive or
negative, of the giving-receiving system which is relevant to the
psychology of the human figures in the poem. The facts that these
monsters hoard treasure instead of using it as an expression of the
reciprocity psychology which informs the human characterizations
of the poem and that Grendel's attack on Heorot is so utterly
gratuitous (because it is not for revenge) are generally coherent
in terms of the system. But because their psychological structures
do not accord with the other character propositions of the poem,
these menaces are extrahuman. It is true that Grendel's dam and
the dragon are motivated by revenge, a sufficiently "human" characteristic in the poem, but even Grendel's dam has simply been
interrupted from her normal activity of hoarding treasure for its
own sake.

One other sample of the problem of character may be drawn
from what appears to be the system operant in *Tom Jones*. Here
the basic, "good-natured" impulse to help others at the cost of
self-interest seems to constitute one pole and the impulse of self-
interest no matter the cost to others its logical opposite. Characterization through such traits as hypocrisy, self-deception, and
self-destructiveness again indicates that the concept of personality
arises and functions in terms of elements constituting the material from which polarization occurs. Thus if there is a villain
in the piece, his personality will not be constructed according to
the same terms which might inform the psychology, say, of the
villain in *Caleb Williams*. This is, of course, to oversimplify complex artistries, but the point is sufficiently illustrated if we can
argue that, however anthropologically relevant, the theories of a
Freud will not structure the characterization of Blifil as they may
the internal monologue of Quentin in chapter 2 of *The Sound
and the Fury*. In Fielding's system, we will agree, Tom has been
Tom and Blifil Blifil since birth, just as we can observe that
Squire Weston, though Tom's opponent at times, is relevant to
the system through his selfishness but is not necessarily a polariza-

tion. According to Freud, all men may, in very different terms, be selfish; but in Fielding's system, Weston moves back and forth, psychologically, between extremes delineated by Tom and Blifil.

Renaissance characterizations structured within the ideational contexts of transcendentalist assumptions may conform to the kinds of laws which we have suggested as applicable to other idea systems. No figure in a play will necessarily emerge as the man of ideal perceptions, but the structuring of a character will be composed of elements according to which the ideal has been conceptualized in the first place. Milton's way with Satan serves as a more obvious later example of this important point in Renaissance writing. From many ancient dialectical points of view, there could be no Satan without God; but for Milton, the details of Satan's perception are fundamentally oriented to transcendental reality, however opposed he is to an acquiescence in the power of God. Satan may be the villain of the epic, but he is constructed as an opposite pole within a characterization system, the basis of which his own words would seem only superficially to deny. His obsession is not a philosophic relativism. It is a conviction that the proposition of hypothetical "personality," while correct, is embodied in the wrong entity. He does not deny transcendentalism; he imagines *himself* as its apex. He is therefore "against God," but as a characterization in a transcendentalist system, his viewpoint and his hostility are constructed according to the terms and grammar of the ideological context within which his creator, Milton, worked.

Because of their basic dialectical clarity, the terms of characterization as they are developed in *Paradise Lost* (or in a morality play) are useful illustrations, but they are useful only if our reference to such strands of the traditional *psychomachia* does not divert attention to purely ethical emphases, for our approach to the creation of figures in Shakespearean tragedy seeks to distinguish as clearly as possible the matter of character from the matter of ethic. Transcendentalism, as a teleology concerned with modes of perception, may obviously be regarded as an ethic; and an author, having specified the characteristics of the transcendental ideal, of the hypothetical "personality," will obviously offer value judgments about how life should be lived in what he is positing as a universe. What we wish to stress here, however, is that a mode of thought does not necessarily imply a set of restricted, specific ethical assertions. Shakespeare could conceivably have invented figures in some play who were consciously occupied only with the sensible world and were contemptuous of hypothetical "personality" ("scornful of God"), while the attitude of the play in question might constantly stress, say, the malice of some power above. Whatever the specific evaluative gestures, the dialectic of the drama itself nevertheless continues to operate within the particular teleological and perceptual context which we have been discussing. Unless characters were introduced who had just read David Hume, the grammar of the play would still remain transcendentalist.

In delineating this point 1 *Tamburlaine* is quite useful for, in contrast to *Doctor Faustus*, Marlowe's earlier play has struck many readers perhaps (including some of Marlowe's contemporaries) as atheistic or at least as iconoclastic of certain Renaissance religious values. Yet it is precisely this quality which may stress the point in hand. If we accept, at least for the sake of argument, an evaluation of the play's ethical stance as anti-Christian, we nevertheless observe a figure who defines his desires, however iconoclastic, in terms of the very gestures of transcendentalist thought. If the audience is indeed meant to approve of Tamburlaine's viewpoint, he is soliciting that approval according to the cognitional assumptions of the age. His own words, when he first attains real power, explain his motivations to his defeated opponent in the very language of these assumptions.

> The thirst of raigne and sweetnes of a crown,
> That causde the eldest sonne of heavenly *Ops*,
> To thrust his doting father from his chaire,
> And place himselfe in the Emperiall heaven,
> Moov'd me to manage armes against thy state.
> What better president than mightie *Jove?*
> Nature that fram'd us of foure Elements,
> Warring within our breasts for regiment,
> Doth teach us all to have aspiring minds:

Our soules, whose faculties can comprehend
The wondrous Architecture of the world:
And measure every wandring plannets course,
Still climing after knowledge infinite,
And alwaies mooving as the restles Spheares
Wils us to weare our selves and never rest,
Untill we reach the ripest fruit of all,
That perfect blisse and sole felicitie,
The sweet fruition of an earthly crowne. [II. vi. 863–80]

In a sense, the speech is almost too good a joke, if it may be
considered that, for in their latter portion Tamburlaine's lines approach caricature, having followed the usual transcendentalist
argument for man's "aspiring" (a word the Scythian indeed uses)
only to end in the bathos of an earthly crown. Mischievous or not,
however, the speech is instructive, for in its delineation of Tamburlaine's character, it does make use of the grammar of transcendentalism to present the Scythian's *weltanschauung*. It does
not necessarily follow that Tamburlaine should then interpret
aspiring for Absolute Being as ontological justification for the
impulse toward the kingship of earth, but since he is a pagan—
he will later be pitted in battle against Christians—it is understandable that his terms will be those of an "Imitation of Jove"
rather than an "Imitation of Christ."

The train of logic which begins with the proposition of man's
earthly restlessness and culminates in the non sequitur of kingship teleology would not necessarily be Marlowe's of course. It is
simply a transcendentalist way to present Tamburlaine's icon-
oclasm, and the clarity and elaboration of this speech in itself is
suggestive both of the potentialities of characterization through
perception theory and of the corollary structures which might be
necessary to support such an endeavor. One thinks of *Edward II*
in comparison, of Marlowe's more complex use of Gaveston as
"goal" for his tragic monarch.

The latent humor which created *Tamburlaine* imparts a certain
clarity to the point with which we are concerned, but if we do not
consider this play amusing, we may be more disposed to accept
the principle in an avowed comedy such as *Volpone* where an

initial speech stands in instructive analogy. We recall the hero paying homage to the gold, which he has instructed Mosca to reveal to the audience.

> Hail the worlds soule, and mine. More glad then is
> The teeming earth, to see the long'd-for sunne
> Peepe through the hornes of the celestiall *ram*,
> Am I, to view thy splendor, darkening his:
> That, lying here, amongst my other hoords,
> Shew'st like a flame, by night; or like the day
> Strooke out of *chaos*, when all darknesse fled
> Unto the center. O thou sonne of SOL,
> (But brighter then thy father) let me kisse,
> With adoration, thee, and every relique
> Of sacred treasure, in this blessed roome.
> Well did wise Poets, by thy glorious name,
> Title that age, which they would have the best;
> Thou being the best of things; and far transcending
> All style of joy, in children, parents, friends,
> Or any other waking dreame on earth. [I. i. 2–18]

By coincidence, the last line again could strike us as especially droll. Jonson has structured the speech so that Volpone winds through the clichés of a transcendentalism which is perhaps more sophisticated than Tamburlaine's and ends by viewing life, through Christian Neo-Platonic eyes, as a "waking dream." But the rationale of Volpone's transcendentalist system is, of course, that the way to arouse from the waking dream is to pierce through the illusion of pseudo-reality in order to behold the true *ens*. This matter is hardly so trivial as an "earthly crown," as for Tamburlaine, but . . . gold. It alone is more firm than the traditional gifts of fortune to which Volpone has alluded: it stands on the level of a Platonic first principle. The comparisons are obvious enough.

Whatever interpretations we might finally accept for these plays, it is not unreasonable to suggest how the kind of characterization structured according to the complex of ideas with which we have been concerned might delineate the movements of these artificial persons. It is easy enough to follow Tamburlaine's vaunting to the point where it is consistent with his premises, as we see them, and for him to acquire a personal grudge against God for the death of Xenocrate. In fact, the Scythian is so well established in this basic, transcendentally oriented attitude that the two parts of the play need only refer to the proposition now and then to maintain it as the plausible basis for the many colorful stage sequences which constitute the bulk of the dramas. Specifically, most scenes enact consequences of Tamburlaine's self-assertion. In Jonson's case we are, however, dealing with a different kind of mind and perhaps with a different point in the development of Renaissance stage characterization. The difference is that Volpone's tendency to worship his own version of reality is used by Jonson as a process. While gold begins as the only true reality, this sense of the true *ens* changes (as transcendentalist thought suggested that it did in all men) to be represented by other things. There is the appropriately named Caelia, for example; and Jonson uses Volpone's vigorous tendencies toward transcendentalist worship to put him out of phase with the other circumstances depicted in the play. Busily creating or imagining heavens and speaking as brilliantly of sensual gratification as Sir Epicure Mammon ever does about his conception of his suprarealities (or as Cicero speaks of "letters"), Volpone becomes unaware that his perception of reality is not the measure of it, and he incurs a comic fall at the hands of Mosca.

This is to lay rather a heavy hand on *Volpone*, but the principle of character structure at issue does emerge, and without much reference to those dimensions which may differentiate comedy from tragedy. The tone of *Volpone*, or of any other comedy, is indeed a complex problem for aesthetic analysis per se; yet despite this difficulty Jonson is useful for indicating how an Elizabethan mind, whether in tragic or comic modes, can "play" with the concepts with which we have been concerned, can arrange them in such a way as to give an illusion of character and even process to a figure who is supposed to provoke humor rather than passion.

And if we can observe this degree of sophistication in Jonsonian comedy, we would be unwise, a priori, to deny it to Shakespearean tragedy.

For the general relevance of such matters to Shakespeare's case, we need only refer to studies of the poet's interest in so-called appearance/reality motifs (embodied, for instance, in Wolfgang Clemen's *Schein und Sein bei Shakespeare*). But appearance/reality is ultimately an oversimplified dichotomy, and while it is certainly an informative generalization about ideas, especially in some of the romantic comedies, it does not speak to the basis of our present interest in Shakespeare's approach to the problem of character structure. Rather, some elements in *Julius Caesar* will serve our purpose, for they more easily indicate specific areas of sophistication in Shakespeare's thinking and emphasize the dramatist's epistemological awareness of what can be derived from different approaches to the general proposition of transcendentalist thought. If we consider, for instance, a motif such as the materialistic doctrines of an Epicurus (which are actually a denial of the transcendentalist way), we find Shakespeare rather more accurate in tracing the possible ramifications of such materialism than many of the sermon writers who so often condemned Epicureanism on irrelevant grounds.

Cassius is no sermonist's voluptuary drowning in pleasures of the senses but rather is an accurate example of how informed Elizabethans might have imagined the classical Epicurean as thinking.[2] Shakespeare reveals a consciousness of the implications of Cassius' position:

> You know, that I held *Epicurus* strong,
> And his Opinion: Now I change my minde,
> And partly credit things that do presage. [2416–18]

[2] For such matters, see especially D. C. Allen, "The Rehabilitation of Epicurus and his Theory of Pleasure in the Early Renaissance," *SP*, XLI (1944), 1–15. Allen notes the conventional condemnation of Epicurus as a voluptuary in Greene, Nashe, and Middleton; but he notes that as early as Erasmus (in his colloquy "Epicureus"), more attention was paid to what Epicurus really implied. See also Seneca's *De Beneficiis*, IV. 2, 4, and 5 (in the divisions of Lodge's translation) for condemnation mixed with a just appraisal of Epicurus' position.

Cassius lists the transcendentalist portents of eagles and ravens before Philippi as the cause of his depression, yet when Messala says "Beleeve not so," he reasserts his Epicureanism and replies defensively, "I but beleve it partly." Shakespeare not only attends to this elementary aspect of the Epicurean position, but he has Cassius, in departure from the Plutarchan source, showing Epicurean contempt for the storms and other atmospheric manifestations which fill the play. When, in a further departure from the source, Cassius is described by Caesar as one who "hears no music" and when Cassius himself uses as the basis for his conspiracy argument the theory of man as a merely physical being (Caesar should not rule because he becomes weakly sick and cannot win swimming races), it is clear that at some point the poet became at least superficially versed in subtleties beyond the standard pastor's condemnations of the Epicurean position.[3]

This attention to Cassius suggests Shakespeare in the act of presenting a Roman character trying to cope with what many in Shakespeare's audience understood was the truth about the universe. What we hear of Brutus' philosophy, then, is also significant. We note his Stoic reaction to Cassius' challenge.

---

[3] In the *"Life of Brutus"*, Shakespeare could have found a detailed description of the Epicurean position on ghosts. See *Shakespeare's Plutarch*, ed. C. F. Tucker Brooke (London, 1909), I, 164–65. Brutus has seen the ghost of Caesar and talks it over with Cassius, who then proceeds to give Brutus what Plutarch calls an Epicurean lecture of some twenty-five lines on how apparitions derive from the disordered subjectivities of men. But the other motifs derive from elsewhere. The distortion of the Epicurean position that man is simply a "reasonable beast" can of course be found in La Primaudaye and elsewhere, but the doctrine of music and the attitude toward storms is only described in another work by Plutarch, *The Moralia*, in the long essay entitled "That a Man cannot Live pleasantly according to the Doctrine of Epicurus." This is the most detailed account in English of Epicureanism which this writer has been able to find dated before 1603. (William Baldwin omitted any reference to Epicurus in his *Treatise of Morall Philosophie*, and neither the *STC* nor the *BMC* list printings of Epicurus or Lucretius in England before 1640.) Recensions of the gist of each essay precede the pieces, and the recension before the Epicurus essay would have informed the reader that Epicurus did not believe in mathematics, music, or other overly subtle topics of presumably Platonic discourse. The essay itself describes the attitude toward atmospheric phenomena and other prodigies.

Bru. O *Cassius,* I am sicke of many greefes.
Cas. Of your Philosophy you make no use,
If you give place to accidentall evils.
Bru. No man beares sorrow better. Portia is dead. [2131–34]

The motif is repeated later when, just after Cassius has revised his own Epicurean conviction regarding prodigies, he asks Brutus:

If we do lose this Battaile, then is this
The very last time we shall speake together:
What are you then determined to do?
Bru. Even by the rule of that Philosophy
By which I did blame *Cato* for the death
Which he did give himselfe, I know not how:
But I do find it Cowardly, and vile,
For feare of what might fall, so to prevent
The time of life, arming my selfe with patience,
To stay the providence of some high powers,
That govern us below. [2439–49]

It would almost seem as if Brutus has stumbled on specifically Christian concepts despite his Stoicism, especially in his condemnation of the noblest Stoic of them all; but Cassius persists:

Then, if we loose this Battaile,
You are contented to be led in Triumph
Thorow the streets of Rome.
Bru. No, *Cassius,* no:
Think not, thou Noble Romane,
That ever *Brutus* will go bound to Rome,
He beares too great a minde. [2450–55]

His inconsistency is not ultimately to the point here, since an interpretation of the play is not the present question. Rather, we argue for what the play reveals about Shakespeare's philosophic awareness. At other times his comprehension is perhaps instinctive, but here it seems to be explicitly defined as he constructs characters in various patterns of relationship to matters associated with transcendentalist discourse. He was apparently capable not only of distinguishing the Epicurean Cassius from his conventional Renaissance-atheist, pseudo-Epicurean brother but also of differentiating Stoicism from Christianity. Further, the poet apparently made it his business to write a play in which Stoic is pitted against Epicurean and in which both are asked to confront storms and prodigies and in Brutus' case, a ghost.

A ghost of course represents an ultimate challenge by the invisible, and we are not surprised when we observe the kinds of reactions it is made to elicit in *Hamlet,* aside from its general influence on events. At the beginning Shakespeare introduces Horatio, who is presented as a "scholar," and who is as skeptical as Plutarch's Cassius about the existence of such things: "Tush, tush, 'twill not appear." Even later his skepticism is not completely gone, for after the ghost's exit, he exclaims:

> Before my God, I might not this believe
> Without the sensible and true avouch
> Of mine owne eyes. [38–73]

And when Hamlet says of this manifestation, "There are more things in Heaven and Earth, *Horatio,* / Than are dream't of in our Philosophy" (863–64), we are perhaps guided to the drift of this statement by recalling the crucial fact that in Renaissance parlance "Philosophy" was not a method but a term referring to the corpus of specifically *classical* ethics, logic, and ontology.[4]

A play such as *The Merchant of Venice* is useful for indicating the degrees of Shakespeare's sophistication in these matters. Here

---

[4] See Lucentio's proposed course of study and Tranio's reply in *Shrew* I. i. 17–40. See also Lafeu in *All's Well* (893–95): "They say miracles are past, and we have our Philosophicall persons, to make moderne and familiar things supernaturall and causelesse." Lear adheres to the distinctions advanced by William Baldwin in his definition preceding his philosophical primer. In this work "philosophy" is the corpus of classical knowledge and is to be divided into ethics, logic, and science—"First let me talk with this philosopher. / What is the cause of thunder?" We recall that to Lear this "philosopher" is alternately a Theban and an Athenian. See also *OED* "philosophy," number 6; the remark in the Malone Society Reprint of *Caesars Revenge,* ll. 2338ff.; and Bacon, "Of Atheism." Cf. Barckley: "it is easily to be seene, how little the study of Phylosophy serveth to the finding out or attaining of the Felicitie of man" (sig. 6).

he attends most carefully and most interestingly to the problem of cognition in terms of transcendentalist thought. Rather than building the kinds of models which we observed in *Tamburlaine* and *Volpone*, he attempts to establish the archetypes of possible variations within this general complex of ideas. In fact, it would seem as if Shakespeare actually challenged himself to differentiate since his theme of the three caskets offers a series of distinctions beyond those available in his presumed sources. It is well known that the caskets theme can be traced to diverse motifs appearing in Gower, Boccaccio, and in the *Gesta Romanorum*, but it is significant that only the *Gesta* tale provides three caskets made of different metals. Shakespeare even diverges from this account, however, for he presents not merely one person who must choose among the three caskets but three characters, each of whom must select one of the three different caskets. This gesture is significant, for regardless of the possible theatrical advantages, the dramatist has ultimately created for himself a situation in which each suitor, each characterization, must at least be minimally relatable to the choice which he finally exercises. We observe, that is, the highly interesting process whereby the poet passes beyond his sources, which merely confine themselves to depicting someone in the act of correct transcendentalist choice. We may speak, if we will, of appearance and reality, but Shakespeare, even in this early play, is really distinguishing among *kinds* of appearance. In a sense, he is trying to differentiate characters by their differing relationships to transcendental tenets. Such a maneuver resembles that used in the structuring of Brutus and Cassius, and the resemblance is too close to be wholly coincidental.

We will agree that if transcendentalist thought had to do with anything, it was concerned with the problem of what men should desire, of choosing rightly. And if we remind ourselves of the premise that all men fundamentally desire the same thing, Shakespeare's comedy schematizes the proposition for our inspection by having different suitors united through their common object of desire, Portia. Furthermore, the play offers epitomes since it furnishes answers. The dramatist could have limited himself simply to a sequence in which Bassanio rejects gold and silver and gives his reasons for doing so, but Shakespeare also offers us depictions of the failures of two of the other suitors. This is significant, for the presentation of Arragon and Morocco in the act and rhetoric of error is a larger artistic effort. The poet attempts to distinguish between two figures in terms of their differing and erroneous approaches toward their common desire. Character, in other words, is distinguished in terms of differing conceptualizations about the same object. The object, Portia, thus becomes complex. Bassanio's Portia is not Arragon's, and Morocco relates not so much to the Portia the audience knows— the girl joking with Nerissa about her suitors—but, as it were, to some notion of Portia. Both Morocco and Arragon regard her as a valuable acquisition; they do not think of her as she herself may be. Yet only the suitor who realizes how Portia is to be grasped mentally and how the way to this entity is to be discerned will gain "union." The union in this play is of course marriage, but when the problem of union-through-correct-concept arises, transcendentalist implications become obtrusive.

The compactness of the scheme and the fact that neither Arragon nor Morocco obtains any "Portia" at all can be misleading for an audience. Each suitor actually has no choice because he faces one specific concept. Having to deal with what we might term the "idea" of Portia and with no one else but Portia, he must determine what way of thinking, what way of looking at things, can gain for him one particular object presented for his contemplation. In a larger scheme, however, there might conceivably be several "Portias," as many as are possibly implicit in the play. If Shakespeare's scheme were strictly allegorical— Spenserian perhaps, or in the general traditions of the *psychomachia*—matters would be clearer if both Arragon and Morocco were rewarded by different kinds of women instead of by nothing. There is the real Portia, to be attained by correct conceptualization of how a real Portia can be united to oneself, and in the suitors' minds there are "Portias" who may or may not coincide with the real one, versions of truth which may or may not be identical with what actually is truth. Those "Portias" are, in another (allegorical) mode, the Duessa or Fidessa which Arragon

or Morocco would win through their individual conceptions of
how one attains.

In the comedy we are confined to the caskets which, as objects
for choice, are complicated entities. Each casket presents a
double problem and perhaps a triple one if we think of the contents and recall the threefold organization of the Renaissance
emblem. The double problem lies in the fact that the chooser
must cope not only with the kind of metal involved but also with
a motto. This complication will be more obvious if we imagine
for the play either three black caskets, each with a different
motto serving as the sole basis for choice, or three caskets of gold,
silver, and lead with no mottos on them at all. Either model
emphasizes the point. In one case, with mottos alone, the suitor
would have to choose a statement applicable to a reasoning
process according to which one seeks to gain something of value.
In the other case, the situation would be more interesting and
more difficult, for to deal with kinds of metal is to deal with
symbology. Lead would not be particularly arcane, for since the
time of Prudentius, virtue has always seemed poor on the outside,
but silver and gold would perhaps be more difficult, if only in
terms of Renaissance theories of decorum. In any event, the
proposition presented to the suitors would appear somewhat as
follows. "If a man thinks that he can unite himself with Portia
by choosing what he believes many men desire, the symbol for
his thought process is gold." And "if a man thinks he can unite
himself with Portia by assuming his desert, the symbol for his
thought process is silver." Thus silver and gold would emerge as
decorous to or representative of different kinds of cognition.

The Merchant of Venice seems to embody a rather complex
schematization emphasizing Shakespeare's tendency, in an early
play, to effect a differentiation of character through various cognitive approaches toward problems inherent in a transcendentalist
dialectic. We observe these matters in the speeches of Morocco
and Arragon, but pertinent, too, is the manner in which Shakespeare dealt with his source for the casket scene. In the *Gesta* the
emperor arranged things rather differently than did Portia's
father.

The Emperour late make iii. vesselles, and the first was of clene goolde, and fulle of precious stonys owtewarde, And withinne fulle of deede bonys; and it hade a superscripcione in theise wordis, *They that chese me shulle finde in me that they servyde.* The secunde vesselle was alle of cleene silver, and full of [earth and wormes] and outwarde it had this superscripsione, *They that chesithe me, shulle finde in me that nature and kinde desirithe.* And the third vesselle was of leed, And with inne was fulle of precious stonys; and with oute was sette this scripture, *They that chese me, shulle finde [in] me that God hathe disposid.*

The damsel who must choose is shown in the process of reasoning, and we will recall that the golden casket leads her to conclude that she has no intrinsic deservings, while the silver casket causes her to observe that what "nature and kinde" tend to desire are "dilectacions of the flessh." She therefore decides that one cannot go too wrong by acting in accordance with what God may dispose, and the *Gesta* conclusion becomes one with the analogues of this tale, the morals of which emphasize that correct choosing depends on submission to God's will.[5]

Shakespeare's deviations from this traditional motif are significant, for if, in ethical terms, the incidents in the *Gesta* emphasize divine providence, he himself defines the conditions of choice in such a way as to make him one with the transcendentalist orientation of his own time. His leaden casket is not a symbol of providence; rather, it is an entity which demands the

[5] See R. Robinson's recension of the *Gesta Romanorum* entitled *A Record of Auncient Histories* (London, 1595; STC 21288), number 32, pass. Geoffrey Bullough, *Narrative and Dramatic Sources of Shakespeare* (London, 1957), I, 513–14 omits "The Morall" and uses *The Old English Versions of the Gesta Romanorum*, ed. Sir F. Madden (London, 1838). This version, re-edited by S. J. H. Herrtage for the Early English Text Society (Extra Series 33) presents two manuscript versions (Harl. 7333 and Addit. 9066) where the phrase "full of precious stonys owtewarde" (Harl.) or "precious stones" (Addit.) describes the outsides of the gold and silver caskets. Harl. is either corrupt or suffers an error in transcription with the result that the silver casket is merely described as "all of cleene silver, and full of precious stonys; and outwarde it had this superscripsion" etc. Bullough prints this version. Addit. 9066 has silver and precious stones on the outside and earth inside. Robinson's recension gives us earth and worms for the contents of the silver casket.

giving of self, the surrender which precedes Plotinian *enosis* with superpersonality and which is paralleled in sublunary affairs by the concept of human love as a motion of self-sacrifice. As for the other metals, their divergence from the source is more subtle and perhaps revelatory of a particularly Shakespearean bent. We can observe these differences because of distinctions advanced by the "Morall" that follows the *Gesta* tale. The golden casket, we are told, represents "some worldly men, both mighty men and rich, which outwardlie shine as gold in riches and pomp of this world." But the silver casket differs subtly and interestingly from its golden counterpart, for by this casket we "ought to understand some Justices and wise men of this world which shine in faire speech but within be full of wormes and earth." Thus the *Gesta* scheme is clear enough. On one hand, a sense of desert equates with gold and dead bones and is an epitome of mighty men; on the other hand, that which nature desires equates with silver, earth, and worms and is an epitome of justices and worldly-wise men.

Clearly, Shakespeare has altered this framework. Bassanio is helpful to us here. He takes gold to symbolize the general ornamentation which hides evil, and as such, it seems clear that gold technically stands for everything implied by those artificial appearances so antithetical to transcendental realities. This being so, what happens to silver is quite different, for although Bassanio dismisses it in a line, calling it a "pale drudge between man and man," there is really more to the silver than this in *The Merchant of Venice*. In the first place, the dramatist has changed the mottos around. In the *Gesta*, sense of deserving is equated with gold; in the *Merchant*, sense of deserving is equated with *silver*. Similarly, the "what many men desire" motif attached to the silver in the *Gesta* is connected to the gold in the *Merchant*. Shakespeare then follows the rest of the source: gold and the death beneath it is the rendering of pompous power, and silver is the rendering of the worldly-wise man. "Oh these deliberate fools," says Portia, "when they do choose, they have the wisdom by their wit to lose." The concept of desert which Shakespeare added to the silver casket and the money symbology established for silver by

Bassanio suggest, however, that the poet had specific ideas when it came to the casket arrangement.

We have suggested that the casket situation presented a three-fold problem. The third element consists of the speeches which Shakespeare has given to each one of the choosers. We have, in sum, observed a process in which the poet, passing beyond the merely moral source presentations, uses his own kinds of caskets not only as symbol but as character-stimuli that elicit from Morocco, Arragon, and Bassanio speeches which indicate three different conceptual frameworks. Morocco and Arragon are not, after all, completely similar persons. Instead, do we not observe Shakespeare suggesting certain distinctions? To choose the golden casket, for example, is to have a personality of the sort which can make the following speeches to Portia.

> Mislike me not for my complexion,
> The shadowed liverie of the burnisht sunne,
> To whom I am a neighbour and neere bred.
> Bring me the fairest creature North-ward borne,
> Where *Phoebus* fire scarce thawes the isicles,
> And let us make incision for your love,
> To prove whose blood is reddest, his or mine.
> I tell thee Ladie this aspect of mine
> Hath feard the valiant, (by my love I swear)
> The best regarded Virgins of our Clime
> Have lov'd it to: I would not change this hue,
> Except to steale your thoughts my gentle queene. [518–29]

The sense of a personal worth is obviously strong:

> By this Symitare
> That slew the Sophie, and a Persian Prince
> That won three fields of Sultan Solyman,
> I would ore-stare the sternest eyes that looke:
> Out-brave the heart most daring on the earth:
> Plucke the yong sucking Cubs from the she Bear,
> Yea, mocke the lion when he rores for pray
> To win the Ladie. But alas, the while
> If *Hercules* and *Lychas* plaic at dice

Which is the better man, the greater throw
May turne by fortune from the weaker hand:
So is *Alcides* beaten by his [p]age,
And so may I, blind Fortune leading me
Misse that which one unworthier may attaine,
And die with grieving. [542–56]

Though Morocco is engaging about the grandeur of his love for
Portia—he will die with grieving—he also is the kind of person
who regards the color of his skin as a sign of intrinsic superiority.
Nevertheless, and interestingly, he does hesitate to rely on the
concept of deserving suggested by the silver casket. Rather, he
chooses gold because it represents what many men desire and because it is appropriate to Portia and to his own "golden mind."

I will survay the inscriptions, backe againe:
What sayes this leaden casket?
Who chooseth me, must give and hazard all he hath.
Must give, for what? For lead, hazard for lead?
This casket threatens[;] men that hazard all
Doe it in hope of faire advantages:
A golden mind stoopes not to showes of drosse,
Ile then nor give nor hazard aught for lead.
What sayes the Silver with her virgin hue?
Who chooseth me, shall get as much as he deserves.
As much as he deserves; pause there Morocho,
And weigh thy value with an even hand,
If thou beest rated by thy estimation
Thou doost deserve enough, and yet enough
May not extend so farre as to the Ladie:
And yet to be afeard of my deserving,
Were but a weake disabling of myself.
As much as I deserve, why that's the Lady.
I doe in birth deserve her, and in fortunes,
In graces, and in qualities of breeding:
But more then these, in love I doe deserve.
What if I stray'd no farther, but chose here?
Let's see once more this saying grav'd in gold
Who chooseth me shall gaine what many men desire:

Why that's the Lady, all the world desires her:
From the foure corners of the earth they come
To kisse this shrine, this mortall breathing Saint.
The Hyrcanion deserts, and the vaste wildes
Of wide Arabia are as throughfares now
For Princes to come view faire *Portia*.
The waterie Kingdome, whose ambitious head
Spets in the face of heaven, is no barre
To stop the forraine spirits, but they come
As ore a brook to see faire *Portia*.
One of these three containes her heavenly picture.
Is't like that Lead containes her? 'twere damnation
To thinke so base a thought, it were too grose
To rib her searecloath in the obscure grave:
Or shall I thinke in Silver she's immur'd
Being ten times undervalued to tride gold?;
O sinfull thought, never so rich a Jem
Was set in worse then gold! They have in England
A coine that beares the figure of an Angell
Stampt in gold, but that's insculpt upon:
But here an Angell in a golden bed
Lies all within. Deliver me the key:
Here doe I choose, and thrive I as I may. [987–1033]

Arragon, on the other hand, exhibits a different attitude in his approach to the contest.

I am enjoind by oath to observe three things;
First, never to unfold to any one
Which casket 'twas I chose; next, if I faile
Of the right casket, never in my life
To wooe a maide in way of marriage:
Lastly, if I doe faile in fortune of my choise,
Immediately to leave you and be gone. [1122–28]

Because we know that everyone who woos Portia must subscribe to these conditions, the speech, in its stressing of the conditions, reveals an incipient literalism. The quality of Arragon's reasoning about the metal in the casket is of a somewhat different mode, however.

Gold, silver, and base lead.
Who chooseth me must give and hazard all he hath.
You shall looke fairer ere I give or hazard.
What sayes the golden chest, ha, let me see:
Who chooseth me, shall gaine what many men desire:
What many men desire, that many may be meant
By the foole multitude that choose by show,
Not learning more then the fond eye doth teach,
Which pries not to th'interior, but like the Martlet
Builds in the weather on the outward wall,
Even in the force and rode of casualtie.
I will not choose what many men desire,
Because I will not jumpe with common spirits,
And ranke me with the barbarous multitudes.
Why then, to thee, thou Silver treasure house,
Tell me once more, what title thou doost beare;
Who chooseth me shall get as much as he deserves:
And well said too; for who shall goe about
To cosen Fortune; and be honourable
Without the stampe of merrit, let none presume
To weare an undeserved dignitie:
O that estates, degrees, and offices,
Were not deriv'd corruptly, and that cleare honour
Were purchast by the merrit of the wearer;
How many then should cover that stand bare?
How many be commanded that command?
How much low pleasantry [sic] would then be gleaned
From the true seede of honor? And how much honor
Pickt from the chaffe and ruine of the times,
To be new varnisht: Well, but to my choise.
Who chooseth me shall get as much as he deserves.
I will assume desert; give me a key for this,
And instantly unlocke my fortunes here. [1132–64]

Arragon has been subtle enough to eschew the gold, aware that
the "fool multitude" choose "by show." But because he has ultimately based his own choice on desert, he has erred in a manner
generally similar though not identical to that of Morocco. Shakespeare would thus seem to be offering rather delicate perceptual
distinctions either imposed upon him by the necessities of the
theatrical situation he created or invented by him for their own

sakes. The two suitors have failed to secure Portia, but this common failure to attain a common goal has been displayed in such a way as to suggest that problems of conceptualization can distinguish character.

To this effect, one could ask: what is it to think "silver" thoughts as opposed to "golden" ones? Shakespeare's intimations in such matters lead us to a way of envisioning what the bases of character could be in the later fictions of his tragedies, for whether "golden" or "silver," both ways of thinking are failures. Bassanio's way triumphs. He presents a solution in the familiar transcendentalist terms which have been the subject of our previous attentions. The inscription on the leaden casket demands sacrifice, and Bassanio's reaction, prompted by the song which warns against judging by the eyes, is in the mainstream: "So may the outward showes be least themselves / The world is still deceiv'd with ornament."

While perfection was the ideal, the dramatist's problem was to portray men who could not, by nature, live up to the philosophical purities proposed by various ethical codes. Thus the ways of the golden and silver caskets suggest to us some Renaissance intellectual propositions about a mind which was less than perfect. Seeking Truth, a quest which he could no more repress in himself than an animal could control his own instincts, imperfect man did not necessarily know where this Truth was to be found or how hypothetical "personality" was to be defined, but he nevertheless made the effort to seek. And if "golden" or "silver" minds could not function so as to locate this Truth in some philosophical heaven, they at least worked toward some version of truth on earth. This truth could be sought in oneself, in others, in riches, or in some way of life—through some substitute which a particular mind would be most prone to create in the evasions of "golden" or "silver" mentalities.

But no one evasion was worse than another, and in Shakespeare especially, we must make ourselves aware of their very equivalence from the transcendentalist viewpoint. There might be characters who would not seek the more obviously material things in life; yet they might seek some intangible (what we might term an "abstraction") that was still far below the level of immaterial

refinement demanded by transcendentalist philosophies. To ideal-
ize honor, courage, or a woman, for example was perhaps to resemble the true idealist more closely than did the miser whose
teleology was one of riches. The sonnet writers quickly discovered
such possibilities in their own games, but divagations all had the
same end. To aim toward honor, toward (Stoic?) virtue, or toward riches, from any ethical viewpoint, could be judged as the
same quality of sin or blindness or mistaking.

We eschew once again the temptation to make ethical judgments, for if we are interested in the art of characterization, the
concerns of evaluation always give place to the concerns of structure. The casket scenes suggest ethical judgment in that both
suitors fail to secure Portia, but our interest lies in the fact that
they fail for different reasons. The suitors need to be analyzed not
in terms of their common goal but in terms of their differing
processes toward this common object of desire. All mortal conceptualizations of "goal" would tend to be wrong or antitranscen-
dental, but the process leading to conceptualization, when
differentiated, would lead to the specificities and individualizations
which we would term Renaissance portrayals of character.

Volpone, for example, made his first appearance worshipping
his gold and providing an almost pedantically accurate text for
our previous observations. But compared to Malvolio, Volpone is
presented as an idealist in that he elevates his gold to the value of
transcendence (always recalling that we are dealing with comedy,
where the touch is going to be much lighter). But it is his brand
of idealism, not his desire for money, which breeds true throughout the play; the process of thought remains consistent while the
ultimate goals do not. When he talks of attaining Caelia, he uses
the same poetic terms before avouched to his gold. But a Malvolio,
who may share the materialistic desires of Volpone, is only interested in a woman, Olivia, as a way to status. He does not have
Volpone's (or Hotspur's) sense of the glorious, a usefully obtrusive trait in the stage pseudotranscendentalist. Malvolio's
process is different; even though he and Volpone are both concerned with money and women, a Malvolio "thinks about things"
in a different way.

6
Shakespeare's Material Men

Questions of process derived from the dialectical modes of transcendentalist thought, as we have seen such processes adumbrated in the previous chapter, offer a way of defining and differentiating among the various forms of characterization in Shakespearean tragedy. Anticipating ourselves, we can even suggest that the tragedies present at least four different kinds of character process, but so saying, we limit ourselves, not the dramatist. Nor would we wish to imply that Shakespeare's art of characterization represents a complete philosophical analysis of all possible intellectual deviations from transcendentalist desiderata for thought in the Renaissance. We speak of four orders of characterization which seem discernible to us. Our discerning them, if our method is valid, may merely be useful for indicating lines of future investigation into the many variations possible to Shakespeare's aesthetic imagination, not only as a writer of tragedies but as an artist whose comic genius warrants equivalent attention.

Shakespeare would appear to have evolved as one type of characterization that kind of hypothetical mind which almost entirely evades the premises of Renaissance transcendentalism. The terms of such a characterization would present an interesting artistic difficulty, for the problem was to depict a believable concatenation of human traits revolving around the proposition of a low ability to abstract. If all men could be regarded as able to "envision," there were yet different degrees. For instance, to propound to oneself goals of worldly ambition demands "envisioning," but such imagining could be argued as less abstractive than the conceptualization, say, of "honour," an entity which Falstaff claims is unreal because it is not available to the senses. Bishop Hall approaches the general problem by arguing that there are three sets of "eyes"—the first, the eyes of sense; the second, the eyes of reason; and the third, the eyes of faith. His example illustrates what is ultimately a distinction of personalities in terms of the levels at which one can "envision."

Tell a plaine Country-man, that the Sunne, or some higher or lesser starre is much bigger than his Cartwheele; or, at least, so many scores bigger than the whole earth; hee laughes thee to scorne. . . . Yet the Scholer, by the eye of reason, doth as plainly see and acknowledge this truth, as that his hand is bigger than his pen. What a thicke mist, yea what a palpable, and more than Egyptian darknesse, doth the naturall man live in! What a world is there, that he doth not see at all![1]

In the universe surrounding such a hypothetical mind, such a character, it is as if "being" is to be defined by the senses and as if one's grasp of this state can be achieved through the materialist realization of acquisitive desires. Accordingly, if a dominant sense of values could be found in such a *weltanschauung*, it would be concerned not, say, with the nearness of the soul to God but with the integrity or notion of wholeness arising from a materially realized sense of the self. And in this mode, the concept of non-being could be defined not as a loss of unity with the transcendental but simply as a loss of unity with those objects perceived by the senses. Recalling that we are describing a possible psychology for certain characters created by a playwright living within a transcendentalist system, the proposition might then be refined as follows. In transcendentalist systems, men are understood as having a "divine thrust," the nature of which they often do not understand. The orientation of our hypothetical character toward physical objects is in this case an orientation toward a substitute definable by visible objects. The striving of such a mind for unity would thus be a striving not toward a merging with some "Personality" but toward objects, as with the miser. Unity would be defined as a oneness with inanimate objects for the sake of realizing a material intimation of selfhood. And it is quantification which might convey notions about the degrees of such attainment. The more money the miser has, the greater he feels he is.

[1] Hall, *Works*, sig. D5ʳ.

It is important to consider such a distinction, for by it we may comprehend not only Shakespeare but the means by which a writer such as Tourneur often presented characterization.

D'am. Borachio, thou art read
In Nature, and her large Philosophie.
Observ'st thou not the very self same course
Of revolution both in Man and Beast?
Bor. The same. For birth, growth, state, decay and death:
Onely, a man's beholding to his Nature
For th'better composition o'the two.
D'am. But where that favour of his Nature, is
Not full and free; you see a man becomes
A foole, as little-knowing as a beast.
Bor. That showes there's nothing in a Man, above
His nature; if there were, considering t'is
His beings excellencie, t'would not yeeld
To Natures weakenesse.
D'am. Then if Death casts up
Our totall summe of joy and happinesse;
Let me have all my sences feasted in
Th'abundant fulness of delight at once,
And with a sweet insensible increase
Of pleasing surfet melt into my dust.
Bor. That revolution is too short me thinkes.
If this life comprehends our happinesse,
How foolish to desire to die so soon?
And if our time runnes home unto the length
Of Nature, how improvident it were
To spend our substance on a minutes pleasure,
And after live an age in misery?
D'Am. So thou conclud'st that pleasure onely flowes
Upon the streame of riches.
Bor. Wealth is Lord
Of all felicitie.
D'Am. Tis, Oracle,
For what's a man that's honest without wealth?
Bor. Both miserable and contemptible.
D'Am. Hee's worse, Borachio. For if charitie
Be an essentiall part of Honestie,

And should be practis'd first upon our selves;
Which must be graunted, then your honest man
That's poore, is most dishonest, for hee is
Uncharitable to the Man, whom hee
Should most respect.[2]

Thus the conversation between Borachio and D'Amville begins
The Atheist's Tragedy. The attitudes depicted here may, in a
sense, seem melodramatic, but the shadings are subtle, at least
from any twentieth-century viewpoint. The pleasures of the body,
so readily grasped at by the significantly named Sir Epicure Mammon in *The Alchemist*, are condemned as not being sufficiently
"lasting," while "Charity" enters the conversation as a misinterpretation. We are familiar with the standard view of what
constituted charity to the self. Because both Borachio and
D'Amville are the villains of the play, the consistency with which
Tourneur carries out the theoretical part of the characterization is
also significant. The talk about man as a superior beast will have
alerted us to Renaissance versions of classical Epicureanism, a
motif which the dramatist pursues.

> D'Am. That power of rule Philosophers ascribe
> To him they call the supreame of the stares;
> Making their influences governours
> Of Sublunarie Creatures; when their selves
> Are senselesse of their operations—
> 　　　　　　　　　*Thunder and lightning.*
> 　　　　　　　　　What!
> Dost start at thunder? Credit my beliefe
> 'Tis a meere effect of Nature. [II. iv. p. 205]

D'Amville proceeds into a highly technical explanation of
thunder, and we recall the Epicurean skepticism of storms as
portents. Later he is irritated by music (V. i.), which he calls
harsh; and finally, in one of the most interesting sequences, when
real ghosts have begun to unbalance his mind and the transcen-

---

[2] Tourneur, *Works*, I. i. p. 176.

dentalist orientation of the play has begun to assert itself, D'Amville is made to react to Charlemont's death. This figure has been given Stoic-Christian soliloquies throughout the play, and as he now dies with a kind of joy, D'Amville gibbers to the judge:

> I would find out by his Anatomie;
> What thing there is in Nature more exact,
> Then in the constitution of my selfe.
> Me thinks, my parts, and my dimentions, are
> As many, as large, as well compos'd as his;
> And yet in me the resolution wants
> To die with that assurance as he does.
> The cause of that in his Anatomie
> I would find out. [V. ii. p. 251]

A materialist view would, of course, define man as no more than a reasonable beast, but members of an audience to whom Tourneur's play may have appealed on an intellectual level would be aware that D'Amville's attitude did not necessarily constitute the Anglo-Catholic settlement. But more importantly, Tourneur's play thus suggests to us not only that Renaissance characterization could have an intellectualist basis but that a particular type which we have suggested as one of Shakespeare's own was not unknown elsewhere on the Jacobean stage. It is, in fact, tempting to speculate on the extent to which Shakespeare may have been influential in this regard, for in certain ways Tourneur suggests some obvious borrowings from *King Lear* not only in the "anatomy" speech we have just quoted but elsewhere. The activities and views of the bastard Spurio in *The Revenger's Tragedy* bear a suspicious resemblance to those of Edmund.

An awareness of views such as those of a D'Amville need not always have produced obviously villainous villains. It was, after all, part of the general Renaissance heritage to contemplate many of the viewpoints we might derive most easily from Tourneur's characters. In fact, the ancient Roman republic offered the picture of a whole civilization oriented to a material goal. It was understood that materialist minds could ultimately see themselves not as heartless rebels but as quite moral persons, a point to be stressed in connection with Shakespeare's own aesthetic practice. The Renaissance reader would constantly have been confronted with such tonalities at every turn in his enforced or voluntary classical browsings: Cicero, Sallust, Livy, Horace—the list is long. These writers held up the materialist ideal of the city, Rome, so eloquently that an Augustine found it necessary to speak, in rebuttal, not of one but of two cities, the second of which was to be imagined as the new, transcendentalist one, the new Jerusalem. The complex classical heritage of the Renaissance not only stressed the moral value of Roman writings but emphasized them to such an extent that a paradox, originally arising from Augustine's observations, was promulgated to the point of cliché. If ancient men led lives of moral austerity and self-sacrifice simply in the service of a terrestrial concept such as "Rome," the modern Christian had good reason to be ashamed if he could not match the pagans even in this virtue.

There was, however, a crucial distinction between moral materialism and the transcendentalist view since Renaissance writers could see how worldy ambition might appear virtuous but should ultimately be taken as the "ape of charitie."

For as that Christian vertue is patient, expecting eternall good, Ambition endureth all for temporall things. Charitie is favourable to the poore, Ambition to the rich, Charitie endureth all for the trueths sake, Ambition for vanitie.[3]

With a knowledge of Rome and what it stood for and with the kinds of distinctions to which we have alluded, a Renaissance playwright in his creation of materialist characters on stage might very well elaborate on the basic definition. He could imagine for his D'Amvilles and Borachios the existence of a belief in some final Truth consonant with their own thought processes. A character could, for instance, suppose a Truth implying the opposite of that surrender which was supposed to cause "merging with God." The natural condition for such a character might then be not love

[3] La Primaudaye quoting St. Bernard, sig. 4I6. Cf. Hall, Works, sig. C^v; and Barnabe Barnes, Foure Bookes of Offices (London, 1606), sig. T3.

but its opposite. When we speculate on this opposite, however, we do well to remember that hate as an opposite would have been a naïveté since hate itself was considered merely an aspect of love. Rather, if we recall the implications of Shakespeare's lead casket, the concept which might more appropriately have come to mind would have been the opposite of what love meant. If love meant surrender, then, in the final analysis, the contrasting concept was something like "acquisition."

The properties of a covetous man are infinit, but principally these: First a covetous man is an Infidel, for he loveth not his brethren, and *he that loveth not, knoweth not God, for God is love* [I Job 4]. Secondly, he is a theefe, for the goods that hee possesseth, are none of his owne, but Gods. Man is only constituted as a steward, and must one day to his perpetuall destruction, yeeld an account thereof.

We are not, of course, concerned with how wicked all this may be but with the polarities involved. In a transcendentalist system the notion of ownership was the obverse of uniting oneself with God. Bishop Hall made the point, also invoking the parable of the steward with his "talent which is death to hide":

If my money were another mans, I could but keepe it: onely the expending shewes it my owne. It is greater glory, comfort, and gaine, to lay it out well, than to keepe it safely. God hath made me, not his Treasurer, but his steward.[4]

The tradition of Fortune lending her gifts was an aspect of this same viewpoint, which ultimately defined the orientation toward acquisition, the "desire of having," as an easily understood basis of materialist conduct.[5]

Constructed on such a principle, a stage character might then be delineated further as holding a consonant set of ethics. Such

---

[4] For the "infidel" quotation, see William Vaughan, *The Golden Grove* (London, 1600), sig. H6; for Hall, see sig. Dᵛ and cf. sig. Cᵛ. See also Richard Barnfield, *The Combat betweene Conscience and Covetousnesse* (London, 1598).

[5] See Barroll, "Structure in Shakespearean Tragedy," *ShakS*, VII (1973).

ethics, ultimately grounded on a desire to have, could be sophisticated enough, to judge by the ancient Romans, to avoid any melodramatic depictions of naïvely lawless and mindless rapacity. The hypothetical character could be imagined as wishing to act reasonably. Such a figure could even be understood as anxious to abrogate his thrusting self-expansion merely for selfish purposes; to avoid losing everything in a welter of anarchy. It would be sensible to act so as to insure that each man would be allowed to control his own segment of the world's goods, no matter how these goods may have originally been acquired.

> They give their vertues onely humane bounds,
> And without God subvert to build againe
>   Refin'd *Ideas*, more than flesh can beare,
>   All foule within, yet speake as God were there.
>
> Mans power to make himselfe good, they maintaine;
> Conclude that Fate is govern'd by the wise;
> Affections they supplant, and not restraine;
> Within our selves, they seat Felicities;
>   With things as vaine, they vanity beat downe
>   And by selfe-ruine, seeke a *Sampsons* crowne.[6]

Like the Romans, such men would necessarily be committed to a kind of order; otherwise, chaos would result, a "chaos" in which material existence would no longer be meaningful. Hence the dominant ethic for such a personal orientation would evolve from the paradox of numbers of materially oriented men faced with the necessity of living together in such a way as to insure order among themselves. The paradox would lie in the fact that the individual dedicated to the proposition of material self-aggrandizement was bound to act against group interest whenever he could, for he sought, after all, a Total Being defined by quantity concepts. Thomas More, among others, imagined this kind of situation and gave form to it when he made Raphael comment on the subject in a comparison of Utopia to other countries.

[6] Fulke Greville, *Poems and Dramas*, I, 197.

In other places they speake stil of the common wealth, but every man procureth his owne private gaine. Here [in Utopia] where nothing is private, the common affaires bee earnestlye loked upon. And truely on both partes they have good cause so to do as they do. For in other countreys who knoweth not that he shall sterve for hunger, onles he make some severall provision for himselfe, though the commen wealthe floryshe never so muche in ryches? And therefore he is compelled even of verye necessitie to have regarde to him selfe, rather then to the people, that is to saye, to other[7]

The basis of such problems is, of course, the concept of ownership which Raphael deplores again and again.

When I compare with them so manye nations ever making newe lawes, yet none of them all well and sufficientlie furnisshed with lawes; where everie man calleth that hee hath gotten, his owne proper and private goods; where so manie newe lawes daylie made bee not sufficient for everie man to enjoye, defend, and know from an other mans that which he calleth his owne. [sig. G4ᵛ]

Moreover,

Where possessions be private, where money beareth all the stroke, it is hard and almost impossible that there the weale-publique may justlye be governed, and prosperously florishe. Unless you thinke thus: that Justice is there executed, where all things come into the hands of evill men, or that prosperitie there florisseth, where all is divided among a fewe. [sig. G4ᵛ]

It is interesting to note Shakespeare's own depiction of such a hypothetical group, as we have defined it here, for he provides some theoretical background for the mentality of an imagined character of the type which we describe. We recall in *Troilus* that Ulysses attempts to explain why the war is not going well by suggesting that the Greeks are divided into as many "several factions" as there are tents on the plain about Troy. To remedy such factionalism, Ulysses brings forward a concept of "degree," without which "the rude son should strike his father dead." We

[7] References are to Thomas More, *Utopia* (London, 1597).

can ultimately define "degree" in Ulysses' terms as proper respect for established prerogatives. But his rationale may interest
us, for as T. W. Baldwin has pointed out, "degree" in this
speech occupies the place usually reserved for "love" in other
systems of order. And if love governs all motion, as we have observed elsewhere, if love also is shown by obedience (the respect
of the son for the father being based on the first commandment of
the second Table, "love thy neighbor"), then Ulysses' speech is
indeed a substitution into conventional Renaissance structures
which usually emphasize love. Mornay is relevant:

In the second Table is contained necessarie precepts for our owne
pollitique societie: for, first of all, such a state cannot be rightly maintained, except there be a kinde of degree and order obserued among
men. [sigs. G10ʳ–G11]

But the tenets of the system emerging from Ulysses' speech are
ultimately and subtly different. This is apparent from the Greek's
animadversion to purely visual matters.

> The Heavens themselves, the Planets and this Center,
> Observe degree, priority, and place,
> Insisture, course, proportion, season, forme,
> Office, and custom, all in line of Order:
> And therefore is the glorious Planet Sol
> In noble eminence, enthron'd and sphear'd
> Amid'st the other, whose med'cinable eye
> Corrects the ill Aspects of Planets evill,
> And postes like the Command'ment of a King,
> Sans check, to good and bad. [544–53]

There is little real transcendentalism here if we contrast Ulysses' astronomy with Lorenzo's talk to Jessica about heavenly
harmony. When "degree" is gone, Ulysses concludes,

> Then everything includes it selfe in Power,
> Power into Will, Will into Appetite,
> And Appetite (an universall Wolfe,

So doubly seconded with Will, and Power)
Must make perforce an universall prey,
And last, eate up himselfe.
Great *Agamemnon:*
This Chaos, when Degree is suffocate,
Followes the choaking. [578–86]

So this degree, "the ladder to all high designs" without which enterprise is sick, hovers glancingly on the edges of conventional transcendentalist recensions but is clearly not the same thing, although it may ape the conventional.

We must not rest then upon the morrall vertues, and make that the chiefe good, which are but steppes to clyme up thereunto, as the wise Heathen taught: for all theyr doctrine, was but to fashion the outward man to civill obedience, making that the end which are but motives to the end. For it is not all one, to be a morrall wise man, and a good Christian.[8]

We are not, of course, interested in whether or not anyone in *Troilus* is a "good Christian," but we are concerned with distinctions such as those suggested by Crosse and with the possible objectivity according to which a Renaissance writer might depict men operating within a different philosophical system. In the case of Ulysses' speech, we are, in the final analysis, presented with a fairly systematic principle of order understandable not necessarily as the Elizabethan "world picture" but as a "reasonable" materialistic orientation. Unless suicidal competition is to ensue, we are told by Ulysses, the principle which must govern the affairs of men is the sanctity of the individual's power among his peers. Degrees in schools, brotherhoods in cities, peaceful commerce, the primogenitive and due of birth, "prerogative of age, crowns, sceptres, laurels"—are all determined by this abstracted principle of degree, a premise which, when scrutinized in context, insures the status quo not for any teleological purpose vis-à-vis the transcendental but for its own sake. It may be true

---

[8] H. Crosse, *The Schoole of Policie* (London, 1605), sig. B2.

that "Troy in our weakness stands, not in her strength," but is not this statement itself ultimately an allusion to the pragmatics of possession? Live as I have indicated, Ulysses seems to say, and you will be able to . . . capture and loot a city. Meanwhile, on the other side, Hector can appeal in terms no more refined (from the transcendentalist point of view) than those which merely claim about Helen:

> these Morall Lawes
> Of Nature, and of Nation, speak alowd
> To have her backe return'd. [1174–76]

Aristotle, his guide, has little effect in restraining Hector "by mere philosophy," as Renaissance writers would have put it, for Hector's final decision speaks for itself. Though intellectually agreeing with Ulysses on "possession,"the Trojan is motivated by quite different principles. If Hector deviates, he deviates from an orientation not necessarily promulgated by Shakespeare the man but imagined by Shakespeare the artist for the sake of the play.

It would therefore not be strange if the poet were to be found pursuing corollaries. If the law itself, in strictly Christian terms, was theoretically an extension of the "'Tables" of the divine law of "love," the quasi-paternalistic instrument described by Vincentio in *Measure* (I. iii), then that concept of law understandable to the strictly materialist mind might hypothetically be based on somewhat different assumptions.

Therefore when I consider and weigh in my minde all these common-wealths, which nowe a dayes any where do florish, so God helpe mee, I can perceive nothing but a certaine conspiracy of rich men procuring their owne commodities, under the name and title of the commen wealth. They invent and devise all meanes and crafts, first how to keep safely without feare of losing, that they have unjustly gathered together, and next how to hire and abuse the worke and labor of the poore for as little money as may be. These devises when the rich men have decreed to bee kept and observed under colour of the comminalitie, that is to say, also of the poore people, then they bee made lawes. [sigs. S4ᵛ–T]

More himself reinforces the view, for he concludes *Utopia* by adopting the position of devil's advocate. He seems to scoff, observing that many Utopian customs are founded "of no good reason":

Cheefely, in that which is the principall foundation of al their ordinances: that is to say, in the communitie of their life and livinge, withoute any occupying of money, by the which thing only all nobilitie, magnificence, wourship, honour and maiestie, the true ornaments and honours, as the common opinion is, of a commonwealth, utterly bee overthrowne and destroyed. [sig. T3]

Any "ideal" that might be imagined as derivable from materialistically oriented men would then be one having to do with maintaining the integrity of the materialistic *ethos*. A mere concern for money was not necessarily the defining consideration here; it involves, rather, a general epistemology of the sort suggested by Lear, who equates quantities of money with degrees of love. Indeed, a specification such as "reimbursement" could be an appropriate *primum mobile* taking several forms. The notion of revenge, for instance, might logically emanate from such a mode of thought. A theory of reimbursement also is implicit in the action which takes away from the aggressor something equivalent to what the aggressor took. In such an imagined universe of the mind, a theory of equivalent deprivation could be the agent which restores the universal order. This "universal order" would be one in which a rough equivalence is maintained, but only among those strong enough to deprive others of their goods. And in such a hypothetical situation, law would operate not as the implementation of a transcendentalist code but as a logical ramification of that general proposition according to which the materialist mind could be imagined as approaching the universe. In a universe ordered not by love but by the principle of material acquisition, deprivation and restoration would have some ontological significance. Ethics would be based on "a kind of exchanging or commutuall justice keeping a precise and religious equalitie of things amongst men."[9] Justice would provide only for the ma-

---

[9] Barnes, *Four Bookes*, sig. V2.

terial integrity of the individual, for within the terms of the hypothesis, it is this material integrity which, after all, defines "being." In opposition or at least in distinction to this system, we will recall that the criterion for justice in transcendentalist systems would be something having to do with the integrity of the soul. Divine justice is visited on the sinner, no matter his financial standing.

To pursue a crucial aspect of this distinction, as we continue to sketch the possibilities for the construction of character with a materialist *weltanschauung*, we can observe the possible differences between the lawful and the legal. In transcendentalist systems, law and legality are theoretically identical, for the primary concern of transcendentalism is whether the human mind is obeying its primal instincts by attempting to merge with "Personality." In such systems, law (*e.g.*, the Ten Commandments) tells the individual how to orient his desires. The Ultimate Judge knows to what extent the conduct of an individual has been lawful, despite any token and legalistic adherence to such laws. One may deceive other humans but not the Ultimate Judge, and we note Claudius reflecting on the fact.

> In the corrupted currants of this world,
> Offences gilded hand may shove by Justice,
> And oft 'tis seene, the wicked prize it selfe
> Buyes out the Law; but 'tis not so above,
> There is no shuffling, there the Action lies
> In his true Nature, and we our selves compell'd,
> Even to the teeth and forehead of our faults,
> To give in evidence. [*Hamlet*, 2333–40]

In a materialist universe, however, the purpose of law would not be the control of emotion but merely the control of material acts. To maintain the possibility of surviving on earth, as Ulysses points out, human beings as a group must avoid the mutual destructiveness of uncontrolled competition. Law in such a situation, assuming aggressive intention, offers purely external control over inner greed.

A materialistic individual would wish to serve himself before the greater abstraction of the group. It would, however, be within the very nature of such men to wish to violate their own laws.

> Must there be still some discord mixt among
> The Harmonie of men, whose moode accords
> Best with Contention, tun'd t'a note of wrong,
> That when war failes, peace must make war with words,
> And b'arm'd unto destruction even as strong,
> As were in ages past our civill swordes;
> Making as deepe, although unbleeding wounds,
> That when as furie failes, wisedome confounds.[10]

In such a context, the very notion of controlling external acts by means of law would contain the grounds for its own circumvention. Material law essentially makes the gesture of drawing a line, of defining a limit to a range of perceptible acts through the threat of force. But the existence of such external and material limits (as opposed to interior and volitional ones) would, in theory, invite the individual to advance as close to the permissible boundary as possible. Since this boundary was a statement of law, a fence not of wires but of words, the concept of the legal as opposed to the lawful would be bound to ensue. As Charron would observe, it is a question of whether laws are to be followed in terms of their intent or in terms of their phrasings, the material manifestation of their intent. And if intent of law could only be expressed by words, was it not possible to prove by words that the verbal barrier of law had not really been invaded? The paradox of materialized "intent" offered the materialist mind something upon which to work.

The *Formalists* doe wholly tie themselves to an outward forme and fashion of life, thinking to be quit of blame in the pursuite of their passions and desires, so they do nothing against the tenour of the lawes, and omit none of their formalities. . . . the extremitie of law is the extremitie of wrong: and as well sayd, God shield us from *Formalists*.[11]

[10] Samuel Daniel, "Epistle to Sir Thomas Egerton," in *Poems*, ed. A. C. Sprague (Cambridge, 1930), 102.

[11] Charron, sigs. L4–L4ᵛ, R7ᵛ, and Sᵛ. Cf. Hall, "The Hypocrite," in *Works*, sigs. R4–R4ᵛ.

Transcendentalist thought required a relativistic attitude toward purely visible things, but symbolic subtlety would not, in theory, be the strong side of a mind oriented away from the assumptions of transcendentalism. Any world view that used sensory perception as the criterion of reality was likely to be especially misled about the whole proposition of language. Francis Bacon is relevant on the point. "There is a great difference between the Idols of the human mind and the Ideas of the divine," he observed and continued, "That is to say, between certain empty dogmas and the true signatures and marks set upon the works of creation as they are found in nature." Of these "idols," we will recall the idols of the marketplace. If the idols of the tribe induced "a false assertion that the sense of man is the measure of things," and if, as Bacon argued, "all perceptions as well of the sense as of the mind are according to the measure of the individual and not according to the measure of the universe," the idols of the marketplace were complementary. They were the most troublesome of all, we gather, for they were "idols which have crept into the understanding through the alliances of words and names." As Bacon asks elsewhere:

And how is it possible, but this should have an operation to discredit learning, even with vulgar capacities, when they see learned mens workes like the first Letter of a Patent or lim[n]ed booke: which though it hath large flourishes, yet it is but a Letter? It seemes to me that *Pygmalions* frenzie is a good embleme or portraiture of this vanitie: for wordes are but the Images of matter, and except they have life of reason and invention: to fall in love with them is all one, as to fall in love with a picture.[12]

---

[12] Bacon, *Advancement of Learning*, sigs. E3ᵛ–E4; and "Novum Organon," in *Works*, IV, 53ff. Our reference to Bacon may appear to take us out of the mainstream of Shakespeare's milieu, but if we are exploring that dubious entity, a "climate of opinion," Bacon has a certain illustrative relevance. As with Montaigne, it is understandable that a mind trained in the transcendentalist tenets of Renaissance theology and philosophy and oriented to eschew the evidence of the senses for some "higher" truth would be ready to derive this kind of skeptical understanding of certain intellectual complexes and even, say, Phyrrhonistic tendencies merely from the suggestions of the transcendental mode. Thus we follow with interest Bacon's

We can look to a vastly more obtrusive area of Elizabethan intellectual interest than Bacon's writings for possible prototypes of the kind of mind whose theoretical structure we have adumbrated here. We have indicated the possibility of a fictional "personality" oriented toward acquisition, with a low order of ability at symbolizing and a conviction of the absoluteness of verbal structures because of a subtle inability to see around the corners of sensible phenomena, and we find a ready-made model in the popular concepts of the Elizabethan Puritan. On this level, it is true, theories about Puritanism might simply resolve themselves to an enumeration of traits derivable from the immediate social situation, criticism leveled at Puritan mercantile activities. Obviously, any conservative writer would object to the principle of a rising middle class along with the usual features of capitalist activity which we take for granted today: we recall the many satires against mercantile greed and the legal dispossession of the moneys or homes of gentlemen. Other aspects of the picture, however, are not without interest. A relative naïveté regarding the concept of loans, leases, and legal agreements, for example, depicted Puritan merchants as "stealing by law."[13] Legalism as a characteristic thus had some depictive focus in notions of Puritan legalism and pietistic hypocrisy.

Because of their separatist tendencies, the Puritans also could be thought of as taking the laws into their own hands or as seeking to abolish the very basis of law in a nation, and Hooker

---

description of the pseudo-Dionysian ranks of angels until he descends to "sensible and material forms" (217), while realizing, elsewhere, that the whole terminology of the "idol" was desirable from a transcendentalist viewpoint which regarded an overemphasis on material forms and human ideas as "idolatry." As for Montaigne, we will recall that his "Apologie of Raymond Sebonde" is a defense of the assertion that "all our wisdome is but folly before God; that of all vanities, man is the greatest; that man, who presumeth of his knowledge, doth not yet know what knowledge is: and that man, who is nothing, if he but thinke to be something, seduceth and deceiveth himselfe. These sentences of the Holy Ghost, doe so lively and manifestly expresse, what I would maintaine, as I should need no other proof against such as with all submission and obeysance would yeeld to his authority" (II, 138–39).

[13] See William Holden, *Anti-Puritan Satire: 1572–1642* (New Haven, 1954), pass.

could accuse them of hypocritically legalistic maneuvers. Thus in Book I of *The Laws of Ecclesiastical Polity*, he begins by discussing the basis of legal theory as a protective device for society and proceeds to challenge the Puritan contention that law had to emanate from one source, the Scriptures. In effect, Hooker reaffirms and promulgates what could be termed a characterization. In his preface, he observes a series of paradoxes which he attributes to Puritan conduct.

They which could not brooke at the first that any man should seeke, no not by law, the recovery of goods injuriously taken or withheld from him, were grown at the last to thinke they could not offer unto God more acceptable sacrifice, then by turning their adversaries cleane out of house and home, and by inriching themselves with all kind of spoyle and pillage; which thing being laid to their charge they had in a readines their answere, that now the time was come, when according to our Saviours promise, *The meeke ones must inherite the earth.* [sig. D3ᵛ]

Statements not only on Puritan avarice and hypocrisy but also on Puritan legalism went hand in hand with imputations of a literal reading of the Bible. William Whitaker agreed with John Calvin that the Catholics were literalistic in their interpretation of the Bible; the Puritans themselves came under the same stricture from the Anglicans. But Hooker, Calvin, and Whitaker, whatever their polemic purposes, presented a *locus* in which literalism as such was part of a more general character complex. These theologians, as well as others, all refer to Augustine's *De Doctrina* on the difference between symbols and signs. In one passage especially pertinent to our general point, Augustine sketches the attitude which induces literal readings:

But the ambiguities of metaphorical words, about which I am next to speak, demand no ordinary care and diligence. In the first place, we must beware of taking a figurative expression literally. For the saying of the apostle applies in this case too: "The letter killeth, but the spirit giveth life" [2 Cor. 3:6]. For when what is said figuratively is taken as if it were said literally, it is understood in a carnal manner.

And nothing is more fittingly called the death of the soul than when that in it which raises it above the brutes, the intelligence namely, is put in subjection to the flesh by a blind adherence to the letter. For he who follows the letter takes figurative words as if they were proper, and does not carry out what is indicated by a proper word into its secondary signification; but, if he hears of the Sabbath, for example, thinks of nothing but the one day out of seven which recurs in constant succession; and when he hears of a sacrifice, does not carry his thoughts beyond the customary offerings of victims from the flock, and of the fruits of the earth. Now it is surely a miserable slavery of the soul to take signs for things, and to be unable to lift the eye of the mind above what is corporeal and created, that it may drink in eternal light.[14]

That Augustine then continues by bringing in idolatry and excessive ceremony as other aspects of such an error would insure his utility to many sixteenth century theologians.

It is therefore understandable that Pico, writing on the qualities of the imagination and stressing the uselessness of a sensorial orientation, would structure an analogy significant for our interests:

Remove the bark of the Sacred Scriptures, lay aside the curtain of the imagination—which is to the bark of the letter what the intellect purified of phantasms is to the spirit hid beneath the bark—and the spirit introduces itself into the soul, and guides it to a divine foretaste, which is a beginning of the future glory to be revealed in us.[15]

But we are not concerned as much with theory here as we are with the "fictions" derived from such theories, and we may reassure ourselves as to the reality of this or some such mode of formal thought in the artistic work of the English Renaissance by recourse to dramatic mentalities. The anonymous author of *The Puritan* (SR, August 6, 1607) presents us with Nicholas:

[14] *De Doctrina*, III, v. See also Hooker, sig. B; Calvin, *Institutes*, IV. xiv. 16; and William Whitaker, *A Disputation on Holy Scripture*, ed. W. Fitzgerald (Cambridge, England, 1849), 494.

[15] Pico della Mirandola, *On the Imagination*, trans. and ed. Harry Caplan (New Haven, 1930), 93.

Nic. Steale my Maisters chaine, quo'the? no, it shal nere bee sayd, that *Nicholas* Saint Tantlings [St. Antlings] committed Bird-lime! *Cap[taine].* Nay, I told you as much; did I not? tho he be a Puritaine, yet he will be a true man.
Nich. Why, Couzen, you know tis written, *thou shalt not steale.*
Cap. Why, and foole, *thou shalt love thy Neighbour,* and helpe him in extremities.
Nich. Masse, I thinke it bee, indeede: in what Chapter's that, Couzen?
Cap. Why, in the first of Charity, the 2. verse.
Nich. The first of Charity, quatha! that's a good jest; there's no such Chapter in my booke!
Cap. No, I knew twas torne out of thy Booke, and that makes so little in thy heart.

. . . .

Nich. Pray, do not wish me to bee hangd: any thing else that I can do, had it beene to rob, I would ha don't; but I must not steale: that's the word, the literall, *thou shalt not steale;* and would you wish me to steale, then?
Pieboard No, faith, that were to much, to speake truth: why, woult thou nim [filch] it from him?
Nich. That I will! [I. iv. 137–68, in C. F. T. Brooke, ed., *The Shakespeare Apocrypha* (London, 1929)]

It is Nicholas' dead master who, as his widow said when reproving her son for not mourning his father, "did deceive all the world to get riches for thee" and "so wisely did quite overthrow the right heir of those lands which now you respect not: up every morning betwixt four and five; so duly at Westminster Hall every term-time, with all his charts and writings."

The humor is gross but illustrative; the same materials in the hands of Jonson, who is memorable for his Puritans, is more brilliant but of the same organization. Subtle suggests that with the newly made gold, it will no longer be necessary for Tribulation and Ananias to

take the start of bonds, broke but one day,
And say, *they were forfeited, by providence.*
Nor shall you need, ore-night to eate huge meales,
To celebrate your next daies fast the better:

The whilst the *Bretheren*, and the *Sisters*, humbled,
Abate the stiffenesse of the flesh. Nor cast
Before your hungrie hearers, scrupulous bones,
As whether a *Christian* may hawke, or hunt;
Or whether, *Matrons, of the holy assembly*,
May lay their haire out, or weare doublets:
Or have that idoll *Starch*, about their linnen.
Ana. It is, indeed, an idoll. [III. ii. 72–83]

The two exit, we will recall, after Subtle has suggested the counterfeiting of Dutch dollars. As Subtle says, "It is no coyning, sir. It is but casting." Whereupon Ananias can conclude, "The *Bretheren* shall approve it lawfull, doubt not." Here again, rapacity, biblical and legal literalism, and pietism are the materials of construction.[16] Law itself is relative. As Ananias observes, "Lawful? / We know no Magistrate."

Shakespeare's familiarity with such hypothetical constructions is readily attested to by *Measure for Measure* and *The Merchant of Venice*. In the former play, Claudio's error leads him into the clutches of Angelo; but the duke, as if aware of Bacon's warning that "penal laws, if they have been sleepers of long, or if they be grown unfit for the present time, be by wise judges confined in the execution," works so as to revive the referents of the decayed symbols which are that law while averting real harm to his subjects. In *The Merchant of Venice*, on the other hand, we are faced with a character who utilizes his victim's belief that a bond will have some symbolic value other than that delimited by the physical writing. Antonio has assumed that the bond was made as a jest, but of course the word "jest" does not actually appear in the document. Portia supports Shylock's world view by carrying his materialistic reasoning all the way through to the finer legalism of shedding blood, a law which also is not written into the bond but which exists "on the books." The duke, one guesses, rejects the whole assumption of the materialist view by *giving* something to Shylock, mercy.

[16] Cf. John Marston, *The Metamorphosis of Pygmalions Image* (London, 1598), sig. D2ʳff.

As Holden has observed (p. 81), Shakespeare did not make any great efforts to characterize Puritanism as such, for although some of his characters have Puritanical traits, they are not as literally founded on the tenets of popular assumption as are the creations of some other playwrights. In fact, we suggest that the character who comes closest to the conventional stage Puritan in Shakespeare's plays is not Malvolio but Shylock the Jew. He is involved in business, lends money, quotes the Bible as justification, sets himself up as a law unto himself, and forecloses on bonds: in fact, if the term "Jew" were extracted from the lines of the play, Shylock would come much closer to the typical stage portrait of a Puritan than would Angelo or Malvolio.

Puritanism was a ready-made mold for a kind of characterization, but there were other archetypes as well. The Pharisees were similarly described; and Joseph Hall, in his first "Character" of a Vice, adduces the "Hypocrite" as a type who combines greed with legality. Shakespeare's own activity, significantly adumbrated in *The Merchant of Venice*, might, as we have observed, have taken its point of departure from distinctions suggested by the tale in the *Gesta*. As we have noted, in its "Morall" the golden casket represents "some worldly men, both mightie men & rich, which outwardly shine as golde in riches and pomps of this world." The silver casket differs from its golden counterpart, for by this silver casket "we ought to understand some Justices & wise men of this world which shine in faire speach but within be full of wormes and earth." We earlier observed Arragon's choice of such a casket, his literalistic review of the rules, and Portia's description of him as a "deliberate" fool. But to the silver casket Shakespeare also transfers, as we have seen, the concept of desert. Removing the earth and worms of the *Gesta*, he substitutes a fool's head. We may with some justification be reminded of the "folly" of the worldly-wise man, while part of the little poem contained in the casket is also relevant:

> Seaven times tried that jud[g]ement is,
> That did never choose amis,
> Some there be that shadowes kisse,
> Such have but a shadowes blisse:

There be fooles alive Iwis
Silver'd o're, and so was this. [1177–82]

Bassanio is led to think of the whole concept of money when he views the silver casket, and the structure of these scenes suggests that there is a relationship of the idea of money and trade to the kind of character complex that Shakespeare might have been building toward in later plays.

To generalize, we may suggest that Shakespeare, wishing to create a character concerned with materialistic concepts, did not confine himself to such immediately obvious matters as the desire for money and property but pursued other ramifications suggested by a prolixity of allied traditions. As a completed structure, such a figure, viewed from transcendentalist positions, could be described as one who initially defined the "self" through unity with material things. But no matter how high the degree of pragmatic cunning, such a mind would be posited as having only a limited ability to deal with abstractions. One aspect of conceptual weakness in such a character would be an affecting of the literal, for distinctions between sign and symbol are not the strengths of such minds, which tend to view the law (or the bond) in a certain way. While a transcendentalist would claim that law is the articulation of a spiritual agreement into visible symbols, the hypothetical character which we describe here would look at matters in another light. In the case of a bond, such a document would become, in effect, the real existence of the agreement rather than a mere representation of intent. Antonio's signature is not simply the symbolic expression of consent but "consent" itself, the "word made flesh." Feste, in *Twelfth Night*, is pertinent on the subject: "Indeede, words are very Rascals, since bonds disgrac'd them" (1232–33).

A bond can be torn up or lost, and it is as if intent itself has disappeared. In the case of general law, a law can still be "on the books" even if the statute itself has lapsed into obsolescence. Yet to the literalist, it would seem as if the referents of a law could still be invoked as long as the physical symbol, the paper-and-ink structure, had not been destroyed. Volition itself apparently could be "materialized" or "stored" like a physical object, even though the transcendentalist view might regard freedom of the will or Christian liberty as freedom from the bondage of the letter of the old law, from the punishment of desert—the death and skull within the golden casket of the *Gesta* and the fool's head within the silver casket of Shakespeare.[17] Since we speak of the transcendentalist view, the genuine-sounding shock and rage exhibited by many Elizabethan and Jacobean playwrights at what for us are such commonplaces as loan interest, mortgage, and bonds might conceivably stem from remnants of a transcendentalist viewpoint, after ample allowance has been made for pique stemming from personal experience.[18]

If such character complexes are to be found in Shakespeare's

[17] Literalism was of course associated with the devil. We recall Antonio's reaction to Shylock's biblical attempts to justify usury: "The devil can cite scripture for his purpose." Cf. Richard III on the same subject (I. iii. 339ff.). In Barnabe Barnes, *The Devil's Charter*, sigs. L4–L4ᵛ, the pope is ultimately deceived by the "Sophistrie" according to which the devil plays on numbers in the charter in such a way that he legally binds the pope to hell. Richard III's speech may be compared: "But then I sigh, and, with a piece of Scripture, Tell them that God bids us do good for evil; / And thus I clothe my naked villainy / With odd old ends stol'n forth of holy writ, / And seem a saint when most I play the devil" (I. iii. 334–38).

[18] Not without interest are the summations of Paul S. Clarkson and Clyde T. Warren, *The Law of Property in Shakespeare and the Elizabethan Drama* (Baltimore, 1942). They conclude on page 88 that "pledges of everyday items of personal property for petty loans must have been far more common than today. . . . There is nothing to indicate, on the other hand, that they [Elizabethan dramatists] had any appreciation of the many legal niceties inherent in the pledgor-pledgee relationship." Cf. pp. 149–62 on "Conveyances by way of Mortgage" for allusions to the whole concept of pledging for loans in Shakespeare's lifetime. Not without relevance was the changing relationship between Chancery and the mortgagor, for they note on page 151 that "by 1630 it is certain that the Chancellor was granting relief from mortgage forfeitures in general, irrespective of special grounds for relief," with the proviso that the mortgagee would pay by a certain date. Forfeitures, we gather, "must necessarily have been very frequent under the strict rules of law in force at the time and prior to the intervention of Chancery to prevent them" (p. 154). Hence they were a great topic of interest to dramatists. In general, we may perhaps view our suggestions as to character type against the larger background of transition from the feudal concept that all ownership rested with the king and that land was held merely by tenure to the time of Shakespeare when, in varying degrees, property theory developed increasing sophistications about the concept of individual ownership.

work, we need not be disturbed by their obvious moralizings. Such characters' literalistic mentalities could reasonably lead them to appeal for justification, to urge that they have acted ethically. In many cases, it is true that they have been made to adhere literally to the premises dominant in a materialistic universe. And such characters in Shakespeare's plays, just as the ancient Romans, could (with their material fervor) be quite moral on this point.

> *Duke.* How shalt thou hope for mercie, rendering none?
> *Shy.* What judgement shall I dread doing no wrong? [1994–95]

There is Ulysses on degree; and there is Shylock on ownership:

> You have among you many a purchast slave,
> Which like your Asses, and your Dogs and Mules,
> You use in abject and in slavish parts,
> Because you bought them. Shall I say to you,
> Let them be free, marrie them to your heires?
> Why sweate they under burthens? Let their beds
> Be made as soft as yours: and let their pallats
> Be season'd with such Viands: you will answer
> The slaves are ours. So do I answer you.
> The pound of flesh which I demand of him
> Is deerely bought, 'tis mine, and I will have it.
> If you deny me; fie upon your Law.
> There is no force in the decrees of Venice;
> I stand for judgement. [1996–2009]

Portia makes a speech about mercy, true; yet Shylock might from his viewpoint ask simply, "what is mercy?" Mercy would have to do with giving, and the kind of character which we describe here would have nothing to do with giving—only with trading, for self-deprivation could be allowed only with a promise of equivalent restitution.

Within this general theory it might be possible, when creating characters, to confine oneself to the equation that any mind not oriented toward transcendentalist aspiration could be taken as immersed in the problem of purely physical acquisition, any desire for riches, food, drink, power, weapons, or horses being offered as evidence of the materialist orientation. But Shakespeare seems to have emphasized his differentiation of a particular class, as we have shown by his attention to the basis of perception. Literalism is the common denominator rather than any concrete objects of desire. With a simplicity of outlook derived from their strong sense that visible entities are absolutes in themselves, members of this class not only exhibit their naïveté through an obtrusive literalism in larger issues but, interestingly, through their inability to comprehend or be amused by the wordplay characteristic of jokes and nonsense.

Such characters also frequently exhibit a tendency toward relatively transparent hypocrisy. Any penchant toward hypocrisy logically derives from the assumption of the literalistic mind that other men can be as effectively deceived by exterior shows as the hypocrite himself. But the connection, though logical, is not inevitable since it may simply be a question of differentiating between effective and ineffective jobs of hypocrisy. Possibly because an audience can, by definition, only see through an ineffective hypocrisy or possibly because Shakespeare made the association for other reasons, discernible hypocrisy is the concomitant characteristic of his character types in this mode. It is as if he shared with Bacon the aphorism that imposture and credulity are two sides of the same coin.

Shakespeare also brought to character structures in this category some traits which may most conveniently be taken as the results not of theory but perhaps of his personal taste and bent in the act of mimesis. In most cases, for instance, these characters are sober minded in the sense that they do not like to drink or indulge in that area of activity which Renaissance writers often termed "pleasure."[19] And, perhaps concomitantly, their mental stances are rendered as somewhat alien to any transcendentalist concepts of love. Rather, they are quite concerned with the notion of their "deservings" or with the "deserts" of others. While

[19] See Barroll, "Anthony and Pleasure," *JEGP*, LVII (1958), 708–20.

this latter bent is comprehensible from the association of desert with trade, both being concepts which posit no outlay without equivalent recompense, such traits do not necessarily follow to the exclusion of other derivative notions. But they do follow in Shakespeare. The miser fondling his gold might be the best or most obvious exemplification of Shakespeare's theories in this area; yet he created no real misers (Shylock is somewhat different, as we shall see). Rather, the poet adhered, with some consistency, to the kind of creation which was essentially an ordering of the foregoing characteristics, whatever the individual ramifications.

That Shakespeare was consistent not only in practice but in what we might guess was his "theory" may be deduced from examining an extremely minor personality in 2 *Henry IV*. This is John of Lancaster who, though the value of his contrast with Hal may not be a minor matter, appears only briefly. Despite the brevity of his role in the play, he is made the subject of Falstaffian commentary. We may recall the fat knight's reflections after a rather unsuccessful interchange with the young prince.

Good faith, this same young sober-blooded Boy doth not love me, nor a man cannot make him laugh: but that's no marvaile, hee drinkes no wine. [2324–27]

Advancing his own theory of personality-through-sherris-sack and contrasting John with Hal, Falstaff notes that Hal "has moderated the cold blood he did naturally inherit of his father" by tempering it with "sherris." The comparison, despite its playful terms, emphasizes Shakespeare's theory of personality differences if we substitute any entity we wish for Falstaff's own ingredient, alcohol. Indeed, the whole argument of character over the three plays has been a sophistication of the fat man's conclusion, for Hal may have cold-blooded qualities, but he is not sober in the sense that John is. John, however, swiftly demonstrates what goes with his sobriety, and in terms pertinent here.

It is John, we recall, who has deceived the rebels into surrender by giving an oath, and then, with the real power now in his hands and the rebels dispersing while his own army is still in formation, by breaking his vow. When the archbishop asks "will you thus break your faith," John answers in a Shylockian adherence to literalisms:

> I pawn'd thee none:
> I promis'd you redresse of these same Grievances
> Whereof you did complaine; which, by mine Honor,
> I will performe, with a most Christian care.
> But for you (Rebels) looke to taste the due
> Meet for Rebellion, and such Acts as yours.
> Most shallowly did you these Armes commence,
> Fondly brought here, and foolishly sent hence.
> Strike up our Drummes, pursue the scatter'd stray,
> Heaven, and not wee, hath safely fought to day. [2223–32]

In his subsequent dealings, John is utterly merciless. No one he encounters is ever pardoned, and he even wishes to run down the already disorganized and scattered "stray" of men merely returning to their homes in joy. The justification of self through God enlarges the picture, and the subsequent encounter with Falstaff completes it.

Since Falstaff, through the series, has often served as a touchstone, we may contrast Hal's tolerance of Falstaff's jokes with John's intolerance of the fat man in this scene. And when Sir John requests a good word at court for his feat of capturing Colville, Lancaster tells him, "I, in my condition, / Shall better speake of you, then you deserve. *Exit.*" Indeed, previously, when Falstaff for once honestly claimed that he captured the prisoner, he was told by John that "it was more of his courtesy than of your deserving." Colville, of course, is sent "to present execution." Finally, John dispatches Westmoreland to the court with news of the battle, promising "Wee with sober speede will follow you."

It is interesting to speculate on the point at which Shakespeare may have decided on this shorthand characterization of a type of personality that begins to appear in his art, but it would strain belief to argue that the poet here wanted to present his audience with a paradigm of his own character theory. It is perhaps useful to speculate, however, that Shakespeare, needing someone in his story for the purpose, invented a personality who might plausibly betray the rebels. Accordingly, John's penchant for operating according to the letter (as opposed to the spirit) of the treaty, his justification of himself by reference to God, and his utter mercilessness were obviously useful. If this is granted, then it is certainly interesting that Shakespeare moved on to fill in, as it were, other traits which would constitute a "whole" personality type. The interview with Falstaff establishes in Lancaster further traits, showing John as obsessed with a concept of "deservings," as impervious to humor, and as a nondrinker. And when Lancaster waxes extremely technical on the subject of Falstaff's exact role in the capture of Colville, we recall, in contrast, that Hal simply surrendered to the fat knight the credit for the death of a far more formidable threat, Hotspur, in a moment when the question of technicalities might have been more tellingly employed.

The existence of Lancaster may thus suggest Shakespeare's method of melting obvious and, if we wish, anti-Puritan strains of thought into the crucible of his own character theory. There is thus Malvolio, who is not strictly a Puritan because he does not quote the Bible, no matter how puritanical he may seem in the modern sense. Yet what Shakespeare had in mind for him may be suggested by isolated lines. "Sometimes he is a kind of Puritan," says Maria of Malvolio, assuming an audience understanding of what she means; and Shakespeare's own association may be derived from a joke he has Sir Andrew bring forward as he says of the duel with Viola:

And't be any way, it must be with Valour, for policie I hate: I had as liefe be a Brownist, as a Politician [*Twelfth Night*, 1410–12]

What's the difference, the audience might ask: the perpetual silliness of Sir Andrew might allow us to assume that point to the joke.

But Malvolio, despite the fact that he might have been understood as a contemporary member of the rising middle class, is significantly constructed, as is John of Lancaster. We gather from several women that he is "sick of self-love," and his name, Malvolio, might from the transcendentalist viewpoint suggest this fact. Malvolio belittles Feste not because he is hostile to the "works of the devil," as it were, but because he is against mirth. He scolds the party group not for frivolous and un-Christian behavior but for not observing decorum. He thinks literally: indeed, this penchant leads to his fall. Simply because the "letter" from Olivia is in her handwriting, he assumes that the physical object is an accurate indication of the spirit behind the writing. Maria stresses this in allusive terms as she reports the success of her plot.

Yond gull *Malvolio* is turned Heathen, a verie Renegatho; for there is no christian that meanes to be saved by beleeving rightly, can ever beleeve such impossible passages of grossenesse. [1448–51]

His erroneous reading is glancingly illumined against the whole background of common doctrine on the subject of scriptural interpretation, a background against which, we recall, Puritans always came under attack for their literal exegeses. And as Shakespeare expounds on the concept in the play, is not "misreading" one of the central motifs in the characterization of Olivia's steward?

"Malvolio," for instance, is not a name mentioned in the pseudoletter; neither is "Olivia." Rather, like Shylock wresting scripture to his purpose, Malvolio seeks to impose an interpretation as if he can make the symbols conform to what he wishes them to represent. This is one aspect of the technique used with the bond and with John's broken oath. "And the end," Malvolio mutters. "What should that Alphabeticall position portend, if I could make that resemble something in me? Softly, *M.O.A.I.*" Stumped by what is, after all, a conventionally constructed Elizabethan anagram, he ponders:

M. But then there is no consonancy in the sequell that suffers under probation: A should follow, but O does.

Finally:
M,O,A,I. This simulation is not as the former: and yet to crush this a little, it would bow to mee, for every one of these Letters are in my name. [1127–47]

His literalism, however, has been apparent ever since he picked up the note and read the posy:

Jove knowes I love; but who, Lips do not moove, no man must know.
No man must know. What followes? The numbers alter'd. [1109–11]

And indeed, they are: "*I may command where I adore,*" etc. But Malvolio's emphasis is one ordinarily devoted to deciphering code, not love letters.

Beyond his literalism, Malvolio also reveals a hypocrisy of sanctimony, for even before he saw the forged letter, he had been thinking of being "Count Malvolio." In this train of thought, he imagined himself not as in the process of romantically relating to Olivia but as leaving her sleeping while he fondles "some rich jewel" and advances to hold forth in state to his houschold. Accordingly, it cannot be said that the letter has altered his personality; the note has merely precipitated the demonstration of Malvolio's drive as a ludicrous campaign based not on love but on greed for money and position. By his very personality, Malvolio is clearly ignorant of (may we say "alien to"?) what is meant by "love." One shows it, he supposes, by wearing silly clothes and simpering. So he casts off his sobriety to attain his worldly ambitions. Because we deal with comedy, he finally incurs comic and appropriate punishment—he is locked up according to rules which he himself would have so literally enforced. Having been fooled into an exhibition of the ludicrous licentiousness which he has so often condemned in others, he is regarded as "mad." Ironically, he initiated this adjective for the same excesses when he burst in upon the partying of Sir Toby, Feste, Maria, and Aguecheek: "My masters, are you mad?" At the end of his ordeal, he finally violates the tone of comedy by exiting not with a rueful laugh of forgiveness but with a vow to "be reveng'd upon the whole pack of you!" He is, as it were, a fuller but not very bright John of Lancaster reduced to the material limitations of his social position.

If Angelo is more complex, the subtleties of his structure emerge as further evidence of these particular principles of one kind of characterization. Like Malvolio, Angelo has no use for humorists, even though Escalus' tolerance of Pompey's diverting chatter might indicate what is acceptable in the play itself. But as he exits, Angelo's reaction to Elbow, Froth, Pompey, and company is:

> Ile take my leave,
> And leave you to the hearing of the cause;
> Hoping youle finde good cause to whip them all.
> [*Measure for Measure*, 587–89]

His pattern is now familiar enough: rigorous theoretical chastity, reviving a law literally applied to a Claudio who is not yet literally married. The deputy can even say to Isabella that her plea is "too late" because Claudio is already legally condemned. He can argue tellingly for law, since that is what he knows, but what he does not know, of course, is himself. We observe him in reaction to a rather interesting kind of temptation as Shakespeare seems to put to himself the question of what happens when a "Malvolio" really falls in love. The poet is prepared to answer since he endows Angelo with soliloquies:

> my Gravitie
> Wherein (let no man heare me) I take pride,
> Could I, with boote, change for an idle plume
> Which the aire beats for vaine. [1011–14]

He is swept from his austere eminence by an emotion with which he cannot, in theory, be too familiar, for love has no place in the acquisitive mind. Accordingly, it is very interesting that he must simply consider his emotion in analogy to Malvolio's taut equation of love with yellow stockings and simpering, "an idle plume." However, Angelo also thinks love is lust, for he offers a kind of recension of the chapbooks which nevertheless endues those clichés with a subtle change:

> what, doe I love her,
> That I desire to heare her speake againe?
> And feast upon her eyes? What is't I dreame on?

Oh cunning enemy, that to catch a Saint,
With Saints dost bait thy hooke: most dangerous
Is that temptation, that doth goad us on
To sinne, in loving vertue. [940–46]

"Ever till now," he ponders, "when men were fond, I smild, and wondered how." His mode of thought is, in a sense, almost pathetic, for the speakers in *The Courtier* might conceivably have approved of the bases of his initial attraction to Isabella. She has stood there arguing almost like a Portia, philosophizing on government and laws, and if he loves her for her virtue, is this not the correct Neo-Platonic path? Clearly, the initial attraction is presented as one stimulated by eloquence and brains:

Never could the Strumpet,
With all her double vigour, Art, and Nature
Once stir my temper: but this vertuous Maid
Subdues me quite. [946–49]

Yet according to the sad quality of Angelo's private universe, this strange new emotion must be wrenched and tortured into the mechanics of a trade-rape. We recall a previous love affair, or at least a betrothal, in which Angelo was to marry Marianna. The ship bearing her dowry and her brother was lost at sea, and thus "the portion and sinew of her fortune, her marriage dowry" as well as her intended husband were lost to her. Angelo, we gather from the duke,

Left her in her teares, and dried not one of them with his comfort: swallowed his vowes whole, pretending in her, discoveries of dishonor: in few, bestow'd her on her owne lamentation, which she yet weares for his sake. [1446–50]

Again we have, as it were, the poet intellectually filling in the outline when he could as easily have suggested that Angelo and Marianna were simply estranged by a lovers' quarrel. Instead, we are to gather that Angelo defined love in terms of money and proceeded by the Shylockian method to justify his reneging.

The outlines are obvious enough, even if conclusions are not. Rather than simply give mercy, as does Escalus for Pompey's first offense, Angelo will "trade" with Isabella for it. At the same time he will evade his side of the bargain in a way logical to the acquisitive mind which knows only force and possession. He also lives by the kinds of quantification which Angelo attributes to heaven when, trying to persuade Isabella, he observes that "Our compell'd sins / Stand more for number than accompt." It also follows that Angelo's material advantage is important enough to lead him to try to wipe out the situation by afterward silencing all parties in order to retain his status which, despite his brief interpretive excursion into "love," is his most important consideration. And in the end, when found out, it is also characteristic of him to say:

> No longer Session hold upon my shame,
> But let my Triall, be mine own Confession:
> Immediate sentence then, and sequent death,
> Is all the grace I beg. [2753–56]

And later he tells Escalus, "I crave death more willingly then mercy, / 'Tis my deserving, and I doe intreat it" (2873–74). We may question whether we are to understand Angelo as trying to evade public shame, a consistent motivation, or whether, as the second passage would seem to emphasize, the deputy's universe continues to be bound by concepts of acquisition and retribution, by a theory of material parity. While not discussing the point at any length here, we can observe that the general emphases in the drama suggest that such concepts are in play. Shakespeare's way with Isabella hints as much.

Isabella can be seen without too much difficulty as Angelo's spiritual twin. And if, Angelo's precontract with Marianna still being in force, he is to be condemned partially by a law which he himself has revived—for he has, willy-nilly, had intercourse with his own fiancée on precontract—then it is up to Isabella, we gather, to get down on her knees to learn the kind of forgiveness which she has previously demanded of Angelo for her brother.

"He dies for Claudio's death," the duke reminds her temptingly; but it is to the credit of this would-be Christian nun that she persists, if only in her own way and if only for Marianna's sake. Significantly, Isabella can never speak of or ask for mercy in Portia's way. Rather, Angelo was easily able to out-argue her on the subject of Claudio merely on legalistic grounds, for Isabella employs Christian philosophy for motives which are not strictly transcendentalist in formulation. Her intolerance of fornication is more rigid when applied to herself than it is when applied to her brother for whom she is, after all, seeking to obtain mercy. But when her brother takes the same attitude toward her possible sexual behavior that she has had toward his, she condemns him to hell in an unforgiving rage at his human fear of death. Finding herself at the end of the play in the old position of imploring pardon for someone, she can as flexibly but as consistently attempt to "reason" mercy for Angelo from the duke. Thinking her brother already executed, we recall her saying to the duke at this juncture:

> my Brother had but Justice,
> In that he did the thing for which he dide.
> For *Angelo*, his Act did not ore-take his bad intent,
> And must be buried but as an intent
> That perish'd by the way: thoughts are no subjects,
> Intents, but meerely thoughts.
> *Mar.* Meerely my Lord. [2841–47]

The duke, presumably to teach her a further lesson (he has already taught her to kneel in behalf of her enemy), must answer her with "Your suite's unprofitable." In the end, Isabella never does "reason" mercy out of the duke as she attempted to reason it out of Angelo. Begging for mercy, Isabella shows the irony of her ambivalent position. As a Christian nun, she should be able to recall Christ's own refusal in the Sermon on the Mount to differentiate between intent and act. In short, the man who commits adultery in his heart is as guilty as the man who actually realizes such a wish. But Isabella shares with Shylock the concept that intent is irrelevant: the difference between Claudio and Angelo, Isabella would have us believe, is that Angelo technically never committed the particular act he meditated, even if he did have intercourse. The duke's implicit lesson presents the other viewpoint. Mercy does not, by definition, arise from the "desert" to be gleaned from the interpretation of some system of retributive morality. Rather, mercy is the function of giving freely. In Portia's words:

> Though Justice be thy plea, consider this,
> That in the course of Justice, none of us
> Should see salvation: we do pray for mercie,
> And that same prayer, doth teach us all to render
> The deeds of mercie. [*Merchant of Venice*, 2109-13]

Isabella at least knew the words, saying as she did to Angelo:

> Why, all the soules that were, were forfeit once,
> And he that might the vantage best have tooke
> Found out the remedie: how would you be,
> If he, which is the top of Judgment, should
> But judge you, as you are? Oh, think on that.
> And mercie then will breathe within your lips
> Like man new made. [*Measure for Measure*, 825-31]

The duke offers the last of his transcendentalist paradoxes. Although Isabella's suit is unprofitable, he will nevertheless pardon Angelo not by reasoning but by fiat—an articulation of the concept of mercy which cannot, by definition, be earned despite deeds or argumentation.

It has been necessary to move rather far afield and to offer an interpretation not of a character but of large segments of a play; but whatever ethical conclusion we agree upon for *Measure for Measure*, we have observed the delineation of characteristics only adumbrated by a figure such as Malvolio. We have seen certain sequences illuminate the various individual facets of one general kind of characterization. If a Malvolio perhaps seems less evil, it is because he is never dropped into the retort reserved for an

Angelo. The steward is never allowed power over Olivia; and for that matter, we do not see Leah present Shylock with the ring which he would not trade for "a wilderness of monkeys," as he quaintly quantifies his love for his dead wife. On the other hand, we never see Angelo in his business dealings, except for the canceled marriage. We never see how he lends money. What we do see in all of these characters is that none of them seems to know what love is. They cannot comprehend this transcendentalist formulation. Isabella may be the exception. She does learn to kneel for the sake of Marianna, but if she is to be the duke's wife, we may assume that she is meant to learn. Given the existence of the transcendentalist thrust in all men, it is not implausible to see Isabella's reluctant plea, however legalistic, as the beginning of the approved mode of using this thrust.

We may argue that we see something like Isabella's development in Shylock, and indeed, we have not really offered this figure our full attention. This is because he does not, except in his more obvious materialisms and literalisms, ultimately belong in the class which we have been discussing. Rather, the more passionate equivocations of some of his passages suggest he is a figure subjected to some transitional techniques. These techniques were to lead to a most mannered and difficult method of characterization with which we will deal not next but last. While we may detect in Shylock a greater warmth than is sometimes apparent in Isabella, we need more specific terms, and such terms can only be refined in our movement away from one end of the theoretical spectrum toward an area in which such entities as warmth and passion do emerge as the dominant structural motifs.

7
Shakespeare's Lovers

Critical writing about Shakespeare's tragic characters often speaks of the "lovers" who have enriched so many of his dramas. The term is not amiss if we expand its definition to include those figures who, unlike a Romeo, are not necessarily limited to a preoccupation with romance. Romeo, we remember, is almost alone among Shakespeare's tragic characters in beginning and ending a play by relating to a woman. A Troilus or an Othello may seem to challenge this statement, but reflection will remind us that while they may be preoccupied with their relationships with lovers, their creator, the poet himself, offers a range of other activities for their audiences to contemplate. Troilus speaks in council or rages over his horse. Othello is seldom required to react directly to Desdemona on stage: he must cope with the Iagos, Cassios, and Brabantios. Thus if we note a grouping which would indeed include Othello and Romeo, and if we also observe that in such a group the women serve not as the primary means of defining these personalities but most often as stimuli for dramatic response, then we can include a Hotspur and a King Henry V when we speak of a second Shakespearean character type. Though Hotspur and Othello may not share an equal preoccupation specifically with women, they do share what we might call an "ardor" not to be found in the Angelos and Malvolios.

In the general intellectual context from which we have approached the larger problem of Shakespearean characterization, we might describe such characters as Romeo or Othello as "aspirers." Our hypothetical picture of the miser may emphasize by contrast the relevant traits implicit in such an orientation. Transcendentalist thought would regard the miser's attempt at ownership as the effort to realize "being" by relating to things visible and manipulable on relatively elementary levels. Shakespeare's aspirers, however, could be regarded as more oriented toward transcendentalist paths. Diagramatically, they may not be set on the one ladder, the one road, the one voyage to the transcendentalist ideal, but they are close enough to be on slightly diverging, almost parallel routes. If we accept the analogy, the problem suggested by such behavior and modes of perception perhaps becomes clearer. These characters do see their optimal directions as being "upward," and we may with some justification take them as "pseudotranscendentalists." They are like those philosophers whose efforts Montaigne terms "nothing else but the extreme indevour of our imagination, toward perfection, every one amplifying the Idea thereof according to his capacitie" (II. 217).

Transcendentalist thought, we recall, would define the proper "self" as, essentially, a proper directing of the individual drive toward Absolute Being. This directing implies a submergence of self to the point at which what remains after appropriate purging of "dross" from the mind can be molded in accord with the ideal "personality." Hence they emphasize service, the best aspirer being paradoxically "elevated" by his willingness to be the best servant. Such a system accordingly produces its characteristic vocabulary: one falls below the standard, or one lives up to it. One is worthy of or one betrays a concept of conduct hovering, as it were, "above" the self. In specific philosophies one might, of course, note a great variety of manners in which to perform "correct" service, but the general shapes of optimal mental behavior would be similar. The importance of a relationship to something envisioned as "outside" and "above" the self would remain constant. And when we isolate this characteristic, we further define the quality constituting this new class of Shakespeare's "people."

It is not completely accurate that Shakespeare planted a pseudotranscendentalist bent primarily in figures who were oriented toward war or women. A Hal is not absorbed in either of these specific subjects; rather, he is preoccupied with his own pseudotranscendental goal, the ideal of kingship. Yet Falstaff has observed in Hal a propensity for "sherris-sack" not shared by his Malvolio-like brother, John. We may, of course, take Falstaff's speech as symbology, but Prince Hal was himself a tradition. As summed up in *The Famous Victories*, Hal's youth was associated with the pleasures of the flesh. If Shakespeare's play never shows

Hal as so directly involved in pleasure, except according to accounts by other characters, we could yet claim for his Hal a sense, if only intellectual, of attraction to the mode itself. He is clearly not John. We may ultimately agree that Hal seems to have to cope with something in his own personality which appears inimical to what an audience knows is his ultimate destiny.

Perhaps war or women or even "pleasure" (like Falstaff's "sherris-sack") thus have representative values. We may ponder the fact that Shakespeare's pseudotranscendentalists are always interested in some kind of "warfare," either with opposing armies or (in that figurative warfare which was an endless Elizabethan joke) with women. Hotspur may strike us as ascetic, but while he might find it an "easy leap" to "pluck bright honor from the pale-faced moon," he can still be parodied by Hal as primarily and compulsively concerned with the care and feeding of horses. While Hotspur's interest in women does seem nil, his contempt for a scented and presumably unmasculine courtier picking his dainty way across a battlefield is eloquent. His cult of virility is itself physicalistic, and Hotspur rings true as a pseudotranscendentalist because of this duality. His sense of the sublimity of service to some elevated concept goes hand in hand with his fascination with one physical side of life. Angelo, by contrast, is instructive. Despite his fall, the deputy cannot really be described as one dedicated to sensual delights. He does not, after all, require that Isabella be his perpetual mistress. On the other hand, he rarely, except in the one obvious instance, seems to see himself as in a conflict. He talks easily from the assurance of a static position.

The story of Troilus, if we see him as more idealistic than Angelo, conveys, however, perpetual war, if only because he is literally a warrior. Lives such as his always emerge as a kind of combat, as if conflict for its own sake is a fundamental gesture of personality. Hal and Hotspur, despite their differences, share this orientation. When Hotspur hears of the defections and latenesses of various contingents before the battle of Shrewesbury, he may seem foolish for saying that to fight with fewer men is to gain the greater glory, but Hal will later make the same gesture.

Will he not, before Agincourt, speak of the happiness of fighting with this small "band of brothers"? It is as if these motions of personality imitate a fundamental tenet of transcendentalist philosophy, the idea of life as constant warfare, as a ceaseless struggle in a *Faerie Queene*–like situation where Acrasia, who tempts to sleep, is the profoundest enemy.

In Shakespearean terms, the similarities and differences between the idealist and the philosophically correct transcendentalist can perhaps be adumbrated by Daniel Dyke, who writes on "the mystery of self-deceiving" and remarks:

> Deceit is, when our *carnall* and worldly desires are accounted of us as *spirituall*. This deceit falleth out in this case, when, in one and the selfe same thing which we desire, there is matter fitte to giue contentment to both these desires.[1]

The distinction is quite pertinent to the class of character we are discussing, for there is a kind of irony in their situation. Such figures create some pseudotranscendental entity outside the self and then, assuming the reality of this entity, perform that somersault which makes it praiseworthy to offer service to such a self-manufactured ideal. It is ultimately for this reason that with some justification we term such figures pseudotranscendentalists, especially if we compare them to the materialists. It is one thing to desire money and power for whatever satisfactions they may offer, but it is another thing to desire some entity in such a way that one sees oneself as performing "service" for it and as being ennobled by this service. In their sense of following something larger than life we detect then a quality of aspiration which defines this new class.

That our distinctions are not purely modern can be deduced from an old and well-established trend of thought in the Renaissance (one reemphasized by the Reformation) concerning the notion of idolatry. According to this concept, the idol was essentially manufactured by the individual who, once having created it, performed the paradox of according it the respect and worship

[1] Dyke, *Self-Deceiving*, sig. X2ᵛ.

usually offered to God. Our interest may be engaged by the fact that although much argumentation had to do with "graven images" in the churches, figurative analogies were also prominent. Thus Hall could say:

Wee are all borne Idolaters, naturally prone to fashion God to some forme of our owne, whether of an humane bodie, or of an admirable light; or if our minde have any other more likely, and pleasing image.

We might then count on La Primaudaye to warn his readers against "making idols of our selves, by sacrificing to our nets, and burning incense to our yearne [yarn]."[2] Shakespeare often refers to the concept, especially in *The Two Gentlemen of Verona*, but his specific familiarity with the traditional way of looking at things in this context may be assumed from his joke in Sonnet 105 where he contradicts himself by creating his object of love not only as eternal but as the Holy Trinity.

> Let not my love be cal'd Idolatrie,
> Nor my beloved as an Idoll show,
> Since all alike my songs and praises be
> To one, of one, still such, and ever so.
> Kinde is my love to day, to morrow kinde,
> Still constant in a wondrous excellence,
> Therefore my verse to constancie confin'de,
> One thing expressing, leaves out difference.
> Faire, kinde, and true, is all my argument,
> Faire, kinde, and true, varrying to other words,
> And in this change is my invention spent,
> Three theams in one, which wondrous scope affords.
>   Faire, kinde, and true, have often liv'd alone.
>   Which three, till now, never kept seate in one. [1609 ed.]

[2] La Primaudaye, sig. 416ᵛ. The allusion is to *Habakkuk*, I, 16. La Primaudaye construes a similarity of fishermen worshipping their fish nets because they provide them with food in preaching against idolatry. For Hall, see sig. 2G6. For other relevant comments on the psychology of idolatry, see Michael Scott, *The Philosophers Banquet* (London, 1614), sig. A2; Isaac Casauban, *The Originall of Idolatires*, trans. A. Darcie (London, 1624), pass.; G. B., *The Narrow Way*, sigs, E–Eᵛ; Charron, sig. T6; and Arthur John Dove, *Polydoron* (London, 1631) sig. A9.

If we were to speak of the "aspirer," we could as easily term him an "idolater" in the realm of ideas. Francis Bacon might summarize the point in his twenty-third aphorism:

There is a great difference between the Idols of the human mind and the Ideas of the divine. That is to say, between certain empty dogmas, and the true signatures and marks set upon the works of creation as they are found in nature.

We will of course recall that Bacon's primary mode of explaining his attack on traditional conceptualizations involved describing four kinds of "idols." We can also consult a Godfrey Goodman, who emphasized that sensory perception was inevitably the parent of idolatry.[3]

In this general class of Shakespearean character, then, we observe that the problem of perception again becomes relevant, especially when one considers the usual concept of acquisition. Oriented differently, other men might "grasp" gold or "own" armies passing in review, falling into the illusion of having achieved a union with Absolute Being through possession. But for the pseudotranscendentalist, the epistemology would be more difficult. In such a case the individual would be trying to merge with an idea, with an hypothesis and an apotheosis, attempting, in one case, "to pluck bright honor." When reduced to definition, however, such aspiration, if it were to be realized by an acquisition, emerges as the wish to be a *kind* of *person*, an image or version of oneself functioning in a particular manner. Hence in the structure of such characters the problem was a dual one: there was the matter of defining the exact nature of that "ideal self" and there was some positing of the means according to which the character feels that he succeeds in identifying with it. On a smaller scale, the pseudotranscendentalist is attempting to become not the ideal "personality" but some alternate version,

---

[3] For the translation of Aphorism XXIII, Book I, see Francis Bacon, "The New Organon," in *Works*, VIII. For Goodman, see *The Creatures Praysing God* (London, 1624). For the general point, see also the various commentaries on the commandment against "graven images."

some hypothetical "personality" manufactured by his own desires. Identifying with some idealized concept of a personality would also be familiar from religious contexts which emphasized holding emotional attitudes deemed characteristic of transcendent "personality." One attained God by the holding of the correct emotions. Kings should try to imitate God by being merciful as well as just, and the piety of any man was to be determined not by how he acted but by how he "felt." In the world of the pseudo-transcendentalist, the same criteria are observed. One "loves" war, for instance, and thus shows his status as ideal warrior; otherwise he is no warrior at all: he is a hypocritical coward. And if correct "feeling" was the test of this kind of acquisition, the test of having attained the ideal, then the concept of "feeling" in this regard actually becomes definitive. How does one know the true Christian? How does one know the true warrior? By his "inmost feelings."

Such terms are crucial to our understanding of this class of character. We observe Othello, who has said:

> I do agnize
> A Naturall and prompt Alacartie [alacrity],
> I find in hardnesse. [579-81]

And in such terms we may understand his later anguish. Toward the middle of the play, he no longer has time for warlike thoughts, for a natural and prompt alacrity in hardness. It is as if, in all conscience, once he is obsessed with his new desire to be a revengeful husband, he must formally acknowledge his lapse from faith, his desertion of the "service" of war, because he is no longer able to give to it his heart and soul.

> Farewell the plumed Troopes, and the bigge Warres,
> That makes Ambition, Vertue! Oh farewell;
> Farewell the neighing Steed, and the shrill Trumpe,
> The Spirit-stirring Drum, th'Ear-piercing Fife,
> The Royall Banner, and all Qualitie,
> Pride, Pompe, and Circumstance of glorious Warre
> And O you mortall Engines, whose rude throates

Th'immortal Joves dread Clamours, counterfet,
Farewell: *Othello's* Occupation's gone. [1992–2000]

"Glorious war" is perhaps one way of looking at the world, but it is not necessarily better or worse than other ways. And if we view the surroundings of the cliché about artillery, the transcendentalist thrust is especially apparent. Othello's "engines" (usually, as in Milton, the devil's work) bring down some of heaven to earth in a situation where ambition is transmuted to virtue and where "occupation" is perhaps more significant if we do not confuse it with its twentieth-century homonym.

But if having the right "feeling" was one conventional means of uniting with the ideal in Shakespeare's characterizations it was also the most elementarily perceived means. The problem of uniting with the ideal could, in theory, entertain endlessly subtle ramifications. When a character wishes to worship something outside himself, we have, for instance, material for that elementary schizophrenia so often adumbrated by those Elizabethan and Jacobean stage figures who insist on referring to themselves in the third person. "Schizophrenia," of course, operates here merely as a figure of speech and not as a cultural counter, but the term most closely describes a kind of problem implicit in the whole transcendentalist picture. "I wot not how," says Montaigne, "we are double in ourselves, that which is the cause that what we believe, we believe it not, and cannot rid our selves of that, which we condemne" (II. 342).

The vocabulary of the "flesh and spirit" or the "body and soul" will come to mind, as will the artistic counterparts. For instance, in the graphics of process, Red Cross moves from an identity as a sickly thrall in the dungeon of Orgoglio to the status of St. George. Yet both are as much the same "person" as is Mankynde in the *Castle of Perseverance,* where the directions suggest to us that Mankynd's "bed schal be under the Castel, and ther schal the sowle lye under the bed tyl he schal ryse and pleye [act]." While we read the *Castle* more often than we hasten to Broadway productions of it, we should nevertheless recall that the audience would have seen Mankynd lying on his bed and dying, after which his soul crawled out from under the bed and addressed his body:

> Body! thou didest brew a byttyr bale,
> To thi lustys whanne gannyst loute!
> Thi sely sowle schal ben a-kale.
> I beye thi dedys with rewly rowte.[4]

Two actors were playing one person. From such elementary beginnings, it seems to have been only a step to portraying the problem of self-knowledge in rather the same terms.

We are all familiar with the *nosce teipsum* tradition as well as with the Renaissance use of the *speculum* analogy according to which the mirror either reveals the ideal or the depressingly actual self. This problem of recognizing the "self" received equivalent dramatization in at least two plays of the 1570s where the main character, Wit, underwent significant transformations. He was seduced by Idleness, reclothed in motley, painted black in the face, and on awaking was recognizable neither to others nor to himself as he looked in a mirror, horrified.[5] The problem of self-knowledge is obviously implicit in the admittedly doctrinal or pedagogic slants of these works, because in the Wit plays, much of the comedy revolves around Wit's unawareness that his face is black or that he is wearing a fool's coat. His rage at not being recognized for "himself" and his incredulity when he finds what he looks like—the "objective correlative" of his various lapses from virtue—suggest dualities capable of such later sophistica-

---

[4] See *Chief Pre-Shakespearean Dramas*, ed. J. Q. Adams (Cambridge, Mass., 1924), 11. 3013ff. of "The Castle of Perseverance." Cf. La Primaudaye, sig. 4G6ᵛ on the struggle of the two selves; and W. C. Curry, *Shakespeare's Philosophical Patterns*, 122ff., for the Thomistic approach to such dualities. The emblem tradition would, of course, constantly represent the two selves as two different persons: see, i. 2. F. Quarles, *Emblemes* (London, 1635), V, 5, emblem 9; G. Whitney, *Emblemes* (London, 1586), sig. T4ᵛ; D. Cramer, *Octaginta Emblemata* (Frankfurt, 1630), emblem 72.

[5] See *The Marriage of Wit and Science*, ed. J. S. Farmer (London, 1909), sigs. D4–E2ᵛ; and (without the specific use of the mirror) *The Marriage of Wit and Wisdome*, ed. J. O. Halliwell (London, 1846).

tions of ancient motifs as the basely transformed Artegal in Spenser's book 5 or the concept of the "King's Two Bodies" in the *Henry IV* plays. In the former case, Artegal has to become ashamed at Britomart's astonishment when viewing his changed looks; and in the latter situation, Shakespeare can present Hal, the ultimate *doppelganger* continually referring to another "self" which he "hides" for the moment. Without attempting to enter into the many controversies regarding these plays, we recall the continuous critical remarks regarding the interchange of Falstaff and Hal in their king-parody scenes, while the possible use of Falstaff as symbol of Hal's desires may suggest Shakespeare's interest in dramatizing the dualisms of personality. Hal's renunciation speech in *2 Henry IV* is pertinent:

> Presume not, that I am the thing I was,
> For heaven doth know (so shall the world perceive)
> That I have turn'd away my former Selfe,
> So will I those that kept me Companie. [3267–70]

Equally interesting is the confrontation with the potentials and terms of second personality as Hal prematurely takes the crown from his father's bed.

> Accusing it, I put it on my Head,
> To try with it (as with an Enemie,
> That had before my face murdred my Father). [2700–2702]

The connotations of a struggle with some other "self" are perhaps not inappropriate to such a pseudotranscendentalist.

Shakespeare is rather specific on this paradox of the contention, as it were, of dual selves, for one such analytical sequence appears in *Troilus* when Achilles is exposed to a "Wit and Science" sequence in the staged group insult. Achilles asks himself why he is being ignored. He understands how men may be left alone when they fall from greatness, but:

> Fortune and I are friends, I doe enjoy
> At ample point, all that I did possesse,

> Save these mens lookes: who do me thinkes finde out
> Something not worth in me such rich beholding,
> As they have often given. [1940–44]

Of course, we realize that this sham actually occurs just because Achilles is so respected, but Achilles' disturbance precipitates the terms of Ulysses' counsel. The latter says he is reading a book which tells that men perceive their virtue "by reflection," not by experiencing what they "own" except through some objective verification:

> no [man] is the Lord of any thing,
> (Though in and of him there is much consisting,)
> Till he communicate his parts to others. [1967–69]

Furthermore, Ulysses argues:

> Nor doth he of himselfe know them for ought,
> Till he behold them formed in th'applause,
> Where they are extended: who like an arch reverb'rate
> The voice againe; or like a gate of steele,
> Fronting the Sunne, receives and renders backe
> His figure, and his heate. [1970–75]

The point would have been argued against in the period by Montaigne, for instance, and by others who would have contended that one should look into some sort of transcendentalist "mirror," into one more equivalent to received ethics than the mere opinion of other men.[6] But Ulysses, for the purpose of persuasion, shares an approach with Cassius, who said to Brutus:

> it is very much lamented Brutus,
> That you have no such Mirrors, as will turne
> Your hidden worthinesse into your eye,
> That you might see your shadow:

---

[6] See Philippe de Mornay, The True Knowledge, pass., for references to Seneca and Socrates who was almost universally regarded as the father of the nosce teipsum tradition.

. . . .
And since you know, you cannot see your selfe
So well as by Reflection; I your Glasse,
Will modestly discover to your selfe
That of your selfe, which you yet know not of. [148–65]

The point in *Troilus* is that Ulysses' line of thought can alarm a person such as Achilles, just as Brutus can conceivably be disturbed by Cassius' machinations. There are, we thus gather from Shakespeare's method, certain characters who espouse a concept of transcendental "self" but nevertheless have difficulty actually *perceiving* it, for after all, it is only a construct of some form of wish fulfillment. There was no Bible, no "Sick Man's Salve" to constantly remind Achilles how to imitate "himself" rather than, say, Christ. Mortal ideals for "imitation" were paradoxically constructed by the object to be imitated, and in a rather shaky mortal hand, we may assume. The consequent difficulty of "seeing" presented a problem characteristic for this kind of figure. The difficulty was that of maintaining a clear view of the self-styled ideal, as clear a view as Hal has when he finally decides that Hotspur is becoming a little tiresome as a potential extension of himself, as ideal prince. "Two starres keepe not their motion in one Sphere," he observes and methodically destroys Hotspur.

But in tragedy, such clarity is presumably hard to come by, and the dualities produced by the effort to worship some idealized figure of the self can produce crises in self-objectification. After too many deviations from one's own standard of idealized behavior, it becomes difficult to know who or what one "is." Actually, this higher "self" is defined by the approval of others as well as by self-approval. Daniel's Cleopatra seems to discover this fact:

Am I the woman whose inventive pride,
Adorn'd like *Isis*, scorn'd mortality?
Is't I would have my frailety so belide,
That flattery could perswade I was not I?
Well, now I see, they but delude that praise us,

> Greatnesse is mockt, prosperity betrayes us.
> And we are but our selves, although this cloud
> Of interposed smoakes make us seeme more:
> These spreading parts of pomp whereof w'are proud
> Are not our parts, but parts of others store.[7]

We may again look at Othello, with whom we began, for he is an especially interesting example of Shakespeare's own grasp on the resultant dualities in this pseudotranscendentalist world view. Lodovico has asked a tormenting question:

> Oh thou *Othello*, that was once so good,
> Falne in the practice of a cursed Slave,
> What shall be saide to thee? [3594–96]

Othello has no real answer, at least until the end when he asks that his story be reported: "Speake of me, as I am." We may waive this ultimate ambiguity to note what follows. He was, for one thing, a lover who was not wise and who now regrets, but we gather he was also something else. There is a verbal picture of a former "self": Othello in Aleppo. This is the Othello who had not yet said farewell to glorious war. But in this same picture there is also a Turk, and the allusion to this pagan carries a singular mode of bifurcation to its highly interesting conclusion. Othello's newly heightened empathy with his former self is carried to such a point that, for the moment at least, he is "outside" in the realm of the quasi transcendental. On the stage, his physical body flashes symbolically as that of the Turk's who "traduc'd the State." This Othello/Turk, murderer of Desdemona, receives the murderous assault, the final struggle and deathblow from the old Othello, the ideal, the transcendental self. One self, as it were, kills the other to reaffirm identity.

Othello's more general situation will raise an important consideration. Much of our passing commentary will have evaded the exact shape of Othello's tragedy and the problems of other

---

[7] See S. Daniel, *Works*, ed. A. B. Grosart (London, 1885), III: *Cleopatra*, II. 3. 42.

such characters if we have not alluded to Desdemona or to her counterparts. Shakespeare's practice in many instances—the obvious exceptions are Hotspur, Hector, and Hal—is to match his pseudotranscendentalists with women. Thus we have suggested that some critics tend to define Shakespeare's "aspirers" primarily as lovers. We again face a chicken-egg situation, as we did when considering the small sketch of John of Lancaster. All lovers would not necessarily have to be pseudotranscendentalists or vice versa, but in tragedies concerning lovers, Shakespeare seems to have found pseudotranscendentalist characters the most useful for his art. The poet was quite clearly concerned, in these love relationships, with constructing character situations wherein the man's dependence on the woman would seem to have "led" him into problems of allegiance, as indicated by Othello's farewell to war.

A woman would be an interesting theoretical solution for the physically oriented pseudotranscendentalist whose notion of "being" seeks not only satisfaction in struggle but whose orientation is to some higher entity outside the self. A woman can obviously operate as a partner in physical pleasures. She can be "fought with" in many Renaissance senses, and more importantly, she can be idealized. It is much easier to consider her "real" than to hold on to the mental vision of an alternate idealized self such as Othello's Aleppo shadow. A man might have been capable of envisioning an ideal self which he could worship and serve according to whatever formally articulated "occupations" he preferred to elevate: but it might have been as difficult to make transcendentalist entities such as honor or warriorship become material as it was to elevate one's own human qualities to the transcendental plane in the first place. If some artificial object— a statue of oneself made of wood, stone, or metal, for instance— might be seen as a rather inept imitation, and if some notion of one's honor was too intangible, then a conceptual solution was to use a human being. To lavish love on a woman thus might be more than physically satisfying if that woman were assumed to be one's own idealized qualities made flesh, a physical objectification of one's supposedly higher self. The chaotic disintegrations of personality with which we are familiar in many of Shakespeare's disillusioned lovers may adumbrate the significance of the woman to character construction in such cases.

Platonic theory would have been a point of departure for such a concept in the Renaissance, for the *Phaedrus* was specific on this subject. We recall that the mutual attraction between certain people was explained in that dialogue by the metaphor which describes human beings as followers of certain gods. Seeking for their god, men really search for its human followers on earth and find in the human lover some trace of the particular god whose spiritual descendant the lover may be. Thus it was possible to say:

Every one chooses his love from the ranks of beauty according to his character, and this he makes his god and fashions and adorns as a sort of image which he is to fall down and worship.

Hence it is also consistent for Plato to say that for man, "the lover is his mirror in whom he is beholding himself, but he is not aware of this," or that in men who love "the qualities of their god they attribute to the beloved wherefore they love him all the more."[8] By whatever means, this dialectic became almost a commonplace in the Renaissance. Thomas Wright specifically followed this train of thought as he observed that "the ground of every mans love of himselfe, is the Identitie of a man with himselfe, for the lover and beloved are all one and the same thing." Hence the argument could proceed:

From the Identitie of our selves and the love thereof, necessarily followeth a certaine love to all them who are united any way unto us, and the stricter this union is, the stricter affection it engendreth, and for that all things united have a kind of resemblance, therefore Philosophers and Divines ground friendship upon similitude.

Chapman could accordingly speak of the function of beauty much as did Spenser, observing that this quality

[8] Plato, *The Dialogues*, trans. B. Jowett (New York, 1937), I, 456–59.

Brings men enricht therewith to beggerie
Unlesse th'enricher be as rich in fayth,
Enamourd (like good selfe-love) with her owne,
Seene in another.

In the same vein, Spenser would observe that the lover

fashions in his higher skill
An heavenlie beautie to his fancies will,
And it embracing in his mind entyre,
The Mirrour of his owne thought doth admyre.

Which seeing now so inly faire to be,
As outward it appeareth to the eye,
And with his spirits proportion to agree,
He thereon fixeth all his fantasie,
And fully setteth his felicitie,
Counting it fairer than it is indeed.[9]

It was inevitable that someone in the Renaissance would see
the possibilities for idolatry imagery in such a described relationship. The lover, after all, manufactures something and then
worships it. Accordingly, John Marston's *Metamorphosis of
Pygmalions Image* could toy with an idea which he delineated
more specifically in *The Scourge of Villanie* (1598) when, in his
satire against amorists, he wrote:

Publius hates vainely to idolatries,
And laughs that Papists honor Images,
And yet (ô madnes) these mine eyes did see
Him melt in moving, plaints obsequiously
. . . .
Unto the picture of a painted lasse.[10]

---

[9] See Spenser, A *Hymne in Honour of Beautie*, 11, 221–30. For Wright,
see sig. P4ᵛ; and for George Chapman, see *Ovids Banquet of Sense* (London, 1595), sig. C3ᵛ. Cf. Samuel Brandon, *The Virtuous Octavia* (London,
1598), sig. E8 (Julia's speech).
[10] John Marston, *The Scourge of Villanie* (London, 1598), sigs. G3–G3ᵛ.

Shakespeare used the concept quite often in connection with love affairs. We recall Helena using the term twice in *All's Well* and Juliet referring to "the god of my idolatry," but a sequence in *Love's Labor's Lost* may indicate the poet's playful familiarity with the theory as more than a figure of speech. Longaville reads a sonnet upon which Berowne will then comment.

Did not the heavenly Rhetoricke of thine eye,
'Gainst whom the world cannot hold argument,
Perswade my heart to this false perjurie?
Vowes for thee broke deserve not punishment.
A Woman I forswore, but I will prove,
Thou being a Goddesse, I forswore not thee.
My Vow was earthly, thou a heavenly Love.
Thy grace being gain'd, cures all disgrace in me.
Vowes are but breath, and breath a vapour is.
Then thou faire Sun, which on my earth doest shine,
Exhalest this vapor-vow, in thee it is:
If broken then, it is no fault of mine:
If by me broke, What foole is not so wise,
To loose an oath, to win a Paradise?

Ber. This is the liver veine, which makes flesh a deity.
A green Goose, a [G]oddesse, pure pure Idolatry.
God amend us, God amend, we are much out o'th'way. [1393–1409]

The point of course lies in the implication as to ways in which Shakespeare might conceivably think of varying relationships between men and women. Clearly, all love affairs are not condemned by the poet as idolatry; the comedies are sufficient proof to the contrary. But the conventional concept of idolatry was one of the intellectual entrées by which Shakespeare's own thinking arrived at a formulation of the problem which his pseudo-transcendentalist types would encounter when they began to unite their personal idealizations with the notion of a woman.

We must state matters thus, for Shakespeare certainly furnishes us the opportunity to distinguish Desdemona's own personality from, say, the thoughts that Othello might have had about her. It is as if the playful talk about idolaters in the comedies assumes a seriousness in connection with the Moor's activities. Desdemona, rather significantly, is Othello's "fair warrior." The Moor even speak Platonically of chaos coming again if his love for her were to disappear. The relationship between Desdemona and Othello's military profession also proceeds through some complexities, for if he sees her as "warrior," he also sees her as a possible agency of Cupid's "toys" in his speech to the senate. In rather subtle ways, Desdemona serves as at once an alternate principle of service and a principle of idealization which summarizes Othello's concept of his military self. When he decides to hate her, he bids farewell to military life, and whether this renunciation represents an election to serve Cupid's toys or an association of military occupation with his love for his wife is a matter for lengthier analysis. The most that can be said here is that the motif of Desdemona as "fair warrior" receives only rudimentary development in the play.

The case of Romeo is atypical in one sense because the militaristic dimension is absent from his portrait and because indications in general are sparse. Yet we can tell certain things. We know that Romeo opens the play loving Rosaline and that he contemplates suicide as preferable to banishment from Juliet. Ultimately, however, the most that could be said in these respects is that Juliet is as enamored with the concept of being in love as is Romeo and hence may be an appropriate concretion of Romeo's ideal self as the "lover." We cannot go beyond this point because Romeo has no other occupation from which Juliet would in theory be diverting him. We cannot "triangulate" the dimensions of a total character concept for, unlike Othello, Romeo has no other ideal form of activity. We do not *know* what his other interests are—except luncheon—when he is not worrying about women.

Troilus' progress is therefore more convincing on the point, for in his play, not only does the whole plot (as Hector suggests) resonate with hints of the idolatry implicit in keeping Helen despite the ghastly toll of lives, but Troilus is specifically presented as a character experiencing spiritual crisis when he knows of Cressida's infidelity. He has personally rejected Helen in and

for herself as a motive for fighting at the very beginning of the
play, but he will later argue that she should be kept because she
is a "theme of honor and renown." The clearly presented distinction between Helen's own character on stage—as well as Cressida's—and the role that these women play representing the personal values of the participants in the war allows us to grasp
points which are only hinted at in *Othello* or *Romeo and Juliet*,
where the women are relatively well-behaved ingenues. In *Troilus*
the women are clearly forced into being symbols, and thus Shakespeare's writing here seems almost a meditation on how pseudotranscendentalists tend to externalize their own ideals into visible
objects which offer such immediate rewards or satisfactions that
their worshipers are always eager to perform service as the conditions of their own personalities. As Fulke Greville put it in his
Of Humane Learning:

> Who those characteristicall Ideas
> Conceives, which science of the Godhead be?
> But in their stead we raise and mould tropheas,
> Formes of opinion, Wit, and Vanity,
> Which we call Arts; and fall in love with these,
> As did Pygmalion with his carvèd tree;
>   For which men, all the life they here enioy,
>   Still fight, as for the Helens of their Troy. [stanza 25]

Hector, of course, has sounded the keynote which will only
be answered by Troilus' most interesting observation that the
"eyes and ears" are "traded pilots" between the "dangerous shores
of will and judgment," thereby scandalizing at least those moral
chapbook writers who might be lurking in Shakespeare's audience.
But Hector's often-quoted observation usefully analyzes the problems existing for the pseudotranscendentalist who places the
burden of his visualized identity on outside concretions.

> 'Tis made Idolatrie,
> To make the service greater then the God,
> And the will dotes that is inclineable

> To what infectiously it selfe affects,
> Without some image of th' affected merit. [1041–45]

Hector, a type of Hotspur, will of course reverse himself, as he must. Since "honor" is his conceptualization of an ideal self, Helen, for his purposes, becomes the symbol not of "woman" but of that which he must defend in himself: "For 'tis a cause that hath no meane dependance, / Upon our joint and severall dignities" (1182–83). But Troilus, with his own problems, seems to occupy Shakespeare's more specific interest in the particular kind of character structure which we study here, for the young warrior is put through a torture which would challenge any pseudotranscendentalist. He has established, at the beginning of the play, that he thinks he is going to "heaven" if he can only possess Cressida; and like Othello, but for other reasons, he has lost an interest in fighting. But in the dark with Ulysses, watching Cressida flirt with Diomedes, Shakespeare treats Troilus' "traded pilots," his eyes and ears, to a small exercise in the problem of sheer visibility. If Cressida represented for Troilus some truth made flesh, the satisfaction of a personal ideal made materially apprehensible, the young warrior's exclamations are now significant.

> This she? no, this is *Diomids Cressida:*
> If beautie have a soule, this is not she:
> If soules guide vowes; if vowes are sanctimonie;
> If sanctimonie be the gods delight:
> If there be rule in unitie it selfe,
> This is not she. [3134–39]

From this we might gather that, for Troilus, Cressida was indeed the soul of beauty and that, for him, she was almost the principle of unity, that Renaissance term of Oneness and Truth materialized only allegorically in the person of Una.[11] Cressida, as an externalization of Troilus' own ideological formulations, has an enormous philosophical burden to bear as a symbol, and herein lies the irony in this sad little scene. Something or some-

---

[11] See Hooker, sig. E.

one may indeed operate as such a symbol, but people do have lives of their own.

A realization of this fact can annihilate the Shakespearean character who insists on externalizing into some visible, apprehensible form the ideal entities he may worship.

> But if I tell how these two did coact;
> Shall I not lye, in publishing a truth?
> Sith yet there is a credence in my heart:
> An esperance so obstinately strong,
> That doth invert that test of eyes and eares;
> As if those organs had deceptious functions,
> Created onely to calumniate.
> Was *Cressed* here?
> *Ulyss.* I cannot conjure Troyan.
> *Tro.* She was not sure.
> *Ulyss.* Most sure she was.
> *Tro.* Why my negation hath no taste of madnesse?
> *Ulyss.* Nor mine, my Lord: *Cressid* was here but now. [3112–24]

Troilus certainly is not mad, but one can be "mad" with appearances. "Seeing" is a complicated matter. Shakespeare suggests just how complicated as his warrior continues to wrestle with what seem to him to be dichotomies.

> O madnesse of discourse!
> That cause sets up, with, and against thy selfe
> [Bifold] authoritie: where reason can revolt
> Without perdition, and losse assume all reason,
> Without revolt. This is, and is not *Cressid*:
> Within my soule there doth conduce a fight
> Of this strange nature, that a thing inseparate,
> Divides more wider than the skye and earth:
> And yet the spacious bredth of this division,
> Admits no Orifex for a point as subtle,
> As *Ariachnes* broken woofe to enter:
> Instance, O instance! strong as Plutoes gates:
> *Cressid* is mine, tied with the bonds of heaven;
> Instance, O instance, strong as heaven it selfe:

The bonds of heaven are slipt, dissolv'd, and loos'd.
And with another knot five finger tied. [3139–54]

May we not, with some justification, return to our earlier suggestion of the schizophrenic overtones to be observed in such a character type? To fasten the terms of one's identity onto some visible object or person can lead to bifurcation, for then, in a sense, personal identity is no stronger or more consistent than is that object which bears the burden of being the symbol.[12] In theory, the danger might be clear if the problem was that of an unfaithful woman, because she would have been defined as an extension of the self betraying the self. Appropriately, Troilus closes his play in pursuit of Diomedes who has, as it were, captured his sense of identity. Shakespeare seems to emphasize this by Diomedes' further capture of Troilus' horse, a theft which diverts Troilus' attention almost comically, but not too comically if we imagine that the horse might be another symbol for Troilus, a symbol of his "soldierly self."

> Oh traitour *Diomed!*
> Turne thy false face thou traitor,
> And pay thy life thou owest me for my horse. [3434–36]

[12] Speaking of bifurcation, it is a curious fact that "amorists," and sometimes those merely interested in the pleasures of the flesh were often spoken of in terms of such dualities. One might assume that misers and murderers could be spoken of as having "better" or "worse" selves as easily as anyone else, but motifs tended to be associated with certain kinds of aberrations, for reasons either owing to traditions of which this writer is ignorant or to psychological sets of associations which would require investigation at great length. See, for example, La Primaudaye, sig. 4C6ᵛ; R. Garnier, *The Tragedie of Antonie*, trans. Countess of Pembroke and ed. Alice Luce (Weimar, 1897), 11. 1188–89; F. Quarles, *Complete Works*, ed. A. B. Grosart (London, 1881), III, 60; Thomas Lodge, *Wits Miserie*, sig. P; Ariosto, *Orlando Furioso*, VII, stanza 47; and Overbury, *Divers More Characters* (London, 1616). See William Alexander Stirling, *Julius Caesar*, the chorus of the fourth act; and Hall, sig. 4T2. Avarice, however, tended to elicit concepts both of incorrect worship and of insatiability. We recall that the latter is continually symbolized by Tantalus, who appears in Spenser's Cave of Mammon; and the former is constantly suggested by idolatry. See Thomas Heywood, *The Hierarchie of the Blessed Angels* (London, 1635), sig. 3D3ᵛ; and Gascoigne, sigs C3–C3ᵛ (Gascoigne invokes both Tantalus and, of course, Ephesians 5).

Cassio may be imagined as joining Shakespeare's group of pseudotranscendentalists, at least in miniature, and curiously, he does seem to "breed true." He has his whore and he gets too drunk, but he also idealizes.

Reputation, Reputation, Reputation: Oh I have lost my Reputation. I have lost the immortall part of myself, and what remaines is bestiall. [1387–89]

This is almost parody, we will agree. It is complemented by the lieutenant's view of Desdemona the "divine," of whom he says that the waves and sands

> As having sence of Beautie, do omit
> Their mortall Natures, letting go safely by
> The Divine Desdemona. [833–35]

Is the logic of Cassio's assent to Iago's suggestion that Desdemona be used as intercessor a logic of character according to which the lieutenant, like his master, tends to believe that idealizations exist in the flesh?

We would give the wrong impression were we to imply that such characters are to be regarded as more foolish than others in Shakespeare. There is, as we have suggested, Hal, just as there is Othello; and if it were a question here of generalizing in any purely ethical terms, we would perhaps agree that such characters, such personality constructions are most often Shakespeare's "good" people, as the Malvolios could never be. The reason perhaps may be that if their paths diverge from the correct transcendentalist ways, aspirers do have a sense that there is something like "aspiration" as a way for human life.

Hamlet is the most interesting case. He is, of course, a complicated character even given the viewpoints suggested here, but elements of the "aspirer" can constantly be detected in his construction. To begin superficially, we are acquainted with the letter in which he describes Ophelia as his "soul's idol." Matter for us is sparse in this particular relationship, however, because we are never told just what Ophelia represents to Hamlet about himself. In the long run, Ophelia is treated as a second Gertrude, as a caricature rather similar to those depictions in various anti-feminist tracts where women are rejected as lecherous, unfaithful, weak, face-painters, etc. It is in others that Hamlet names those qualities in which he reposes a specifically self-defining faith. Most obviously, his father is an extremely useful figure, for Hamlet senior is dead when the play opens. He thus operates not as a person but as a memory, as, in effect, an insubstantial entity, the very stuff of transcendentalism. Since the father does not now really exist in the flesh, Hamlet is able to picture him, to objectify himself through an entity which actually has, by death, transcended reality. The young prince's descriptions of the dead king do not necessarily accord with anything that we can independently know about the deceased ruler, but they do accord with those characteristics which Hamlet described as existing in an "ideal man" when he discussed the concept with Horatio. A number of such descriptions are couched in the rhetoric of transcendentalism, and one statement in addition emphasizes "seeing."

> My father. me thinkes I see my father.
> *Hor.* Oh where my Lord?
> *Ham.* In my minds eye (*Horatio*).
> *Hor.* I saw him once; he was a goodly King.
> *Ham.* He was a man, take him for all in all:
> I shall not look upon his like againe. [372–77]

We are later treated to many definitions of "man" by Hamlet, just as the play presents us with many variations upon the problem of "seeing." That Horatio should present Hamlet with an irony—"My lord, I think I saw him yesternight"—is perhaps a sufficient commentary on whether or not Hamlet senior is as unique as his son would claim. The appearance of the ghost does, after all, present Hamlet with a paradoxical substantial, a material immaterial being, the ideal made "flesh."

If the father, in Hamlet's mind, takes on the stature of transcendence, he also becomes figurative. He is "Hyperion to a satyr" in comparison to Claudius, while Claudius is "no more like my father than I to Hercules." The prince's imaginings regarding his father are restated at some length in the queen's closet, again with some significant accentuation on the visual.

> Look heere upon this Picture, and on this,
> The counterfet presentment of two Brothers:
> See what a grace was seated on his Brow,
> *Hyperions* curles, the front of *Jove* himselfe,
> An eye like Mars, to threaten or command
> A Station like the Herald Mercurie
> New lighted on a heaven-kissing hill:
> A Combination and a forme indeed,
> Where every God did seeme to set his Seale,
> To give the world assurance of a man. [2437–46]

Can transcendence go further, even though the word "man" again echoes through the play? But Hamlet is essentially a searcher in these stages, for just before this scene we begin to suspect that while the father serves as an objectification of the ideal, sometimes Horatio may, too.

> *Ham. Horatio*, thou art eene as just a man
> As ere my Conversation coap'd withall.
> *Hor.* Oh, my deere Lord.
> *Ham.* Nay, do not think I flatter:
> . . . .
>   Dost thou heare,
> Since my deere Soule was Mistris of my choise,
> And could of men distinguish, her election
> Hath seal'd thee for herselfe. For thou hast bene
> As one in suffering all, that suffers nothing.
> A man that Fortunes buffets, and Rewards
> Hath 'tane with equall Thankes. And blest are those,
> Whose Blood and Judgement are so well co-mingled,
> That they are not a Pipe for Fortunes finger,
> To sound what stop she please. Give me that man
> That is not Passions Slave, and I will weare him

In my hearts Core: I, in my Heart of heart,
As I do thee. Something too much of this. [1904–25]

It is Hamlet's trait to magnify those he loves into paragons,
just as he denigrates those he distrusts into whores and villains.
He shows it in this speech, and we will see Horatio attempt to
commit suicide, suggesting that he might at times be passion's
slave. However, that is not necessarily Horatio's fault. He is a
human being, despite Hamlet's idealized picture, just as the
father, despite Hamlet's idealism, suggests in his "reincarnation"
as ghost that fleshly entitics are not exactly such absolutes as one
would have them. Rather, we may most usefully equate Hamlet's
portraits of the people whom he admires with his wishes for
himself, with his quest for a version of both mental and physical
perfection, a quest which is challenged when circumstances force
him into specific definitions.

Finally, the pseudotranscendentalist, like Hemingway's characters, may be identified through his sense of a "code." Haunted
by the difficulty of that ideal to which he is attempting to adhere
despite his epistemological confusions, he is often squirming in
paroxyms of shame. Complementary to this, perhaps, is the desire to be "justified" in the end. This urge "to have one's story
told" is not really characteristic of all of Shakespeare's tragic
figures. We find it in Othello and Hamlet and even Timon, but
we find it most poignantly absent in Hotspur. He has died in
such a way that his story must be one of failure: his very defeat
annihilates that leap to pluck bright honor from the moon. His
death effectually separates him from his ideal self, the fame of
continuous military victory.

Oh *Harry*, thou hast rob'd me of my youth:
I better brooke the losse of brittle life,
Then those proud Titles thou hast wonne of me,
They wound my thoghts worse, then the sword my flesh. [3042–45]

And of course, such theft has been exactly Hal's purpose: there
is another who now requires these realizations.

8
Tragic Actors

"The Superstitious," observed Joseph Hall, "hath too many gods; the Profane man hath none at all, unlesse perhaps himselfe be his own deitie, and the world his heaven" (sig. R5). In a modern sense, we could not invoke the adjective "profane" very usefully for any of Shakespeare's tragic characterizations, but the distinctions implicit in this kind of thinking by the poet's contemporaries suggest an interesting and complex figuration with which one must deal in the study of Shakespearean tragedy. We have previously suggested two other modes of characterization in the poet's dramas, the "Angelo" and the "Troilus" archetypes, and as far as such terminology can be utilized in this kind of discourse, we can say that here we encounter still another such "type."

On reflection, we might observe that the Angelos and the Troiluses ultimately conform to rather large and conventional partitionings. Johannine or Pauline trichotomies are fairly obvious in this context: the temptations of the world, of the flesh, and of the devil; or lust of the flesh, lust of the eyes, and pride of life. A simplistic categorization clearly places Troilus in some kind of Castle-of-Perseverance staging, on the platform of the "flesh," while Angelo shows a more obvious preference for the "world." But such distinctions are only useful for purposes of clarification and do not account for the complexities of the influence of Renaissance traditions upon Shakespeare. Therefore, if we suggest that a third kind of character which we would describe is more closely allied to the "platform of the Devil" or "pride of life," we recognize hoary distinctions and suggest an attempt to differentiate, but we do not thereby offer definition. Rather, let us take "pride" as an unsophisticated keynote, a *topos* by which to suggest what a sophisticated Renaissance artist might have been stimulated to build from the ancillary traditions surrounding these ancient notions.

In the context of generalized transcendentalism, we have

guessed that the search for hypothetical "personality" could be taken as obscured not only by the limitations of the senses but by the limitations of the intellect, as when the pseudotranscendentalist was said to be deceived by such an immaterial entity as honor into assuming that here was a "something" to which he might aspire. And even if another order of intellect was satisfied with more obviously material objects, riches and political power, these two kinds of character did have structural affinities, a mode of relating the self to something considered "exterior." Even if Desdemona was much more than an appealing wife in Othello's eyes and if money was something more than counters for the exchange of goods in Shylock's mind, the principle remains basically the same. In one kind of vocabulary, such men sought strange gods; in another, they dabbled in "appearance" while ignoring "reality."

But there could be, conceivably, a kind of mentality not impelled to relate to such externals at all. If we think in terms of equations, the *third* one of the following statements might epitomize a theoretical basis for the intellectual orientation we here seek to describe. "My existence is 'proved' because I have many belongings"; "my existence is 'proved' because I am the ideal soldier"; "my existence is 'proved' because . . . I am." Such an orientation would become useful later in Cartesian contexts, but within the traditions with which we deal here, this was, of course, the sin of Lucifer, the sin of pride.

Such a reference will locate this particular complex of thought in tradition, but followed much farther, the ancillary ethical statements hardly serve as distinctions useful for any theory of characterization. The Devil, after all, was the father of all the sins. By the same token, pride, Satan's characteristic, having caused the fall of man through his desire in Eden to be "as gods," could be described as a trait *fundamental* to all mankind: we need only recall the position of "pride" in both Marlowe's and Spenser's parades of the Seven Deadly Sins. Since all mankind, to use another analogy, could be described as seeking its heaven on earth, an Othello is proud, an Angelo is proud, as were all men who placed more confidence in their own endeavors than in God or other philosophical versions of Supreme Being. Nevertheless, the operations of Lucifer might distinguish through myth some of the character traits which we would advance here.

Satan wished specifically to displace God, not to worship some substitute. The irony, from the transcendentalist point of view, was the fact that while the Lucifer mentality assumed the validity of its own private existence, the only kind of possible "being" was by participation with the Real. In these terms, however, it was possible to distinguish something in the whole human phenomenon other than pride. One could speak of the kind of mind for which the sense of identity was not satisfied by merging but by remaining self-sufficient. On more mundane levels, such a mind would not need to identify with any sublunary entities.[1] But on this same mundane level, transcendentalist thought would stress that man, whatever he might think, was indeed incomplete without God and that when entertaining any concept of actual ontological self-sufficiency, he was perhaps more deeply deluded than when he was thinking other kinds of sublunary thoughts. To avoid suggesting any ethical prejudgments in such analysis, however, we may remind ourselves not of the usual religious moralisms but perhaps of attitudes toward the Stoics, for we have seen that their assumptions, if not their practices, drew fire. Their emphasis on taking refuge in the self incurred inevitable criticism from transcendentalist thought, for the Christian-Platonist would question the very validity of the independence suggested by Stoicism. "Self" could ultimately have no transcendental definition unless by participation, and in hypothetical "personality."

No matter the precise strands of theory involved, the kind of characterization which we seek to define was perhaps the oldest known to the Elizabethan stage if we consider the several traditions that contributed to the concept of pride. If we recall the vast importance of Terentian comedy not only for the schools but for the stage in the middle of the sixteenth century, we of course realize that Thraso, the braggart soldier of *The Eunuch*, was well

[1] See John Donne, *The Sermons*, ed. G. R. Potter and E. M. Simpson (Berkeley, 1955), sermon 14 pass.; and Montaigne, II, xvi ("Of Glorie").

enough known for his name to pass into the language, Shakespeare using the term "thrasonical" at least twice.[2] *Ralph Roister Doister* would offer, in the title character, another early equivalent. But the Terentian tradition, from our point of view, would have to be taken at the most as ancillary; and when it came to specific types, Shakespeare was equally ready to refer to Herod as exemplar, and with logical reason. The Bible (and the play cycles which biblical stories produced) offered something more than the merely laughable braggart: such figures as Pharoah, Augustus, Herod, and Pontius Pilate.

We are all familiar with these traditions, but we may well reflect on the artistic situation established by the custom of dramatizing such biblical stories in the cycle plays. No matter what the reason, the moment such potentates were presented on the stage in a traditional story, a condition of characterization was thereby established. By definition, such tyrants would ultimately meet frustration to the greater glory of God, and whether or not such defeats were actually presented on the stage, the audience could view the potentates within the context of a wider knowledge which produced paradox. The greater the self-esteem of the tyrant, the greater the disparity between his knowledge and that of the audience. He could be watched as a boaster from the very beginning, a boaster who, sooner or later, would receive his due no matter the magnitude of his self-esteem. Accordingly, his speeches about his own glory would, by definition, never *convince*, and the audience would see the boasting not so much as a factor determining events but as a demonstration. By contrast, any serious self-inflation from a character in an early seventeenth-century tragedy would not necessarily be looked upon with comparable objectivity, for he just might turn out to be the hero—Bussy D'Ambois, perhaps. But a Herod, appearing just after a scene in which the three wise men have been speaking of a "New King," would incite attention of a different sort. The

[2] For the general and well-known association, say, of Armado to Terentian influences, see T. W. Baldwin, *Shakespeare's Five-Act Structure* (Urbana, 1947), 391 and 550–53. Cf. Daniel C. Boughner, *The Braggart in Renaissance Comedy* (Minneapolis, 1954), pass.

audience would not consider this Herod a crucial factor in the story, and it would not need to ask itself whether his claims to greatness were to be taken seriously.

In these terms, the effect on the playwright becomes significant, for the unknown writers of the cycle plays were faced, a priori, with an interesting technical problem. Herod must boast. But boasting, when one comes to write the lines for a character, is not a completely simple principle of imagined discourse. If it is a question of hyperbole, one can expound one's greatness in five lines. If one listed the number of realms which one commanded, matters could perhaps be drawn out at greater length. But if boasting was as complex as Terence hinted that it might be in his various comedies or as complex as we now surmise in its manifestation of personality directions, the principle of bragging might not have been an easy one to translate into any lengthy series of speeches throughout a whole play. Hence we observe, either by cause or because of traditions not too well known to us, that a Herod or a Pharoah passed, for the most part, through rather specific phases in his dramatic life on the stage. One comes on the boards and proclaims one's greatness. One is then told by a messenger that there is someone greater; this produces anger. One then takes steps to wipe out the competition, but fails. One then loses one's temper again. Where individual authors wished their own specific emphases is adumbrated by one tradition, that of the "raging" Herod. In fact, these rages suggest the important manipulation of a general principle. To describe these biblical tyrants so was to depict delusion. It was also to show reactions against any contradiction of such delusion by the greater, sacramental world of the cycle play itself. To generalize, we have the outlines of the basic characterizational problem applicable to a *King Lear*.

Shakespeare's fundamental familiarity with such situations is suggested by Henry V's ferocious threat to the inhabitants of Harfleur as he says that they will see

> Your naked Infants spitted upon Pikes,
> Whiles the mad Mothers, with their howles confus'd,

Do breake the Clouds: as did the Wives of Jewry,
At *Herod's* bloody-hunting slaughter-men. [1297–1300]

We know that scenes depicting the Slaughter of the Innocents
were prominent and sometimes comic in the cycle plays, but from
the histrionic point of view, Hamlet's remark is more suggestive.
He associates Herod with passion since if one is too prone to
"tear a passion to tatters, to very rags," this "out-herods Herod."
Even Falstaff becomes unwittingly involved when Mistress Page,
reading his letter and commenting on his soldierly pretentions,
exclaims "What a Herod of Jewry this is!" Perhaps all of this was
hearsay for Shakespeare, although Hardin Craig has emphasized
the persistence of cycle-plays into the seventeenth century; but
Shakespeare's association of Herod with what is, essentially, a
technique of personality presentation is not without significance
for us.[3] Some of the speeches of these Herods suggest, by cause or
effect, the development of those personality theories which a
dramatist might have employed to depict a character whose
orientation would be termed "prideful."

The effort to subtilize boasting in such plays was already apparent in the elementary use of three traits from which even
Pontius Pilate was not immune. There was the usual demand
from the Herod-figure that everyone stand "still as a stone" in
his presence. Then there was the rage at messengers. This trait
was perhaps dimly recalled by Shakespeare, whose Cleopatra
rages at her messenger and elicits the remark from him that when
she is in such moods, "Herod himself" dares not approach her.
Finally there was the frustration at the knowledge that the infant
Christ has escaped into Egypt. But (not necessarily in chronolog-
ical development) some Herods were given personalities which
vaunted even beyond the specific situation, beyond their consciousness of their political predominance in Palestine. Thus in
the Masons' and Goldsmiths' play in the old York cycle, Herod
introduced himself in this manner:

[3] Hardin Craig, *English Religious Drama* (Oxford, 1955), 377–86.

The clowdes clapped in clerenes that ther clematis in-closis,
Jubiter and Jovis, Martis and Mercury emyde,
Raykand overe my rialte on rawe me reioyses,
Blonderande ther blastis, to blaw when I bidde.
Saturne my subgett, that sotilly is hidde,
I list at my liking and layes him full lowe;
The rakke of the rede skye full rappely I ridde,
Thondres full thrallye by thousandes I thrawe when me likis;
Venus his voice to me awe
That princes to play in hym pikis.

The prince of planetis that proudely is pight
Sall brace furth his bemes that oure belde blithes,
The mone at my myght he mosteres his might;
And kaissaris in castellis grete kindines me kithes,
Lordis and ladis loo luffely me lithes,
For I am fairer of face and fressher on folde
(The soth if I saie sall) sevene and sexti sithis,
Than glorious gulles that gayer [is] than golde in price;
How thikne ye ther tales that I talde,
I am worthy, witty, and wise!⁴

We can see this as a perhaps naïve yet conventional dramatization of what transcendentalist thought might describe as the
prideful intellect. It is therefore with little surprise that we observe emphasis on merely personal beauty and see it repeated
rather blatantly by another Herod:

Behold my contenance and my colur,
    Brightur then the sun in the meddis of *the* dey.
Where can you have a more grettur succur

---

⁴ *York Plays*, ed. L. T. Smith (Oxford, 1885), 123–24. Cf. for generalized
self-glorification such oratory as Lucifer's before his fall (see page 4) and
Pontius Pilate's speech on pages 307–8. Cf. also, Play XIV in *Towneley
Plays*, ed. George England, EETS, ES LXXI (1897), 140ff.; and Augustus
Caesar, Play IX, 78ff. This is finally carried to the extreme of the pageant
of the Shearmen and Taylors in the Coventry Corpus Christi plays where
Herod announces that he has made heaven and hell, defeated Magog and
Madroke, is the cause of thunder and lightning, and is prince of purgatory.
See *Two Coventry Corpus Christi Plays*, ed. Hardin Craig, EETS, ES
LXXXVII (1931), 17–18.

Then to behold my person that is soo gaye?
My fawcun and my fassion, with my gorgis araye,—
He thatt had the grace all-wey ther-on to thinke,
Live the [he] myght all-wey with-owt othur meyte or drinke.
[*Two Coventry*, 18]

While this is amusingly absurd, one of the Coventry plays is perhaps more subtle. In this play there is very little "raging." In fact, Herod enters the stage on his horse and presents us with a picture of cheerful and rather inoffensive conceit.

As a lord in ryalte in non Region so riche
And ruler of all remys I ride in ryal a-ray
Ther is no lord of lond in lordchep to me liche
non lofflyere non lofsummere evir lasting is my lay.

Of bewte and of boldnes I here ever-more the belle
Of main and of might I master every man
I dinge with my dowtines the devil down to helle
Ffor bothe of hevin and of herth I am king sertain.
I am the comelyeste kinge clad in gleteringe golde
Ya and the semelyeste sire that may be-stride a stede
I welde att my will all wightis upon molde.

Ya and wurthely I am wrappid in a wurthy wede
Ye knightes so comely bothe curteys and kene
To my paleis wil I passe. Full prest I yow plith
Ye dukis so dowty ffolwe me be-dene
On to my ryal paleys the way lith ful right.

Wyghtly fro my stede I skippe down in hast
to myn heigh hallis I haste me in my way
Ye minstrell of mirth blowe up a good blast
Whill I go to chawmere and chaunge myn array.[5]

If we agree that the writers of these plays were attempting to answer a technical challenge, the problem of depicting pride, then what is sometimes carelessly called "raging" in Herod may emerge

[5] See *Ludus Coventrieae*, ed. K. S. Block, EETS, OS CXX (London, 1922), 151ff. Cf. *York Plays*, 308 (Pilate's speech).

as a somewhat more complex problem in depiction. This can be observed from the usual crux which confronted the mystery writers, for ultimately, Herod had to face reality—the escape of Jesus to Egypt or the frustration of having the wise men tell him that there was a king greater than he—just as Pharoah had to face the frustration of Moses' power. And, as we would expect, the matter was never too interestingly handled: here was the place for Herod, or Pharoah, simply to "rage." We may note the attempt to depict rather more complex reactions in Towneley XVI, *Herod the Great*, as the king speaks to his people, first threatening them regarding their obedience and then voicing his worry about that Boy.

> My name springis far and nere / the doughtiest, men me call,
> That ever ran with spere / A lord and king ryall;
> what joy is me to here / A lad to sesse my stall!
> If I this crowne may bere / that boy shall by for all.
>   I anger;
> I wote not what dewill me alys,
> They teyn me so with talys,
> That by gottis dere nalis,
>   I will peasse no langer.
>
> what dewill! me thynke I brast / ffor anger and for tein.
>   [*Towneley Plays*, 169]

We will of course refrain from reading too much into such sequences, for the very artificiality creates accidental structures. While he is raging, Herod still has to act as a bearer of news, just as do the other characters; and there is some indication that ejaculations of rage and frustration must alternate with these "news items." It is nevertheless interesting to note the changes from grief to joy to self-assertion and back to grief again when these reactions are tucked in between the necessary biblical information, as in the tenth Chester play.[6]

What happens to Herod, Pharoah, Pilate, and Augustus Caesar never happened to a Thraso, whose amiable self-promulgation

[6] *Chester Plays*, ed. Hermann Deimling, EETS, ES LXII (1892), 186–88.

was bland by comparison to the fulminations of the biblical figures. This was natural, for the writers of the religious plays confronted a different problem in depiction, the question of presenting that huge kind of pride which theoretically sought to rival God for the domination of all existence. We thus note a natural expansion of the one trait always implicit in cycle presentations. There was a tendency to exploit the ultimate lack of realism in the outlook of a Herod (who, in one case, could be made to say that he governed all the Zodiac), and the makers of moralities often seized on this divagation, not necessarily because it was suggested by the stories but perhaps because transcendentalist thought defined pride itself as ultimately unrealistic since it ran directly counter to what was thought to be reality in the transcendental sense. In *Hickscorner* this unreality is unequivocally conveyed by Freewill, whose self-esteem and activity suggest that he is not "free" in the "Christian liberty" sense.

> Am I not a goodly person?
> I trow you know not such a guest.
> What, sirs! I tell you my name is Freewill;
> I may choose whether I do good or ill;
> But for all that, I will do as me list.

The doctrinal contradiction is amusing and anticipatory of Angelo's "Look, what I will not, that I cannot do"; but Freewill's remarks are perhaps commented upon in his play by the statement that he and "imagination" are good friends. Only in imagination, we may conclude, is the headstrong pride of man justified.

The point is also made in secular drama, as we observe in the activities of Thersites. More obviously a Thraso than Freewill, he is in the grip of his military dream as he says in soliloquy, "How, sirrah, approach, Sir Launcelot du Lake. / What, renne ye away, and for fear quake?" He similarly challenges in imagination Gawain and "Kay the crabbed" and concludes:

> If no man will with me battle take,
> A voyage to hell quickly I will make,
> And there I will beat the devil and his dame,

And bring the souls away: I fully intend the same.
After that in hell I have ruffled so,
Straight to old Purgatory will I go.
I will clean that, [and] so purge [it] round about,
That we shall need no pardons to help them out.
If I have not fight enough this ways,
I will climb to heaven and fet away Peter's keys;
I will keep them myself and let in a great rout;
What, should such a fisher keep good fellows out?[7]

We may have here elements of the *miles gloriosus*: after all, when actually threatened, Thersites runs to his mother for protection. But do we not also have a secular boaster making a conventionally Herodian speech? If so, we observe a technical variation from the cycle play in Thersites' enactment of obvious self-delusions. These are presented as material for the audience to sift. For instance, when Thersites is threatened by one man and has run to his mother, he tells her that "a thousand horsemen do persecute me." At another point he exclaims "what a monster do I see now" when a snail approaches. Delusion has thus influenced his rudimentary perception not only by the building of imaginary defeated foes but also by the magnification of those objects actually presented before his eyes and, importantly, before the eyes of the audience.

The kind of characterization which thus seems to have been associated with pride may interest us if only because these fictitious individuals represented one of the oldest acting traditions available to players (and perhaps writers). Elements in such a character complex would have been transmitted to them either through the mystery or morality or through school training in the acting of classical Roman comedy.[8] The basis of such a character complex, furthermore, is apparent. The keynote was simply talk or, if we like, soliloquy. The trait of pride would seem to have demanded the exploratory treatment that a Lechery or a Judas

[7] *Six Anonymous Plays*, ed. J. S. Farmer, 1st ser. (London, 1905), 201–2. For Freewill in *Hickscorner*, see p. 132.

[8] For discussions on the subject, apart from the problem of Roman comedy, see Robert Withington, "Braggart, Devil, and Vice," *Speculum*, XI (1936), 124–29.

Escariot did not, since the presentation of these latter figures might require merely a statement of aims and the enacting of some representative behavior. However, the Herods or other "types" of the proud man would be required, when conveying pride, to *say* something "proud." And it was in this "saying" that any dramatic empiricism may have encountered its earliest challenge to subtlety. The response, we have suggested, utilized what could be termed a theory of pride. We might speculate on the ramifications of such theory in order to prepare ourselves for what a superior dramatist might have such a character talk "about."

If, according to transcendentalist views, man was impelled by a "spark"—affections which made him yearn to be united with Entity—and if frail man was too prone to errors of perception, substituting riches, honor, power, soldiership and the like for that which should be his true goal, how was one to think of the mind which performed quite another kind of substitution? If one yearned for Absolute Being and assumed that the yearning itself was an expression of attainment, if one thus placed one's ontological reliance on a sense of the intrinsic superiority of the self, as did Satan, then the problem of external controls might be somewhat complex. Such a mind ultimately would have less grasp of cause and effect than did those which had at least semivisible substitutes for Absolute Being. A Shylock might be mistaken in his evaluation of gold, but he would at least know when he had lost "control" of gold, no matter how irrelevant gold itself might be in the ultimate scheme of things. And he would at least have something toward which to work, just as Romeo could be momentarily happy if his criterion of happiness-through-love could for the time being be satisfied by a Juliet. But even the early Herods show the complex implications for perception-depiction in a reliance on mere self. They fly into rages when their messengers tell them that there is a king greater than they are: they often call their messengers liars. They must, for what is the criterion for knowing superiority? One must return to a sense of purely abstract assertion—"I am because I am." The terms of remaining within one's own concept of self are not, say, another brave deed, another conquest, or another lover. The terms can only be the grammar of a mental assertion or reassertion: "—am I not Herod?"

The insistence on one's greatness simply because one is great is an attitude more difficult than self-assertion through, say, soldiership. Instead of depicting a "proud" character by delineating specific goals and the attempt to attain or retain them, this technique had to cope with the problem that the goal, in effect, did not exist. Rather, since such a mind would consider itself as "arrived," it was a question, in drama, of dealing with the very cognitive materials which would be available to a character who was convinced that he always retained that status by which he defined his existence. In this sense, such a characterization could pose a real challenge to any author's theory of human psychology. A Herod might be the unsophisticated answer, a Thraso the comic answer—characterization in terms of final comic punishment rendered—but the theoretical problem remained constant. Since it was a question of portraying effect, not cause, of presenting the effort to remain in the attitude that one has achieved one's goal, not the effort to achieve some goal, a sophisticated dramatist who wished to delineate something other than a proud buffoon would have had to analyze, whether by intuition or by conscious reasoning, the technique of depicting such a mental stance.

In theory, it might be guessed that this kind of character, by definition, explored external phenomena rather less deductively than his gold- or honor-seeking brothers. The relationship of such a mind to externally perceptible realities would be such as to leave unaltered a personal preconception of a situation. Externals would not operate as a check on self-envisionment but rather as a confirmation of an already generalized sense of superiority. As a human being, this figure would of course need to operate to a certain extent in terms of outside facts, but these externals would be organized by him into ideational groups which would simply bear witness to his own reality—his being or consciousness, if we will—as "great." Such a figure would not, like Troilus, serve a pseudotranscendental entity; rather, this new figure would see himself existing in a transcendentalist system in which he was the Chief Entity. If the heavens and the earth declare the glory of God in one system, then, in a personal system, they could very well declare the glory of the self.

It would then follow that any idea complex—say, honor—would be useful and would be adhered to only as long as it served all such purposes. But when any of these concepts ceased to be psychologically useful as the conceptualization, the objectification of the greatness that one wished to see in oneself, then, with the utmost sincerity, some other entity could be espoused for the purpose of self-realization. One way or the other, as it were, the heavens must declare the glory of this "god." Importantly, it would be just at this juncture that our new kind of character would part company with a Hotspur. Hotspur adheres to his idealization to the end: he worships it and he does not desert his god, for his is a way of thought which wishes primarily to serve. But this new kind of character will assume the service of or will identify with any entity only as long as it defines his own greatness.

It is for these reasons that such characters may finally appear "theatrical" at times. Yet if they do indeed assume "roles," they do not do so from frivolity but for the purpose of cognitive survival within the terms of their own epistemological systems. It is also useful to remind ourselves that there might have been a close relationship between just this kind of characterization and the problem of stage acting itself. Shakespeare, as an actor, may have been stimulated to these resemblances between life and art. But we compare this new character only to a certain kind of actor, that player not sufficiently detached from his art to be able to practice it objectively, one who feels a personal sense of identity only when he is safely within a role. Furthermore, if such an actor were to assume that the applause was not for his histrionic ability but for himself "as" the personage he was enacting, he would be a fitting image of the character type we describe here. Regarding his assumption of various roles as proof of his superiority, refusing all roles except those which might command respect for greatness, and feeling that he is nothing except when he is within such a role, this kind of character would also represent an interesting and (on the part of the playwright) perhaps conscious departure from an old tradition in ethics which utilized the concept of the stage as a transcendentalist parable.

The *Theatrum Mundi* motif insisted upon an opposite kind of difference between transient and ultimate realities.[9] By this *topos*, man was like an actor on the stage of the world. Playing the role of king or beggar, he had to work at his part until the end when all actors would be returned to their intrinsic equality in that great tyring house in the sky. Accordingly, all sublunary "roles" were illusion, and "backstage" was Reality. The teleological error which this metaphor pointed at occurred when the human being, the actor in this transient world, mistook his "role" on "this great stage" for Reality itself. The kind of character which we here describe pursued such an error, attempting, as it were, to reverse the direction of the *Theatrum* cliché. The greater the vigor with which one played the role, the greater its actuality, as if the stage of the world was Reality's arena.

In another sense, whatever reality existed for such a character could only be defined, perhaps even created, by virtue of the strength of wishing for it, by virtue of emotion itself. We might attest that we are not deviating into anachronism in our speculations on Shakespeare's method by recalling what the poet himself might have come to understand about the profession of the stage actor. We do not of course know what method of acting was used in the early seventeenth century as the best approach to stage impersonation, but a Hamlet tends to equate histrionics with this ability to "create" not gesture but emotion.

> Is it not monstrous that this Player heere,
> But in a Fixion, in a dreame of Passion,
> Could force his soule so to his own conceit,
> That from her working, all his visage warm'd;
> Teares in his eyes, distraction in's Aspect,

[9] For an ancient *locus*, see that section of book 3 in John of Salisbury's *Policraticus* translated as *Frivolities of Courtiers* by Joseph B. Pike (Minneapolis, 1938).

A broken voice, and his whole Function suiting
With formes to his Conceit? And all for nothing?
For Hecuba? [1591–98]

Thomas Wright was aware of this approach, as were some of the rhetoricians, and he observes the similarity of a good actor to a good orator:

He that will act well, must of necessitie stir up first that affect in himselfe, he intendeth to imprint in the hearts of his hearers; and the more vehement the passion is, the more excellent action is like to ensue. [sig. N]

The points are generally illustrative: one generates emotion to convince oneself so that one can then convince others. The first term relates to our present problem, for it seems to have been understood that the power of "conceit" (concept) enabled a mind to maintain the self-induced realities by which the personality was to be defined. In the moralistic sphere, this notion of the mind was also understood as the cognitional temptation of one who, as Charron observed,

setleth himselfe in himselfe, and in such sort conceits himselfe and whatsoever he hath, that he preferres it before all, and thinks nothing comparable to his owne.

Although "these kinde of people" are no wiser than those who constantly strive for that which they cannot have, Charron observes, "yet they are at least more happie."

The proof of his own transcendence for such a character would essentially be circular: what he perceived confirmed his own belief, as with Thersites who magnifies the snail. What such a character would ultimately require was, then, not actually proof but reaffirmation. And if emotion confirmed reality, the process of confirmation was a bridge made of redefinitions. It was in such a connection that Montaigne would say with Wittgenstein that "most of the occasions of this worlds troubles are Grammatical."

If the mere roles these men assumed to themselves, the terms in which they thought, served to create what they wished independently of any check from external reality, then, in Bacon's formulation, they would "studie words, and not matter,"

Pygmalions frenzie is a good embleme or portraiture of this vanitie: for wordes are but the Images of matter, and except they have life of reason and invention: to fall in love with them, is all one, as to fall in love with a Picture.[10]

We may interest ourselves in an element of this erroneous process as Shakespeare himself would seem to have analyzed the matter. In the plays we often detect this motif when we observe a character imbued with a strong sense of decorum. He seems to insist on the "appropriate," not for the purposes of etiquette but for the ordering of what he regards as reality. Again, the problem of the actor comes to mind as well as the many Renaissance tracts on the role of decorum in poetry.[11] The concept of the decorous would be crucial and relevant because of the nature of what decorum itself in theory requires. It demanded that one given class of phenomena be associated with another, that one class of visible objects be used to represent a particular invisible entity: gold for kingship or, in Neo-Senecan drama, "kingly speech" for a king. But because the objects used for representation were not *indifferent*—old rags could not "decorate" the palace—the concept of decorum did not involve the process of symbology in its pure sense in which case any object, as long as it was understood as a symbol, might serve. But when one begins talking of decorous symbols, then into the argument drifts the assumption that there is an *intrinsic* relationship between symbol and thing symbolized. Logically, "decorum" abandons the domain of "symbol" for the domain of "sign," and ultimately, a decorous symbol is a basic contradiction in terms. Hence, when a class of characters insists

---

[10] For Charron, see sig. L2; for Montaigne, see II. xii. 233; and for Bacon, see *Of the Proficiencie and Advancement of Learning*, sigs. E3ᵛ–E4 and 2P.
[11] See, for example, George Puttenham, *The Arte of English Poesie* (London, 1589), III, Chaps. 23 and 24.

on "decorum" or "appropriateness" as the ordering concept, much might be inferred from the mind so oriented.

At the very least, an obsession with decorum would suggest a tendency to confuse symbol with sign, to equate a representation with the reality being symbolized. We might guess that any insistence on the decorous was ultimately an insistence that all symbols, strangely, were to "partake of the nature of" that which they symbolize. And if some character in drama operates in this cognitive manner, it may even be possible for us to assume that his ability to distinguish between the realities and fictions around him is being rendered as weak. By insisting on a decorum, he may rather insist that reality be ordered according to that structure of symbology in terms of which his own mind may move. Reality may finally be ordered for him through the process of metaphor. Hamlet is exemplary when he reminds us of some contemporary insistences that an actor's impersonation had to be decorous. By not sawing the air too much (as people often do in real life) or by not being "too tame" (as people often are), Hamlet's actor is being required not to be the symbol of some person or to represent in any pure sense but to "be" the person via the bridge of appropriateness. By such imitation one presumably "becomes" that which is imitated. Hamlet desires on his stage not a style but a person, the mirror held up to nature as he defines nature.[12]

If a poet were primarily interested in writing philosophical treatises, then we might observe his presentation of exemplary figures enacting modes of thought with rigid consistency. But since Shakespeare was a dramatist, his figures in the class we describe here are never mad enough to believe that all exterior phenomena necessarily attest to the validity of their own preconceptions. In most cases the poet rendered matters plausible by

---

[12] That Shakespeare was aware of such distinctions may be inferred from his tacit departure from Ben Jonson in the matter of the various dramatic decorums and also by the fact that when decorum is mentioned in Shakespeare's plays, the characters make jokes about the concept. Hamlet's notion of imitation may be isolated if we consult R. P. McKeon, "Concepts of Imitation in Antiquity," in *Critics and Criticism* (Chicago, 1952).

insulating the perceptual world of his characters: most frequently
these figures are kings. They come on stage already equipped with
that potentially unrealistic sense of self which, in other Shakespearean characters, has to be rendered to the audience by more
subtle technical means. For a Lear to speak of his greatness in
terms of his monarchic status would, after all, be a simpler artistic
proposition than for some figure who was not a king to speak of
his "self" in terms of some undefined greatness. Kingship can
protect a character from immediate punishment by reality. It is
only when the poet has manipulated events to the point where
these kings are driven to rely solely on the terms of their own
personalities that their *weltanschauungen* become obvious.

A contrast of Henry V with Richard II is instructive here. The
Hals show that it is possible to relate to kingship rather as someone else, some pseudotranscendentalist, might deal with the concept of soldiership. There is the ideal and then, according to the
terms of pseudotranscendentalism, there is the "code" to which
one adheres in order to be able to identify with the figure of the
warrior or, in this case, the figure of the king. The whole *Henry
IV / V* sequence, in this sense, seems to pose the problem, with
Hal as its focus, of the terms of the code: how does one live up
to the (Tudor) ideal? With Richard, however, the question
arises as to whether a bad king still remains a king. There is an
obvious disparity between the king role as societal function and
the king role as attestation of some quasi-transcendental personal
validity. But with certain of Shakespeare's tragic figures "I am a
king" becomes a statement having the same "grammatical" value
as "I am a man." For Coriolanus to say "I am a warrior" is in
theory for him to mean that "I do those things which allow me
to claim this title." But "I am a king" can often tend to suggest,
in the mouths of some of Shakespeare's characters, not that "I
have a contract with society" but a statement of the same order
as "it is a cat," "that is a stone," or "this is a tree." Such thinking
is not characteristic of Shakespeare's kings only, however. Any
character who confuses function with being would be an equivalent.

Henry V is an interesting contrast. Harry has presumably "arrived." If he wishes, he can easily become his other self, his kingship, but Shakespeare has him remain transcendentalist. Hal seems to realize that continual mental exercise is the price of identifying with the ideal kingly *persona*, just as continual combat, Ulysses suggests, must enable Achilles to maintain his grip on the ideal status of warrior. In *Henry* V the constant exercise is mental for the simple reason that there is no real rebellion; we have, rather, an impression in the play of endless definition, of endless justification. The chorus is sufficiently instructive:

> So swift a pace has Thought, that even now
> You may imagine him upon Black-Heath:
> Where, that his Lords desire him, to have borne
> His bruised Helmet, and his bended Sword
> Before him, through the Citie: he forbids it,
> Being free from vain-nesse, and selfe-glorious pride;
> Giving full Trophee, Signall, and Ostent,
> Quite from himselfe to God. [2865–72]

Say what we will about possible ironies within the play itself, we may yet adhere to the supposition that Harry demonstrates an Othello-like interest in a principle: the man has to act in such-and-such a way in order to conform to the idealistic definition of a king, just as the warrior must be brave to conform to the soldierly ethic.

In his exposition of Hal as perhaps the most justifiable pseudo-transcendentalist possible in Tudor society, Shakespeare also has his character speak at length on the easier view, adopting as he does a theme that is almost *topos* regarding the subject of "Ceremonie."

> And what have Kings, that Privates have not too,
> Save Ceremonie, save generall Ceremonie?
> And what art thou, thou idoll Ceremonie?
> What kind of God art thou? that suffer'st more
> Of mortall griefes, then do thy worshippers.
> What are thy Rents? what are they Commings in?
> O Ceremonie, shew me but thy worth.

What? is thy Soule of Adoration?
Art thou aught else but Place, Degree, and Forme,
Creating awe and feare in other men?
. . . .
Can'st thou, when thou command'st the beggers knee,
Command the health of it? No, thou prowd Dreame,
That play'st so subtilly with a Kings repose.
I am a King that find thee: and I know,
'Tis not the Balme, the Scepter, and the Ball,
The Sword, the Mase, the Crowne Imperiall,
The enter-tissued Robe of Gold and Pearle,
The farsed title running 'fore the King,
The Throne he sits on: nor the Tide of Pompe,
That beates upon the high shore of this World:
No, not at all these, thrice-gorgeous Ceremonie;
Not all these, laid in Bed majesticall,
Can sleep so soundly, as the wretched slave:
. . . .
And but for Ceremonie, such a Wretch,
Winding up Dayes with toile, and Nights with sleepe,
Had the fore-hand and vantage of a King. [2088–2130]

The easier view in question, of course, would be that which is
espoused by Bates and Williams who, in this curious sequence,
appear content to lay all responsibility on the king. If they did
not, they would hardly last out another Homily on Obedience.
But the tables are turned. While a king often confuses his "self"
with ceremony, in *Henry V* it is the subjects who are curiously the
victims of the error. Harry sees his own symbolic role more clearly
than they do. Understanding that to be a king is not to be a
different order of being, he is not the callow fool greedy for the
golden round and using the specious kinds of reasons attributed
to him initially by his dying father. He may have other vices, not
our concern here, but on "kingship" he sees clearly and, more
importantly, he shows us that Shakespeare himself was sufficiently
analytical on the general subject to justify our notions regarding
the class of character which we explore here.

If the basis of such characterization is the tendency to reinterpret external phenomena in order to retain a sense of personal

validity, depictional requisites become clear, for reinterpretation is a mental process. If this process is to be the keystone of a characterization, it follows that the technical problem for the dramatist is the depiction on a stage not of physical activity but of thinking. That is to say, if speculative thought were to be the material out of which a character was to be molded, and if such thought had to be presented to an audience in a playhouse, then these characters had to be shown as subject to purely verbal modes of seventeenth-century irrationality. The words had to reenact a process of purely hypothetical confusion in thought, and since a merely visible action on stage could, at best, be ambiguous by itself, this new kind of character could only reveal the details of any complex ratiocination through the word patterns than an audience could hear.

Julius Caesar is an early illustration of the problem—an interesting one, too, in that we have here a character who wishes to be "king" in a context where "kings" can not exist, in the time of the late Roman republic. The poet has created a situation which requires the depiction of some plausible motivation for such a kind of wishing, and Shakespeare's way with Caesar is significant. To a greater extent than with Brutus, the poet constructs a Caesar who rather obtrusively thinks in terms of symbols which have only the referents that he himself will allow to them. Proceeding almost completely in terms of words, not of things, his proto-Cartesian effort to achieve self-definition operates in purely symbolic reorganizations of reality. That the Roman leader allows himself to believe in such rebuildings of reality becomes a significant artistic maneuver when viewed from our present context.

> Danger knowes full well
> That *Cæsar* is more dangerous then he.
> We [are] two Lions litter'd in one day,
> And I the elder and more terrible,
> And *Cæsar* shall go foorth. [1034–38]

Such purely verbal self-deceit becomes more obvious in Caesar's talk about Cassius. We observe the initial reaction of fear and

then Caesar's mode of changing his own perception, of rein-
terpreting via verbalist structures, again to skirt the concept of
danger.

> Such men as he, be never at hearts ease,
> Whiles they behold a greater then themselves,
> And therefore are they very dangerous.
> I rather tell thee what is to be fear'd,
> Then what I feare: for always I am *Cæsar*.
> Come on my right hand, for this ear is deafe,
> And tell me truely, what thou thinkist of him. [310–16]

The concept of self also must be reinforced by such verbalist assertion. If the parody of such assertion is the shallow and ridicu-
lous boast, a more serious situation is the eloquent attempt to
build identity with the bricks of words used not as symbols but
as signs, not as indicators but as creators.

> I could be well mov'd, if I were as you,
> If I could pray to moove, Prayers would moove me:
> But I am constant as the Northerne Starre,
> Of whose true fixt, and resting quality,
> There is no fellow in the Firmament.
> The Skies are painted with unnumbred sparkes,
> They are all Fire and every one doth shine:
> But, there's but one in all doth hold his place.
> So, in the World; 'Tis furnish'd well with Men,
> And Men are Flesh and Blood, and apprehensive;
> Yet in the number, I do know but One
> That unassaileable holds on his Ranke,
> Unshak'd of Motion: and that I am he,
> Let me a little shew it, even in this:
> That I was constant *Cimber* should be banish'd,
> And constant do remaine to keepe him so. [1266–81]

Richard II is the most obvious application of Shakespeare's approach to the problem of depicting such types, for unlike Caesar,
who is struck down in the middle of the play, Richard is forced

to retreat throughout the play, to reinterpret. His case resembles Lear's even if the latter's is much more complexly presented. In both instances, men who are convinced of the ultimate defining power of kingship come up against political pragmatisms. Such challenges tend to precipitate internal crises in self-definition, and it is in such friction that "characterization" comes into full play. Richard's own case may strike us as fairly obvious and as such is the more useful example. We have, for instance, his own private "sacramental universe" in which objects of perception signify, not symbolize, the validity of the self.

> knowest thou not,
> That when the searching Eye of Heaven is hid
> Behind the Globe, that lights the lower World,
> Then Theeves and Robbers range abroad unseene,
> In Murthers and in out-rage bloody here:
> But when from under this Terrestrial Ball
> He fires the prowd tops of the Easterne Pines,
> And darts his Lightning through ev'ry guiltie hole,
> Then Murthers, Treasons, and detested, sinnes
> (The cloake of Night being pluckt from off their backs)
> Stand bare and naked, trembling at themselves.
> So when this Theefe, this Traitor *Bullingbrooke*,
> Who all this while hath revell'd in the Night,
> [Whilst we were wandering with the Antipodes]
> Shall see us rising in our Throne, the East,
> His Treasons will sit blushing in his face,
> Not able to endure the sight of Day;
> But selfe-affrighted tremble at his sinne. [1392–1407]

We are reminded of Caesar's way. He fears Cassius, but he does not adopt the method of a Macbeth by moving to eliminate this source of fear. Rather, the answering move is to attempt a reorganization of reality in which the dictator "becomes" figuratively, and thus literally, all-powerful. And if Caesar's preference for Decius' more flattering interpretation of the fountain dream may adumbrate a tendency, its specification, we recall, is again that symbols have only one necessary meaning and hence slide over into the area of signs. Similarly, Lear assumes the storm is in his "corner" because it serves him as symbol.

When driven from the first notion of identity, when only a madman would assume that kingship had any practical relevance to one's own situation, such characters then, very significantly, are made to begin floating out in search of new identities, new realizations by which they can conceive of themselves, new roles, if we wish. It is not a question of pretending to others but of convincing the self. Lear, the powerless king, contemplates Poor Tom.

Is man no more then this? Consider him well. Thou ow'st the Worme no Silke; the Beast, no Hide; the Sheepe, no Wooll; the Cat, no perfume. Ha? Here's three on's are sophisticated. Thou art the thing it selfe; unaccommodated man, is no more but such a poore, bare, forked Animall as thou art. Off, off, you Lendings: Come, unbutton heere. [1882–89]

It is as if one hastens to "become" this new *ding an sich*, recalling Richard's own variations but with a characteristic play on words. Richard does attain for a moment, in the last lines, a sense of what the truth for such characters really is.

> Thus play I in one [person], many people,
> And none contented. Sometimes am I King;
> Then treason makes me wish my selfe a Beggar,
> And so I am. Then crushing penurie,
> Perswades me, I was better when a King:
> Then am I king'd again: and by and by,
> Thinke that I am un-king'd by Bullingbrooke,
> And straight am nothing. But what ere I am,
> Nor I, nor any man that but man is,
> With nothing shall be pleas'd, till he be eas'd
> With being nothing. [2697–2707]

One of the more interesting traits which Shakespeare advances in the depiction of such characters is what we have before termed their insistence on the appropriate, the decorous. The absorption of certain characters in the concept is presented to us as a personality symptom or, if we wish, as one of the plausible characteristics with which the poet wished to endow a figure so that the major shape of his personality would be discernible. In fact, we can understand the appeal of a character to decorum (or to any synonym of the concept) at times when the concept does not appear relevant as a reiteration of his basic epistemological assumptions. The matter becomes most pertinent and most complicated, for instance, when decorum enters the area of the emotions: "Of comfort no man speake / Let's talke of Graves, of Wormes, and Epitaphs" (1504–1505). Richard, sensing the disappearance of his power, can talk this way, even stating that "I live with Bread like you, feel Want, taste Griefe, need Friends." "Let me wipe it first, it smelles of Mortality." Against such statements we are asked to contrast Richard's sun image or Lear's constant resumption of kingly roles in his madness despite his momentary adoption of the role of worm. On the simplest level, it is as if these characters must, in the midst of misfortune, adopt the role, say, of Archetypal Unfortunate, it being better to be something than nothing. But more complexly, as we have also noted, one must "feel" the role. We are left to ponder Richard's statement: "Goe to Flint Castle, there Ile pine away, / A King, woes slave, shall Kingly Woe obey" (1569–70).

Emotion, per se, has a certain definitive power in these cases because the characters are deriving a sense of being from the fact of feeling. But even emotional self-knowledge therefore becomes somewhat illusive: when "I wish" merges with "I am," the role can induce the emotion, as with Hamlet's actor. In fact, it is as if the role has not been defined unless the proper emotion has been captured. Is it necessary to take off all one's clothes before one feels "more sinned against than sinning" or to lose Bushy, Bagot, and Green as well as an army before saying "I live with bread like you, taste grief, need friends"? Is it necessary to "go forth" to the senate in order to prove to oneself one's courage?

The questions are difficult, of course, and who can tell whether they have even been solved today? But with Shakespeare's attention to them, the role of decorum in the matter of the emotions would seem clear. Given one's case, one has to feel what one believes to be the appropriate emotion; otherwise one is not well into the role. And if one is not well into the role, one cannot "be" one of the specific aspects of that chameleon "personality" which grounds its proof of superior identity on its realization of an existence which evades facts by reasserting other kinds of superiority.

Since all humans are humans and do indeed have "real" emotions, the obverse (as Coriolanus discovers) is that emotional self-knowledge in such figures is sketchy at best. Does the physical manifestation cause the emotion, or does an emotion cause the physical manifestation? We can return to our point of departure, Hamlet's contemplation of the actor on the subject of Hecuba, for after his remark, we recall the rest of the well-known soliloquy.

> Yet I,
> A dull and muddy-metled Rascall, peake
> Like John-a-dreames, unpregnant of my cause,
> And can say nothing: No, not for a King,
> Upon whose property, and most deere life,
> A damn'd defeate was made. Am I a Coward?
> Who calls me Villaine? breakes my pate a-crosse?
> Plucks off my Beard, and blowes it in my face?
> Tweakes me by' th' Nose? gives me the Lie i'th'Throate,
> As deepe as to the Lungs? Who does me this?
> Ha? Why, I should take it: for it cannot be,
> But I am Pigeon-liver'd, and lacke Gall
> To make Oppression bitter, or ere this,
> I should have fatted all the Region Kites,
> With this slaves Offall, bloudy: a bawdy villaine,
> Remorseless, Treacherous, letcherous, kindless villaine!
> Oh Vengeance!
> [Why?] What an Asse am I? I sure, this is most brave,
> That I, the sonne of [a dear father] murthered,
> Prompted to my Revenge by Heaven, and Hell,
> Must (like a Whore) unpacke my heart with words,
> And fall a Cursing like a very Drab,
> A scullion? [1606–28]

Hamlet ponders some interesting questions. Does he not feel sorrow? If he does regret the death of his father, why can he not work up at least as much passion as the actor did over Hecuba? We therefore note Hamlet trying to "generate" a role by uttering a string of adjectives, trying to make himself "feel." He seems to become partially aware of the paradox. One wonders, ultimately, whether part of Hamlet's problem, as Shakespeare presents it, may not be caused by a notion that feeling is caused primarily by its manifestations.

Macbeth's dilemma is similar, is it not, as he hears of the death of his wife? The sequence is significantly introduced by the cry of women.

> What is that noise?
>> *A cry within of Women.*
> Sey. It is the cry of women, my good Lord.
> Macb. I have almost forgot the taste of Feares.
> The time ha's beene, my sences would have cool'd
> To hear a Night-shrieke, and my Fell of haire
> Would at a dismall treatise rowze, and stirre
> As life were in't. I have supt full with horrors,
> Direness familiar to my slaughterous thoughts
> Cannot once start me. Wherefore was that cry?
> Sey. The Queene (my Lord) is dead.
> Macb. She should have died hereafter;
> There would have been a time for such a word: [2327–39]

Macbeth's reaction to the queen's death, as well as to the cry of women, seems to him to be "nothing" because he cannot react in the way he has described above. He thinks he is not horrified because, quite simply, his hair is not standing on end. But is not what follows tantamount to an emotional reaction?

> Out, out, breefe Candle,
> Life's but a walking Shadow, a poor Player,
> That struts and frets his hour upon the Stage,
> And then is heard no more. It is a Tale

Told by an ideot, full of sound and fury
Signifying nothing. [2344–49]

We can certainly take this curious and subtle parody of the transcendentalist metaphor as reaction whether the hair stands on
end or not. That life seems meaningless after the news of the
death of a wife is, after all, hardly a conclusion for which a purely
intellectual analysis may be held ultimately responsible.

Lear shows how this confusion of emotion can lead to misapprehension of the self as, ironically, his various sarcastic postures
to his recalcitrant daughters give way to an invocation to his
gods. "Touch me with Noble anger," he exclaims, betraying his
orientation by his endowment of ethical quality to an emotion.

And let not womens weapons, water drops,
Staine my mans cheeks. No you unnaturall Hags,
I will have such revenges on you both,
That all the world shall—I will do such things,
What they are yet, I know not, but they shalbe
The terrors of the earth! you think Ile weepe,
No, Ile not weepe, I have full cause of weeping,
But this heart shall break into a hundred thousands flawes
Or ere Ile weepe. [1576–85]

The poet depicts this king, who relies on a theory of intrinsic
superiority, as wishing for one emotion while he physically experiences another. Whether Lear is sorrowful but wants to be
angry or whether he is angry but wants to be sorrowful is a matter that we cannot discuss here. It is enough to observe that, like
Hamlet and Macbeth (who, however, experience such problems
only fleetingly), the old king is constantly depicted in the confusions attendant on the difference between self-conscious and
unpremeditated feeling, a confusion which dogs him throughout
his play.

There are also such characters who are not kings, and interestingly enough, we find one in the drama with which we initiated
the present series of examples, in *Julius Caesar* where Brutus
presents a problem more complex than, but reminiscent of, some

of the early Herods. Let us assume an interpretation according to which Brutus has decided to kill Caesar with rather ambivalent motivation since Brutus has remarked that he knows of no reason why Caesar deserves death. In this context, which would also include Brutus' observation before his suicide that he did not kill Caesar with half so good a will as he now kills himself, some salient motifs delineate Brutus as a rudimentary example of the character type which we have been discussing. Such characters as Lear or Richard II might ultimately be placed in a very general category of pride (as opposed to some category of "service to an external ideal"), but Brutus especially shows that pride as an organizing concept has only limited utility for the "blueprint" of such characters. If we approach Shakespeare's Roman Stoic by inspecting his speech to the conspirators, once he has decided on his course, we find clearly delineated and now-familiar traits which transcend Pride.

> For *Antony*, is but a Limbe of *Cæsar*.
> Let's be Sacrificers, but not Butchers *Caius*:
> We all stand up against the spirit of *Cæsar*,
> And in the Spirit of men, there is no blood:
> O that we then could come by *Cæsars* Spirit,
> And not dismember *Cæsar*! But (alas)
> *Cæsar* must bleed for it. And gentle Friends,
> Let's kill him Boldly, but not Wrathfully:
> Let's carve him, as a Dish fit for the Gods,
> Not hew him as a Carkasse fit for Hounds:
> And let our Hearts, as subtle Masters do,
> Stirre up their Servants to an acte of Rage,
> And after seeme to chide 'em. This shall make
> Our purpose Necessary, and not Envious.
> Which so appearing to the common eyes,
> We shall be call'd Purgers, not Murderers.
> And for *Marke Antony*, thinke not of him:
> For he can do no more than *Cæsars* Arme
> When *Cæsars* head is off. [798–816]

The density of this speech is high, but the most obvious aspect, the conclusion to spare Antony, offers some leverage with which

to work because the structure of the play will tell us that Brutus
was absolutely wrong in his assessment of Antony. Brutus' incorrect conclusion was arrived at, ultimately, by metaphor, was it
not? Antony may figuratively be a "limb" of Caesar, and within
the metaphor the "arm" cannot function when the "head" is
cut off; but there is obviously a line where metaphor must cease
and reality begin. Brutus' reasoning might then strike us as fantastic, not necessarily because Antony is misjudged but because of
the process according to which he is misjudged. Herod in his own
way was fantastic—only a maniac would claim to be god of
earth, heaven, hell, and weather—but in the cognitions of such
characters the fantastic is the mode. Thus it is sufficient to say
that within this general context Brutus merely offers a different
criterion for cognition. We are to gather, since there is no "blood"
in the "spirit" of Caesar, that blood should not be shed in
actuality.

In this sequence Brutus has a formula for emotional orientation, too. In one sense, the conspirators are going to act in a
play: they will play "purgers." In this playlet, one organizes the
self much as the actor who spoke of Hecuba appeared to in Hamlet's eyes. The heart (traditionally the seat of the affections) must
operate in a specified way. It will stand behind the deed, stirring
up the affections to the violence requisite and afterward regain-
ing control. One will kill "boldly" but not "wrathfully." This is
much like telling a troop of actors to engage in a real fist fight on
stage and then not to run amuck because they must remember
they are only acting. Physical assassination is not a fiction. It is
as if, because one wishes to murder but does not wish to see himself as "murderer," the emotions are organized to receive different names. Perception is filtered into metaphor, and decorum
becomes the ultimate principle to which Brutus appeals throughout the play. The symbology of the murder must be the ritual of
sacrifice, not the tearing-to-pieces by the pack. Presumably, if
one thinks this way, then so it will, in truth, be. In a similar vein
Brutus speaks about Antony.

> *Cass.* Yet I feare him;
> For in the ingrafted love he beares to *Cæsar*.

Bru. Alas, good *Cassius*, do not think of him:
If he love *Cæsar*, all that he can do
Is to himselfe; take thought, and die for *Cæsar*,
And that were much he should: for he is given
To sports, to wildnesse, and much company. [817–23]

It is unclear here whether or not Shakespeare intends Brutus to mean that Antony is too poor or immoral an object for this noble sacrifice, but the last two lines are sufficiently instructive. In this curious equation, Antony should do the right thing, the decorous thing, either by actually killing himself or by pining away simply because he is so lewd (or because he should not outlive Caesar, or because a lewd man should not continue to live after a man like Caesar has died).

Since various scholars have commented on other aspects of this character, we need only indicate how Brutus may further exemplify the traits under general discussion. A sense of elevation for which Cassius later serves as a foil is apparent in the following passage:

There is no terror, *Cassius*, in your threats:
For I am Arm'd so strong in Honesty,
That they passe by me, as the idle winde,
Which I respect not. I did send to you
For certaine summes of Gold, which you deny'd me
For I can raise no money by vile meanes. [2043–48]

And so forth. Cassius can, we gather, raise money by vile means, but he has been reproved by Brutus for doing so, even though Cassius is now reproved for not presenting some of it to Brutus.

The two sequences regarding Portia's death are also instructive. When Messala reports what Brutus already knows, that Portia died, he acts ignorant of the fact and urges Messala to tell news he is obviously unwilling to impart. So finally:

Bru. Now as you are a Roman tell me true.
Mes. Then like a Roman, beare the truth I tell,
For certaine she is dead, and by strange manner.
Bru. Why, farewell *Portia*. We must die, *Messala*:

With meditating that she must die once,
I have the patience to endure it now.
Mes. Even so great men, great losses should indure. [2183–89]

This is perhaps precisely Brutus' decorous point, but Cassius' comment is not irrelevant: "I have as much of this in Art as you, / But yet my Nature could not beare it so." [2190–91]

"Well, to our worke alive," answers Brutus, and he immediately proposes the march to Phillipi, the justification for which is rather like his justification for sparing Antony earlier. The speech is a famous and resonant one but is hardly to their immediate point.

> There is a Tide in the affaires of men,
> Which taken at the Flood, leades on to Fortune:
> Omitted, all the voyage of their life,
> Is bound in Shallowes, and in Miseries. [2217–20]

This is, of course, true enough—once it has been established that the particular tide in a particular affair at hand is indeed "at the flood." It is not, as the subsequent battle proves. Has not Brutus again acted in terms of a purely verbalist way of thought, confusing metaphor with reality?

Such confusion, as with the actor, ultimately confuses the self. We recall that Cassius asks Brutus if he will kill himself in defeat. Brutus finds such an action (again) "vile," but when Cassius draws him an evocative picture of being led in triumph, Brutus reverses his field abruptly.

> No, *Cassius*, no:
> Think not, thou Noble Romane,
> That ever *Brutus* will go bound to Rome,
> He beares too great a minde. [2453–55]

The death speech will reiterate these confusions of the character whose sense of identity depends, paradoxically (at least according to transcendentalist recensions) on "itself" and not on some exterior ideal.

My heart doth joy, that yet in all my life,
I found no man, but he was true to me.
I shall have glory by this loosing day
More then *Octavius*, and *Marke Antony*,
By this vile Conquest shall attaine unto. [2679–83]

"Glory," of course, was the true object of desire, but can it really be said that Antony was "true" to Brutus after being allowed the pulpit in a typically Brutean gentlemen's agreement? And can we ignore Brutus' own charge against Cassius in the quarrel scene?

The bent of the play's structure would here seem apparent. With his claim to glory and true loyalties, Brutus manufactures a greatness according to his own definition, since he has failed to cope with the external realities of the play. In those definitions, what emerges in Brutus' mind is a bivalued universe so characteristic of the thinking of this class of Shakespearean figure. On one side are those who support Brutus and his honor; on the other are those who may be termed "vile": they are of the class which opposes the definitions with which Brutus has surrounded himself. They are the enemies of Brutus, but for Brutus, of course, they are more than that. By being his enemies, they are the enemies of virtue, truth, and goodness.

Richard II plays a scene which would appear to summarize all the motifs with which we have associated this class of figures, and his speech allows us to see how the many traits can unite into that whole which will convey the logical relationship of the varying elements in this general character complex.

Give me that Glasse, and therein will I reade.
No deeper wrinckles yet? hath Sorrow strucke
So many Blowes upon this Face of mine,
And made no deeper Wounds? Oh flatt'ring glasse,
Like to my followers in prosperitie,
Thou do'st beguile me. Was this Face, the Face
That every day, under his House-hold Roofe
Did keepe ten thousand men? Was this the Face,
That like the Sunne, did make beholders winke?

Was this the Face, which fac'd so many follies,
That was at last out-fac'd by Bullingbrooke?
A brittle Glory shineth in this Face,
As brittle as the Glory, is the Face,
For there it is, crackt in an hundred shivers.
Marke, silent King, the Morall of this sport,
How soone my Sorrow hath destroy'd my Face.
Boling. The shadow of your Sorrow hath destroy'd
The shadow of your Face.
Rich. Say that againe.
The shadow of my Sorrow: Ha, let's see,
'Tis very true, my Griefe lies all within,
And these externall manners of Laments
Are meerely shadowes, to the unseene Griefe
That swells with silence in the tortur'd Soule.
There lies the substance. [2199–2223]

That the deposition scene of which this sequence is a part was added to the play in the 1608 quarto might in itself arouse interest. Although speculation has it that the scene was suppressed until it was finally allowed to appear under the supposedly greater liberalism of a James I,[13] it is no less plausible to suggest that Shakespeare's approach to this kind of character in 1608 might have developed beyond what was in the deposition scene in 1597.

The sequence, we will agree, points rather specifically at Richard's problems in conceptualization, and Bolingbroke aids us by his remark. Richard's point is that his sorrowful impetuosity, his dashing of the mirror, can be an indication that his sorrow has destroyed his mirrored face. However, Bolingbroke suggests the subtlety, that it is an unreal sorrow which has destroyed that unreal, mirrored face. Richard, of course, seizes the term "shadow" to suggest that the whole action, like Hamlet's customary suit of solemn black, is a mere indication of huge internal sorrow, but we can also follow Bolingbroke. Expecting to "see" sorrow, to find some literal manifestation of it, Richard has called

[13] See Hinman's introduction to *Richard II*, Shakespeare Quarto Facsimiles, No. 13 (Oxford, 1966); and Chambers, *William Shakespeare* (Oxford, 1930), I, 350 ff.

for the mirror in which he hopes visually to apprehend himself in the role of Sorrowful. But there are no lines in the face; emotion, as Lear learns, cannot necessarily be "seen." The curious and interesting development in the sequence is that Richard has accordingly found it necessary to insist on an appropriate accompaniment to his sorrow. The "moral" of his "sport" is to convey to us that sorrow has indeed destroyed his face, even if it has not. The symbolic statement, as it were, establishes the fact. The action must be performed to make the sorrow real, for the moral we are asked to draw is not that Richard is sorrowful but that this emotion has a visual reality.

There are of course ironies. This rich speech is suggestive in the various definitions offered by Richard regarding the nature of his face. It was the sun again with glory shining in it, as if kingly glory were itself a visible attribute. It is tantamount to his kingship, and if destroyed not by Bolingbroke but, as Richard has said, by his own sorrow, the implications are not without interest. Since the face has last been compared to regality, Richard in effect says that it is this kingly element which sorrow has destroyed. There is more truth in this than Richard realizes, for he has abandoned the role of king to assume another role, that of the Sorrowing Sufferer, the victim of the transitory quality of life.

Ultimately, this kind of Shakespearean character must react to protect itself when threatened with identity annihilation. The move from King to Sufferer is one such maneuver: we have seen Lear perform it. And has not Richard described himself as "Christ" to Bolingbroke's "Judas" and Northumberland's "Pilate"? The move is as predictable as Richard's need to realize, to make real his state through the visualities of the broken mirror and, later, through the audibilities of the music when "time is broke and no proportion kept." And thus the music also becomes something else. It is a remnant of a would-be sacramental universe where the heavens declare the glory of Richard. It becomes a showpiece, a decoration, a "brooch": "For 'tis a signe of love, and love to *Richard* / Is a strange Brooch, in this all-hating world" (2731–32).

9
Shakespeare's Villains

Assuming that all men try to know themselves in terms of some symbology achieved by an individual effort at self-objectification, we saw, in chapter 3, that there are no grounds for any rigid prediction as to what specific conceptualizations a given character might choose. A Macbeth might wish to be king—why a king? Troilus wishes for Cressida—why a woman? There are no real answers, and indeed, in Shakespeare's plays one cannot admit this kind of question. Often, a particular desire, such as Romeo's for a lover, is rendered as a *donné* which cannot be challenged in the immediate aesthetic situation. It seems enough to posit someone such as Troilus who reposes his faith in a woman rather than in, say, an ideal father. The play will then proceed to construct Troilus as a pseudotranscendentalist. It is therefore interesting to note certain characters depicted as unable to have confidence in *any* particular conceptualization. This class, in general, comprises most of those figures usually taken as Shakespeare's "villains."

To describe them in this manner does not really do justice to the artistic issue, for an Angelo might strike us as "villainous" enough. Therefore, we again eschew ethical evaluations and instead define these characters by the way in which Shakespeare conducts them through their searchings for a conceptualization of "identity." They exhibit dissatisfaction with the goals they do gain; they sometimes seem insatiable; they toy with various modes of conceptualizing themselves to themselves. And if their waverings are, in effect, their character modes, their dissatisfactions are eloquent examples of Shakespeare's fundamental theory regarding this general problem of human desire, which is itself the axiom of all his structures. The indecisions of these characters attest to the inefficacy of all goals for satisfying or even objectifying the mysteries of human thrust.

These Shakespearean figures are closer to those who pursue riches and political power than to other types, but they do differ from the Malvolios and the Angelos in having, as it were, a stronger transcendentalist imagination. Perhaps for this reason they remind us of the Romeos; there is "aspiration." Furthermore, although it does not seem implicit in any theory, such characters are initially presented as suffering under a sense of what can only be described as rejection. Seemingly prevented by such rejection from realizing their "selves" in some objectification, they are depicted (in some analogy to the "king types" which we have hitherto discussed) as driven to merely verbal assertions of their own worth.

> Three Great-ones of the Cittie,
> (In personall suite to make me his Lieutenant)
> Off-capt to him: and by the faith of man
> I know my price, I am worth no worsse a place. [12–15]

Because these characters do not have the trappings of kingship or because their aspirations may simply be posited by the dramatist as too restless, they have some trouble achieving that concept of the validity of the self as "rightly" expressed. They speak of their deservings, but it is often uncertain what they think they deserve. Most often, if their abstracted sense of their own validity does depend on some perceptible confirmation, it depends on being esteemed and loved by other people, usually by *one* person. Accordingly, the converse occurs. When they have problems, these characters focus their troubles on the figure of one person who then becomes the fancied enemy. This dependence on people is interestingly attested to by the great pleasure these characters seem to derive from pretending just that intensity and delicacy of love for which they seem to long and for which they seem ready to sacrifice everything.

Perhaps a key to their longing for esteem and love lies in the fact that these figures are pictured as despising themselves, as considering themselves nothing. There was, of course, the Renaissance proposition that man was nothing because he was without transcendent personality, without "God." However, when these characters advance to any generalized solution to the problem of aspiration, they repose a paradoxical confidence in human beings. They are, if we wish, idolaters who expect more self-definition from the love of a human being than would ordinarily be possible. Their burning hate betrays their dependence, and their anger is perhaps rendered even greater by the fact that other humans are not, after all, the *primum mobile*. In fact, they are more undependable than, say, an abstract ideal of soldiership. But because of their burning hate, we can understand how such figures would make useful villains. It is as if Shakespeare sometimes used such a theory of personality when he needed a character to be in personal vendetta against someone else in a play. In such cases, the poet may have accordingly created our fourth kind of figure as the most plausible for the situation.

It is interesting that such characters are often depicted as almost self-conscious materialists, the classical Epicureans of Shakespeare's plays (Edmund's praise of bastardy being the most obvious case in point). We also have Iago's significant definition of love:

we have Reason to coole our raging Motions, our carnall Stings, or unbitted Lusts: whereof I take this, that you call Love, to be a Sect or scien.
Rod. It cannot be.
Iago. It is meerly a Lust of the blood, and a permission of the will. Come, be a man. [682–88]

To be "a man" is, of course, to put money into one's purse. And it is as if Shakespeare intends that such characters see no way, in their world outlooks, to the transcendental possibilities for human nature made available by familiar traditions. Consequently, such figures are allowed only a limited awareness of the very proof afforded by their discontent that there could be in man something beyond purely materialistic orientations. The imaginativeness, the conviviality, and even the sense of humor that Shakespeare depicts in such types serves to refute the very kind of generalization that these villains put forward about the limitations of mankind.

The figure who might be indicative of this type is curiously and significantly mischaracterized by Julius Caesar. When he speaks of Cassius, does not Caesar really draw the picture of an Angelo?

> I do not know the man I should avoid
> So soone as that spare *Cassius*. He reades much,
> He is a great Observer, and he lookes
> Quite through the Deeds of men. He loves no Playes,
> As thou dost *Antony*: he heares no Musicke.
> Seldom he smiles, and smiles in such a sort
> As if he mock'd himselfe, and scorn'd his spirit
> That could be mov'd to smile at any thing.
> Such men as he, be never at hearts ease,
> Whiles they behold a greater then themselves,
> And therefore are they very dangerous. [302–12]

Perhaps more indicative of Caesar's inability to cope with the situation around him than of Cassius' character, this judgment contains the seeds of its self-refutation merely in its conclusions regarding Antony. At the same time, the juxtaposition of a lean and hungry Cassius to men who sleep at night, fat and sleek, seems more applicable to a Malvolio than to the Cassius we observe in the play. In fact, when we note Mark Antony's cynicism and greed in the proscription scene, we can conclude that Shakespeare need not have been as simple as he has made his Caesar on this point.

Cassius' earliest speeches move in directions not accounted for by Caesar's analysis.

> *Brutus*, I do observe you now of late:
> I have not from your eyes, that gentlenesse
> And shew of Love, as I was wont to have:
> You bear too stubborne, and too strange a hand
> Over your Friend, that loves you. [123–27]

If we argue that here is the evolution of an approach meant to be the seduction of Brutus, Cassius' later remarks in soliloquy do not allow us to rest so easy.

Well *Brutus,* thou art Noble: yet I see,
Thy Honorable Mettle may be wrought
From that it is dispos'd: therefore it is meet,
That Noble Mindes keepe ever with their likes:
For who so firme, that cannot be seduc'd?
Cæsar doth beare me hard, but he loves *Brutus.*
If I were *Brutus* now, and he were *Cassius,*
He should not humor me. [415–22]

The resonance of cliché is in the first few lines, if we assume that Cassius is merely the *simpliste* villain (whatever that is); but it is worth noticing that another figure, one whom we have regarded as rather more complexly conceived, thinks along the same lines. "Were I the Moore," he protests to Roderigo, "I would not be *Iago*":

In following him, I follow but my selfe.
Heaven is my Judge, not I for love and duty,
But seeming so, for my peculiar end.
For when my outward Action doth demonstrate
The native act, and figure of my heart
In Complement externe, 'tis not long after
That I will weare my heart upon my sleeve
For Dawes to pecke at. [63–70]

All this may well be so, but we observe with interest that even after he has obtained all that Cassio ever possessed in the way of rank, prestige, and personal trust from Othello, Iago can still be moved to say

If *Cassio* do remaine,
He hath a daily beauty in his life,
That makes me ugly. [3100–3102]

Such characters as Cassius and Iago are precipitated into their activities because they "love not wisely but too well." Their problem, initially, is to handle kinds of rejection which they cannot understand. And it is significant that they must immediately react with a burning hate, for as we have suggested, this response demonstrates a profound dependence. To be rejected, after all, is not to have ceased to exist, unless one's sense of identity depends on a definition of one's own validity by someone else. What is the difference between Othello's plotting against Desdemona and Iago's plotting against Othello? In these respects it is significant that while the Oedipus complex has been suggested as in some way relevant to Hamlet, homosexuality has often been speculated in the problems of Iago. While we would not espouse such twentieth-century terminology in connection with the work of an English Renaissance playwright, what provoked such formulations is important. It can certainly be said that Iago and Cassius are not indifferent to those who reject them. Iago is even put into the position of proving to Roderigo that he hates Othello. And, by reacting so violently, it would appear that, like the lovers of another Shakespearean class, this group of villains derives some identity not from a sense of certain talents but from a relationship. It is as if praise and love could confirm one's fundamental sense of existence.

Cassius' vindictive words about Caesar are, of course, an important motif throughout the early parts of his play, but it is useful to compare them to that statement by Cassius that he would hold firm if anyone tried to seduce him from allegiance to Caesar. Exiled, as it were, from a potential relationship with those who may help to "identify" them, such characters are really quite lost. Although they are ready to worship, they are not ready to do so within the Elizabethan "world picture." In their quests for the absolute, they seek satisfaction from someone whom they ultimately have put on the transcendental plane but who will not give them back some symbolic status to make that relationship concrete and thus real. Robbed of this feeling, they are cast adrift, seeking identity in themselves by adopting role after role.

They also reduce all men and all transcendentalist gestures to the realm of illusion. Such modes have, after all, not worked out for them. Cassius will accordingly emphasize the fact that Caesar is no more of a man than he himself is. Nothing is innately superior: once a man loses a swimming race, he has demonstrated his inability to lord it over others. The fault is not in our stars but "in ourselves, that we are underlings." But while he is so reductive about men, does not Cassius finally follow Brutus as slavishly as he condemns others for following Caesar?

The first half of *Julius Caesar*—few will quarrel with such a bifurcation of the play—concludes the presentation in what we may term "Cassius A" of elements common to his class of character. The bold walk through the storm, the exposing of the chest to lightning, the reduction of all phenomena to a Lucretian materialism—all are viewpoints shared with Edmund in his deification of Nature and with Iago in his sermon on individual validity as dependent on nothing but the self. "Virtue! a fig! 'tis in ourselves that we are thus or thus," says Iago. He and his "brothers" see a universe essentially meaningless, essentially "atranscendental," for they can find nothing on earth that satisfies their yearning. But with the second half of *Julius Caesar* comes a slightly different Cassius whose other traits indicate an interesting Shakespearean phenomenon, the presence of a character type in transition, a partially digested concept by the poet of that kind of figure which will finally be integrated in the persons of Iago and Edmund.

Yet in the first half of the play Cassius has shown a certain tendency to assume roles even to himself: Machiavellian schemer, defier of the elements, and perhaps even, swept by Brutus' rhetoric, patriotic assassin and Stoic poseur.

> *Bru.* Fates, we will know your pleasures:
> That we shall die, we know, 'tis but the time
> And drawing dayes out, that men stand upon.
> *Cass.* Why he that cuts off twenty yeares of life,
> Cuts off so many yeares of fearing death. [1313–17]

After Brutus has suggested the ceremonial bath in blood, it is Cassius who sees the possibilities of role in a way different from Brutus' perception.

> Stoop then, and wash. How many Ages hence
> Shall this our lofty Scene be acted over,

In State unborne, and Accents yet unknowne?
Bru. How many times shall *Cæsar* bleed in sport,
That now on *Pompeyes* Basis lie along
No worthier then the dust?
Cass. So oft as that shall be,
So often shall the knot of us be call'd,
The Men that gave their Country liberty. [1326–39]

In the second half of the play, Cassius is challenged by another potential alienation. It is not illogical that he should stand culpable of taking bribes and of supporting those of his subordinates who do, but the result on stage is that the audience is presented with a possible repetition of the situation which opened the play. "*Brutus*, this sober forme of yours, hides wrongs," Cassius observes, and one might reasonably expect menace as he is pushed to say "*Brutus*, baite not me, Ile not indure it." Caesar certainly experienced the truth of such a statement, but in this half of the play, when Brutus begins acting like Caesar vis-à-vis Cassius, the audience watches Cassius actually back down before the tantrums of a mere man who desires the ends without being faced with the means. Cassius' threat that Brutus had better moderate his language of chastisement is answered by Brutus' peroration:

When *Marcus Brutus* growes so Covetous,
To locke such Rascall Counters from his Friends,
Be ready Gods with all your Thunder-bolts,
Dash him to pieces. [2056–59]

And with friendship thus put on the basis of money, Cassius seems to wilt.

Cas. I deny'd you not.
Bru. You did.
Cas. I did not. He was but a Foole
That brought my answer back. *Brutus* hath riv'd my hart:
A Friend should beare his Friends infirmities;
But *Brutus* makes mine greater then they are.
Bru. I do not, till you practice them on me.

Cas. You love me not.
Bru. I do not like your faults.
Cas. A friendly eye could never see such faults. [2060–69]

This half-humbug, half-significant persistence concludes with Cassius' melodramatic gesture of baring his chest a second time in the play and giving Brutus the dagger. But he says:

Strike, as thou did'st at *Cæsar*: for I know
When thou did'st hate him worst, thou lov'st him better
Than ever thou loved'st *Cassius*. [2084–86]

And when they make up, Cassius observes,

Have you not love enough to bear with me,
When that rash humour which my Mother gave me
Makes me forgetfull. [2102–4]

Cassius has claimed that he was an older soldier, and it follows hard upon this sequence that he would sorely be tempted again as he and Brutus debate strategy. With Brutus forcing his quasi-metaphysical view of the ripeness of time over Cassius' advice, he can only interject "Heare me, good Brother" between speeches and end with curious monosyllabic taciturnity: "Then with your will go on: Wee'l along / Our selves, and meet them at *Philippi*." Brutus asks if there is no more to say. "No more, good night. / Early to morrow we will rise, and hence." But as Cassius departs:

Oh my deere brother:
This was an ill beginning of the night:
Never come such division 'tweene our souls:
Let it not *Brutus*. [2224–39]

At this point in the play, Cassius has very little to gain from hypocrisy. Indeed, he possesses an army and territories. Yet his great concern for Brutus' opinion and his use of the term "love" so constantly argue a specific direction of his emotions. We could suggest that, needing Brutus' army for the impending attack, he must still pose as friendly, but the significant fact of Cassius' characterization is that he has constantly deferred to Brutus' political opinions, even when knowing that this deference is not wise. This tendency, especially in the plot to kill Caesar, is partially explainable as the attempt to keep Brutus in the plan, but in the second half of the play such motivation is irrelevant. Given the stakes before Philippi, nothing is to be gained in the realm of politics or avarice from Cassius' submission. It is merely a way of avoiding personal conflict with Brutus.

Cassius' later depression, when he is alone, emphasizes this personal problem.

> Give me thy hand *Messala:*
> Be thou my witnesse, that against my will,
> (As *Pompey* was) am I compell'd to set
> Upon one battell all our Liberties.

The next two lines, however, are in interesting juxtaposition to what preceded: "You know, that I held *Epicurus* strong, / And his Opinion: Now I change my minde" (2412–18). Whatever has prompted this vacillation in materialist belief may not be articulated in Cassius' mind, but his actions have shown us that he has not lately been led by the logic of such a view. His emotions seem to have told him of a greater reality. We may ask, for instance, how he has actually been "compell'd" to the strategy which he considers poor. An answer may emerge in the manner of his death, for Shakespeare deviates from Plutarch in his description of the suicide. The biographer observed that it was the "taking" of Titinius which made Cassius think that the battle was lost, but Shakespeare's character phrases matters somewhat differently as he prepares to die: "O Coward that I am, to live so long, / To see my best Friend tane before my face" (2515–16). The problem of love, as G. Wilson Knight has observed, is a problem in the play as a whole, but we might submit that it is crucial to the analysis of the character class which contains a Cassius.[1]

[1] See *The Imperial Theme,* "The Eroticism of *Julius Caesar*" (Oxford, 1931).

The bifurcation of Cassius, all Machiavelli in the first half of the play and all sensitivity in the second half, is interesting evidence of the development of the kind of figure which we here discuss, and similar developmental activity may be found in other early plays. We recall an Aaron in *Titus Andronicus* who, though mouthing profaneness, offering long recitals of the spectacular evil he has done, and taking a frankly atheistic position, yet emerges as almost selfless in his anxiety for and devotion to his illegitimate child.

> My mistress is my mistress: this my selfe
> The vigour, and the picture of my youth:
> This, before all the world I do preferre. [1790–92]

There is Shylock, too, a more artistically interesting figure. We have suggested that he belongs to a class of characters such as Angelo, especially since Shakespeare presents the problem of literalistic perception as one of his salient traits. Nevertheless, we note that like Cassius and Iago, Shylock burns in hatred. In terms of business dealings, Antonio is a hindrance to Shylock; but we will agree that spitting and spurning are at least plausible motivations for Shylock to want to cut Antonio's heart out. We have, in fact, a reaction to a rejection. Recalling Shylock's tendency to adopt roles and, by definition, his "atheism" formally realized in his Renaissance status as a Jew, we also note in him many earmarks of a Cassius. Shylock's remark to Jessica when no Christians are present may strike us as suggestive.

> I am bid forth to supper *Jessica*,
> There are my Keyes: but wherefore should I go?
> I am not bid for love, they flatt[er] me,
> But yet Ile go in hate, to feede upon
> The prodigall Christian. [848–52]

We are accustomed to this reversal with the Cassiuses—if not love, then hate. It is also of great interest to observe another trait which Shylock does not share with the Angelos and the Malvolios. He is not humorless. Summing up Launcelot Gobbo in one instance, he observes:

> The patch is kinde enough, but a huge feeder:
> Snaile-slow in profit, and he sleepes by day
> More then the wilde-cat. [883–85]

Our experience with Launcelot might incline us to agree, but there is further significance for Shylock's own character in this listing of Launcelot's faults. We might wonder how Launcelot managed to lead the kind of life he did with Shylock. When the Jew tries to convince Launcelot that his job with Bassanio will be harder, do we not raise an eyebrow at the fact that Launcelot was retained at all in Shylock's service?

> Well, thou shall see, thy eyes shall be thy judge,
> The difference of old *Shylocke* and *Bassanio*;
> What Jessica, thou shalt not gurmandize,
> As thou hast done with me, what, Jessica?
> And sleepe, and snore, and rend apparrell out. [836–40]

Whatever the truth of the matter—and we must remember that Launcelot himself may not be definitive on the subject, being sufficiently superstitious about Jews to upset Jessica with the statement that she is damned—Shylock's final judgment of Launcelot may have some significance for assessing Shakespeare's intentions here. Recalling Malvolio on the subject of Feste or Angelo on the subject of Pompey, we might agree that Shylock is not an enemy to humor. In fact, it can be suggested that even Shylock's villainous sense of humor in the bond scenes shows him as the potential member of a class of characters distinguished by this trait. We recall Aaron's heavy-handed and macabre jokes as well as his would-be tricks. We also recall a deliberate differentiation between Brutus and Cassius in this respect. The two are exposed to a stimulus. Their quarreling has been interrupted by a sudden entrance:

> *Cass.* How now? What's the matter?
> *Poet.* For shame you Generals; what do you mean?

> Love, and be Friends, as two such men should bee,
> For I have seene more yeeres I'me sure then yee.
> *Cass.* Ha, ha, how vildely doth this Cynicke rhyme?
> *Bru.* Get you hence sirrah: Sawcy Fellow, hence.
> *Cass.* Beare with him *Brutus*, 'tis his fashion.
> *Bru.* Ile know his humor, when he knowes his time:
> What should the Warres do with these Jigging Fooles?
> Companion, hence.
> *Cass.* Away, away be gone. *Exit Poet.* [2114–24]

A sense of what is funny would seem to indicate high levels of awareness through the ability to perceive paradox, and Shakespeare's villains are famous for this trait. Perhaps it is the possession of this sense which defines their real intelligence and imparts the illusion of humanity to so many of their portraits. A Brutus, it seems, cannot laugh.

It is interesting that many of these characters are given real handicaps. Shakespeare's actions in this respect render such intelligent and warped figures if not tragic then ultimately pathetic, for they are often at greater disadvantages than others. And these very handicaps sometimes serve as the terms in which these characters will, as it were, resolve their searchings for something to "be." Aaron is a Moor and thus black: we hear much from him in defense of the beauty and appropriateness of this "devil color." He wishes to be a kind of devil, to take rest in this conceptualization. "If there be devils," he remarks skeptically, "would I were a devil." Edmund is a bastard, and though Phillip the Bastard in *King John* is not overly sensitive about a situation which makes him related to Richard I, Edmund can be discovered alone on stage resolving the matter in his mind by taking refuge in a anti-social position, constructing a superior virile identity from this fact of being a bastard until he moves on to other roles. Shylock is a Jew. Richard III is a hunchback. "Dogs bark at me as I halt by them," he says, and his search for a "way" may anticipate Edmund's.

> Why, I (in this weake piping time of Peace)
> Have no delight to passe away the time,

Unlesse to see my Shadow in the Sunne,
And descant on mine owne Deformity.
And therefore, since I cannot prove a Lover,
To entertaine these fair well spoken dayes,
I am determined to prove a Villaine,
And hate the idle pleasure of these dayes. [26–33]

Perhaps so, but we may know him from his initial commentary on his inability "to strut before a wanton ambling nymph" to his sharp and mocking self-disparagement after his wooing of Anne. Speaking of Edward, he describes him as

A sweeter, and a lovelier Gentleman,
Fram'd in that prodigallity of Nature:
Yong, Valiant, Wise, and (no doubt) right Royal,
The spacious World cannot againe affoord:
And will she yet abase her eyes on me,
That cropt the Golden prime of this sweet Prince,
And made her Widdow to a wofull Bed?
On me, whose all not equals Edward's moiety?
On me, that halts, and am mishapen thus?
My Dukedom, to a Beggerly denier!
I do mistake my person all this while:
Upon my life, she findes (although I cannot)
Myselfe to be a marv'llous proper man. [439–51]

We might speculate, if we had the leisure, on the implications for the play here. Is it not possible, for instance, that Richard is his own chief despiser? Yet his self-hate may not be justified, at least as far as his physical appearance is concerned, for he can be attractive to Anne. His basic problems reemerge in his remark before his last battle.

There is no Creature loves me;
And if I die, no soule shall pittie me.
Nay, wherefore should they? Since that I my Selfe,
Finde in my Selfe, no pittie to my Selfe. [3662–65]

Never satisfied because they are too intelligent to be convinced of the reality of their self-conceptualizations, such figures go on to

judge their inability to convince themselves of some earthly validity as in itself a kind of nonexistence.

> What? do I feare my selfe? There's none else by,
> *Richard* loves *Richard*, that is, I am I.
> Is there a Murtherer heere? No; Yes, I am:
> Then flye; What, from my Selfe? Great reason: why?
> Lest I revenge. What? my Selfe upon my Selfe? [3644–48]

Hamlet is an interesting case in these respects, for although we
have suggested that he takes his final rest in the attitude of the
pseudotranscendentalist, do we not have many of the essentials of
the villain type in his structuring? There is much in his external
situation which might encourage us in this view: is he not forced
to plot against others and, by a demi-commitment to murder, to
become a potential villain? To proceed further in this vein is,
however, to play with words. Let us suggest that in Hamlet the
"formula" for a Cassius or a Richard III is used but is put to a
different purpose. It is not odd that this should be so, for clearly
the complexities in the characterization of the villain type have
great potentialities. If we were more certain of Shakespeare's
chronology, we might even suggest that by the time he wrote
Hamlet, the "Cassius" type and the "Malvolio" type were those
best established in his art and that in *Hamlet* we observe an
"Angelo" (Claudius) beginning the play by preaching to a "Cassius" (Hamlet) the Christian virtues of overcoming grief for one's
dead father.

Rather than devote excessive space to the discussion of such a
controversial character, let us indicate certain gross resemblances
and potentialities. Hamlet may be the villain who eventually finds
himself. We have described the "Cassius" type as one who is not
satisfied in the various roles that he tries on for himself because
his intelligence does not allow him to be convinced of their validity. There is nothing to be said against the possibility that such a
figure could finally be allowed to discover for himself a proper
conceptualization, however, and Hamlet's may be the case. The

transcendentalist orientation of such a character is always fairly strong, his concern for love being one of his important motivations. Accordingly, to take a rest in pseudotranscendental attitudes is not an inconsistent move. In Hamlet we find self-contempt, the absence of a sense of self, and the tendency to adopt roles as a way of coping with reality. We also find philosophical skepticism and a keen sense of humor. If we put an Edmund in Hamlet's position, we might have different results only because Hamlet is even more cautious about giving final belief.

Hamlet is initially presented as a malcontent suffering under a sense of rejection, and we cannot, by a kind of critical somersault, attribute this discontent to the fact that his father has been murdered. It has not been sufficiently emphasized that the well known scene contrasting Hamlet's mourning black with the regalia of the coronation celebration serves to accentuate a rebellious discontent which is justified by information gathered later but which is not justified at the time that the play begins. Hamlet has not yet heard from the ghost; he nevertheless contemplates suicide. And if there is a basic and initial discontent, can we not trace much of it to the problem of love, a matter so strong in the thinking of a Cassius? Hamlet's relationships with Gertrude and Ophelia suggest this as does, of course, his devotion to his dead father, but the matter is emphasized by means of Ophelia. If we are to rely at all upon her report, whatever the remote reaches of Hamlet's possible "strategy," do we not observe a certain dependence?

> He took me by the wrist, and held me hard;
> Then goes he to the length of all his arme;
> And, with his other hand thus o're his brow,
> He fals to such perusall of my face,
> As he would draw it. Long stay'd he so,
> At last, a little shaking of mine Arme:
> And thrice his head thus waving up and downe;
> He rais'd a sigh, so pittious and profound,
> That it did seeme to shatter all his bulke,
> And end his being. [984–93]

When Hamlet is barred from discourse with Ophelia, he is cut off not only from his father but from someone else. This gradual withdrawal of love from him is ironically reinforced by Ophelia herself as she performs a gesture in which the king and Polonius did not instruct her.

> *Oph.* My Lord, I have Remembrances of yours,
> That I have longed long to re-deliver.
> I pray you now, receive them.
> *Ham.* No, no, I never gave you aught. [1748–51]

Confronted as he is with Ophelia returning his gifts, he may be surprised at her reason—"rich gifts wax poor when givers prove unkind"—for it does not betoken rejection. He thus may be sincere when he warns her away from him, the terms being interestingly of a piece with the self-condemnation which is his salient trait throughout the play.

I am very proud, revengefull, Ambitious, with more offences at my becke, then I have thoughts to put them in, imagination to give them shape, or time to acte them in. What should such Fellowes as I do, crawling between Heaven and Earth. We are arrant Knaves all, beleeve none of us. Goe thy wayes to a Nunnery. [1779–85]

He may or may not glimpse Polonius now; but when his mood of self-abasement changes to a spirit of reviling, his conclusion— "I say we will have no more Marriages"—may be sarcastic, yet it also betokens disillusionment with one of the traditional modes and bonds of love. The almost deliberate bawdiness to Ophelia before the mousetrap play may be an aspect of this sensitivity, for his "country manners," while they may be meant as a sarcastic exaggeration of Polonius' conventional fears, also create the hypothetical situation to satisfy Hamlet's ultimate definition of women as undependable in the matter of love. They are simply sex machines. Except for Horatio, one gathers, there is no dependability. Hence knowing what we do about Rosencrantz and Guildenstern, Hamlet's welcome to them is pathetic in the ambivalence of its attitudes.

Begger that I am, I am even poore in thankes; but I thanke you:
and sure deare friends my thanks are too deare a halfepenny; were you
not sent for? Is it your owne inclining? Is it a free visitation?
[1319–22]

Indeed, he perceives a welter of broken love relationships. It is
therefore not surprising that thoughts of suicide, of self-annihila-
tion (perhaps), should alternate with decisions as to the role one
should enact—from that of avenger with thoughts that must be
bloody or worth nothing, to that of lover laying competitive claim
on top of the coffin, to who feels the greatest sorrow for Ophelia's
death. From the transcendentalist point of view, Hamlet's ultimate salvation may derive from his weariness with role seeking,
his tired decision to allow events to lead him. It is a decision
which makes him deviate from the characters in the "villain"
class who must ultimately grasp something.

Iago and Edmund are the most fully developed of these figures,
although Iago's course is perhaps the most complex. His search
for "reasons" has elicited much comment, but can we not just as
logically speak in terms of his search for role? Denied lieutenancy,
he toys with the concept of the Machiavellian who ever makes his
fool his purse and thinks of himself as a Hamlet figure when, in
his own insecurity about marriage, he conceives of Aemelia as an
adulteress. Finally, he hardens into what seems the most auda-
cious conceptualization.

> How am I then a Villaine,
> To Counsell Cassio to this paralell course,
> Directly to his good? Divinitie of hell,
> When divels will their blackest sinnes put on,
> They do suggest at first with heavenly shewes,
> As I do now [1474–79]

The interchange toward the end of the play is even more significant in these respects.

> Oth. I look down towards his feet; but that's a Fable.
> If that thou bee'st a Divell, I cannot kill thee.

Lod. Wrench his Sword from him.
Iago. I bleed Sir, but not kill'd. [3588–91]

If he is tauntingly suggesting that Othello has proved the point, then Iago would seem to have solved his problem of identity by the very opposite of an *imitatio Christi.* In a sense more complexly investigated by Shakespeare than the case of Richard III, Iago has identified himself by resorting to a conceptualization of self as villain and even devil. But because Iago wishes simply to call himself this, we need not take him at his word any more than we take Richard II at his word when he suggests that he is Christ.

Shakespeare would seem to present us with complementary halves in such characterizations. On the one hand, there is no assurance of identity, for it depends on the love or esteem of someone else. On the other hand, we observe the at least rhetorical grounding of the ego in just that disadvantage according to which one fancies oneself to be rejected. Morocco in *The Merchant of Venice* adumbrates this motif, which may have become part of Shakespeare's characterization stock. "Mislike me not for my complexion," he can say to Portia, but then he can go on to argue how superior this complexion actually makes him. That the motif is early can be inferred from the poet's way with Aaron as he snatches his newborn son away from Demetrius and Chiron.

> What, what, ye sanguine, shallow harted Boyes,
> Ye white-lim'd walls, ye Ale-house painted signes,
> Cole-blacke is better then another hue,
> In that it scornes to beare another hue;
> For all the water in the Ocean,
> Can never turne the Swans blacke legs to white,
> Although she lave them hourely in the flood.
> [*Titus Andronicus,* 1780–86]

On the other hand, when he proudly confesses his atrocities, there is the following interchange:

> *Goth.* What canst thou say all this and never blush?
> *Aar.* Ay, like a black Dogge, as the saying is. [2237–38]

The activity of the play certainly does not lend itself to great complexity of character, but Aaron's way looks forward to Richard's decision to espouse the deformity which he feels makes peacetime a time of rejection and to Edmund's decision to be lawless because he was born outside the law. It is as if a definition of the self is based on a decision to "properly" love oneself, as Iago would put it, by loving what one is physically. The error is akin to Richard II's, for he derives his identity from being a king. Both types depend on superficial means of self-definition, and both types, too, can seek other identities, "becoming" other things with histrionic ease yet almost believing their own acting.

Edmund, finally, does not radically depart from the tenor of this character class. At the finish, he rather quixotically says to Edgar, "If thou'rt noble, I do forgive thee." Does he not enact with some pathetic fatuity the very role from which his birth has barred him and at which he has accordingly scoffed? But he has attained rank in his own mind to such an extent that the ancient pomp and ceremony of the tournament lures him as it would the most romantic schoolgirl. Goneril has pointed out for us the fact that Edmund did not have to answer this challenge from someone unknown, but despite this information (or in its context) Shakespeare has endowed Edmund with a need to adopt the pseudoaristocratic pose.

It may be too "modern" to speak of Edmund's relationship to his status as bastard, if we again think of Phillip the Bastard in *King John*, but clearly a sense of inferiority and rejection is an important part of Edmund's character. "Some good I mean to do, spite of mine own nature," he says, paralleling Cassius' and Iago's self-concepts as fundamentally depraved and inferior. Since it is already too late to save Cordelia and Lear, Edmund's remark can only have relevance to the play in terms of what it tells us about him. Thus his ultimate sense of triumph is not without its pathos. Though to himself inferior, he can conclude about the deaths of Goneril and Regan,

> Yet *Edmund* was belov'd:
> The one the other poison'd for my sake,
> And after slew herselfe. [3196–98]

It is perhaps a final irony of his own situation that he misunderstands the nature of desire so badly that he takes these actions to be signs of love, but his remark affirms the fundamental preoccupation of this class of characters with their desperate and thwarted search for a love which will enable them to stop despising themselves. And we cannot really take our ease in simply calling them villains, if Hamlet is acceptable as testimony. Such character structure is fluidly conceived in order to serve many purposes. Thus we must certainly question how sophisticated any mere concept of "villainy" really might be within the general context of the patterns we have been tracing.

10
The Concept of Character in Shakespearean Tragedy

I t is clear that we differ with the observations of A. C. Bradley, whose *Shakespearean Tragedy* derived its approach from principles consonant with the psychological and ethical generalities not of Renaissance transcendentalism but of a nineteenth-century Anglo-Hegelianism.[1] This system of thought led him to recognize Shakespeare's characters as engaged in the attempted exercise of a superhumanity, it is true, but what seems to have followed from the argument is that Shakespeare's tragic heroes were to be accepted as rendered, to be interpreted a priori as men of demonstrated and even transcendent validity. Given the proposition of their innate grandeur, what followed was the inevitable formulation of another kind of process which was to be regarded as the "tragedy" which these heroes endured.

To glance momentarily at the forested trees of such traditionally undefined terminology, Bradleyan tragedy occurs because the hero suffers misfortune and unhappiness in his play and because, accordingly, certain conclusions are generated from this suffering. But these conclusions are not derived from propositions about character; they derive from ethical assumptions. Having accepted the superhuman status of the hero, the audience is also to accept his ultimate ethical validity. His process is accordingly to be viewed as an engagement and combat with some purely external principle. The hero is pitted against some idea of "evil," either in the life around him or in the hostility of the cosmos. Within this orientation, any questions about character will assume a certain and predictable shape. Othello being so noble, how could he have come to kill Desdemona? Lear being so sinned against, what does his archetypical suffering force him to utter in a madness which must, as if by definition, be taken as axiom in his comments on the nature of a universe that prostrates both him and his good daughter?

[1] See A. C. Bradley, *Shakespearean Tradgedy* (London, 1904), lecture 1.

Along the vector of tragic character in which the transcendent validity of the hero is to be assumed and where, in the combat, it is the "vile world" which triumphs, distortion would appear to prevail further in the critical attempt to assess the terms of Shakespeare's mimesis because the hero's defeat must be rationalized with premises regarding his stature. Is it not characteristically argued that though evil has indeed prevailed, the hero has paradoxically triumphed? In his speeches of defiance at the given situation or in his speeches of indifferent surrender, this kind of hero has asserted himself, for the concept of the transcendent tragic hero prefers such self-assertion to the complex of ideas which are taken to have beaten him down. One views a play such as *Lear*, therefore, as an expression of Shakespeare's pessimism, if only because the materials for the final dialectical gesture required by the critical system are so ambiguous: Lear's death-in-joy/sorrow at Cordelia's breathing immobility. Otherwise, the concept of transcendence in Shakespeare's tragic heroes arcs into an inescapable circle, for whichever the direction of argument, to begin at any point in this system is to arrive at another point on the limb. The moment, for example, that any character is to be regarded as an archetype—Othello the Ideal Warrior—it follows that, as archetype, he is "larger than life," even "transcendent." He is thus better than life and, by definition, cannot be defeated by it, even if he dies.

But if the term *tragedy* is to be invoked at all in connection with the concept of character, Bradleyan and Bradley-influenced systems of dealing with the transcendental aspirations of the Shakespearean tragic hero imply, rather, modes of what must be termed the "comic." The concept of assertion, the notion of the hero as archetype and as statement of ethical position may remind us of the manner in which *nova comoedia* generalized "character." To create that conflict between value positions whose resolution would accord with ethical norms was the essence of one Renaissance comic tradition. According to it, oppositions between such archetypes as the *senex*, parasite, and *matrona* evolved into a victory for those in the group representing the principles with which the audience might side (*Volpone* would indicate the more sophisticated examples). But the force of statement inherent in a characterization system that might generate a *pedantius*, *meretrix*, or *miles gloriosus* is equalled, is it not, by the notion of tragic archetypes which delineates such transcendencies as Othello the Warrior or Hamlet the Thinker? If such archetypes are also to be involved in that kind of tragedy which must end in the paradox of a personal triumph, and if even one such tragedy, *Lear*, is not so constructed and thus must be termed pessimistic, we will note little difference between such tragedy and most concepts of comedy. There is, of course, the matter of mood and feeling, but this is as much as to say that the texture of an *Othello* would approach more closely the definition of *comoedia* implicit in Dante than that which is to be inferred from a *Roister Doister*. In the end, the thrust of the Bradleyan approach to tragic characterization cannot evade its inevitable direction toward conundrum, whatever the texture of the resulting comic tragedy.

Our search is for a more serviceable statement about that problem of tragic character in Shakespeare which seems more usefully investigated not through some concept of the philosophical role of the tragic hero in the drama-as-essay but through the attempt to recover some notion of the psychological organizations conceivably familiar to Shakespeare and his contemporaries. Accordingly, to approach the dilemma of superhumanity which seems to be an issue in the gesture of Shakespeare's characterizations will be to agree with the Bradleyan position only as it were from the nebulous proximities of remote and deviating coastlines. Let us assume that there was current in Shakespeare's culture a general picture of man as unable to attain to a higher level toward which he was understood to be striving through solely human means. Our sense of the problem of a tragic character in the cultural context where Transcendental Being was a familiar and consistently defined concept will thus differ from that espoused by the author of *Shakespearean Tragedy*.

However, to differ is not necessarily to embrace an opposite pole that might render Shakespeare's tragic heroes as slaves of passion, as archetypes playing out the elementary definitions inherent in some (although not all) medieval and Renaissance *exempla.* Nor is any easy pseudo-Hegelian synthesis derivable from the foregoing remarks. If any generalization is possible, rather, it may be formulable as a statement about the resultant technical complexities inherent in any approach to dramatic characterization which is the product of a society oriented toward transcendentalist assumptions. The concept of Absolute Being must ultimately regard the mind's very attempt at self-differentiation as ethical deviance. If the Proclean character of most Renaissance philosophies assumed this deviant propensity as innate in the personality (indeed, as definitive of the sublunary condition) then what, from the purely aesthetic viewpoint, remained as the material for the process of character manipulation in drama? It is from this viewpoint that a Bradley or a Campbell, though important for the sensitivities of their individual interpretations, become not antithetical but extraneous to the scope of our own inquiry.

This is not, however, to suggest that we even consider approaching Shakespeare's tragedies as specific essays in Christian or other transcendentalist doctrines. Nor do we propose to view Shakespearean dramas as morality plays, even though such a form was part of the tradition received by Elizabethan and Jacobean dramatists. We understand the chief purpose of morality drama as the promulgation of received doctrine and the direction of its structure as an effort to demonstrate why doctrine indeed must be followed. Hence a morality is, in effect, an animated essay in which such a concept as "Infidelitie" may be concretized by the human actor but in which the activity of the figure on stage is directed by an author's concept of the intellectual relationship of such (animated) concepts *qua* concepts. In this sense, the human actor would himself actually be irrelevant to the process. The morality play need not be viewed; it can be read for its content. Stage presentation may raise the power of its persuasion but will not alter the burden of its dialectical conclusions.

Thus the morality tradition could not, in our eyes, logically modulate into what we might call Elizabethan drama, although Spivack might so argue. Even though certain conventions of stage presentation might indeed carry over, the assumption underlying the structure of a morality would be totally different from the assumption underlying any play which is not a morality. In other kinds of plays, it was obviously a question of imitating human beings. Whatever the criteria for imitation, the dramatist, as he began his task, had, by definition, a different concept of the aesthetic issues involved. It was initially a question of whether he was to animate a received intellectual concept such as Sloth or whether he was inventing a hypothetical person whose traits might include sloth. The invented person embodies a concept, and the ultimate result of any characterization on stage is likely to suggest the playwright's notion of human beings. However, the distinction we stress has to do with the difference between presenting on stage a concept as concept or a concept as it might be suggested in the behavior of a figure to be imagined as a human being. It is true that human beings acting in a play could certainly achieve extremely propagandistic results, but we should not confuse similarity of effect with similarity of cause. To bring on stage a morality character whose name is Greed-With-Insecurity-But-With-Love-For-Mankind is perhaps to become complex; nevertheless, a specific mode of representation is hereby betokened. To present a character merely named Othello is to play another game completely, no matter how morality-like Othello's play may strike us.

Our own view is that characterizations are structures determined by such cultural generalizations as might have surrounded any given dramatic artist in the history of world literature. In this study we have been dealing with a society which could structure for the stage an Everyman created according to the assumption that the individual life begins in specific personal transgression against a cosmic postulate for the workings of the human mind. The problem we have encountered is that if a society sought to draw from the Everyman assumption some idea of the tragic, such an idea would have its own characteristic difficulties. Any dramatic statement of tragic process or even of tragic causation in human action risked redundancy through the inevitable logic raised by the idea of a first cause, man's fallen condition.

The art of other civilizations might conceivably view man as beginning in perfection and wandering into error through the interposition of cosmic or societal forces, but the transcendentalist postulate differed. After all, if men, by definition, begin life in "error," depictions of character cannot logically operate (as they might in other societies) to exhibit an encounter with some cosmic or societal force which would shatter the equilibrium of any generalized man—an accidental marriage to one's own mother; the question of how to deal properly with the Clytemaestra-Aegisthus combination responsible for the murder of one's father. Rather, in the transcendentalistically-oriented society, individual crises or tragic causations function within a concept of man's fallen condition. And in such a cultural context, the translation of psychological assumption into the mimesis of dramatic causation and process will espouse the redundancies of an appeal to the root concept of original sin or its ideological synonyms, unless characterization weds itself to the notion of a tragic drama through different kinds of *inventio*.

Human mimesis could be realized on the stage, for instance, through a search into the imaginable ramifications of original sin or human blindness. Given a notion of an a priori human aberration, the dramatist, however complex his ultimate conceptions, might see as his task of characterization the very arrangement of such intertangled strands of human motivation as might reasonably or at least plausibly stem from that proposition of an inborn and universal lack of rapport with the mental attitudes appropriate to the plane of transcendental cognition. Confining his portraiture, however, to such strictly evaluative notions as nobility or, on the other hand, lustfulness of the flesh or the eyes, a Renaissance dramatist might achieve the purpose of sermon but not necessarily the invention of persons. To be a maker in the medieval sense or a poet in the Greek sense that Sidney understood, the playwright ultimately had to construct something in the way of a process according to which humans were describable not through the evaluation of archetypes but through their aspirations to their individual goals. In short, this process would involve their personalities regardless of whether or not, from transcendentalist viewpoints, these efforts were erroneous.

We have suggested a description of how Shakespeare dealt with these matters, but in a transcendentalist context there were theoretically so many ways to error that it is little wonder that each step in these paths of error is not accounted for in Shakespeare's total technique or in his tragedies. But if our delineations have not seemed to account for all of the poet's tragic characterizations, if theory has not seemed complemented by what we take to be the facts of a given tragedy, we may partially explain this by the changes in emphasis imparted through a consideration of possible stages in the imagined transcendentalist mental process. In fact, process might be crucial to individuation if all men were to be regarded as unable to thrust "correctly" toward the transcendental and if all men were regarded as unable to cope with the symbolic awarenesses demanded by transcendentalistic philosophies. There could be generalized groupings of kinds of failure in conceptualization, but process would individualize further.

To glance at this matter, let us analyze the theoretical stages posed by a transcendentalist version of mental activity. One is born with certain talents or abilities. One then decides what will objectify these abilities into some symbol according to which one can see oneself as superior. One takes steps to attain whatever material or situation constitutes the body of this symbol—riches, kingship, reputation, a woman—and having attained it, one defends the possession of it, either retaining or losing it. Thus the misinterpretation of the symbol, the quality of one's own talents, and the adequacy of one set of talents to attain a desired symbol can emphasize character, as can a continued inability to discover the satisfying symbol. If we can suggest, for instance, that a character such as Richard II is related to a class, we can explain seeming exceptions in terms of stages in process. Richard is related to Julius Caesar, Brutus, Lear, Falstaff, Hector, Lady Macbeth, and Coriolanus; but if the presence of Coriolanus puzzles us, it is perhaps because of his stage in the process. As secure as Richard in his role, Coriolanus is yet forced into the position of seeking a symbol, the consulship, which he assumes is to be awarded as a sort of military medal, even though we are reminded by the presence of the populace and Menenius on stage of the other talents that a consul might find more useful. His death in Corioles emphasizes his failure to realize that the world is not organized according to his desires, for after the fiasco of the consulship, he assumes first that the deletion of Rome is a proper objective correlative and then that his filial emotions are sufficient to dissolve a Volscian military campaign. Indeed, his neurotic refusal to adopt the role of petitioner to the common people suggests his relationship, by obverse, to Richard II. Emulating Alexander, who spared the house of a man who once entertained him in Thebes, Coriolanus makes the same gesture but forgets the important detail of the man's name: it is the role which is important. It is his work, his warriorship, which is misleading, for he seems to "do" things, as Richard II does not. We may finally compare him to other Shakespearean warriors by noting that he does not place soldiership on a pedestal and consider it a state to which he must aspire. Soldiership is not his ideal; he simply is the Soldier.

Similarly, when we speak of a class suggested by Othello, exception may be taken if we claim that this class is composed of Romeo, Cassio, Troilus, Hal, and Macbeth, for it would seem that the last character is hardly comparable. But perhaps we again must take into account the problem of a step in a theoretical process. "What a man dare, I dare" seems to be the basis of Macbeth's striving. He is no Coriolanus, but he is an Othello plotting against a Desdemona. Macbeth, like Coriolanus, is put into the position of having to seek a symbol for which he is not adequate. And just as Coriolanus assumes that the consulship is the appropriate symbol of his soldiership, so Macbeth seeks the kingship with the same misunderstanding but with different premises. Importantly, he never feels that he deserves kingship. He aspires to it as a symbol of that manly soldiership which is his pseudotranscendental ideal. The play presents the dilemma of this soldier trying to accomplish an unsoldierly, unmanly task buttressed only by the battlefield virtues. The symbol, once attained, is never adequate: "To be thus is nothing but to be safely thus." We note in him the bewildered realization that symbols are not, after all, definitive or adequate to articulate what is really desired. Does he not reveal this in his despair, showing us what he assumed he was obtaining? He did not want to kill Duncan because

> He hath Honour'd me of late, and I have bought
> Golden Opinions from all sorts of people,
> Which would be worne now in their newest glosse,
> Not cast aside so soone. [508–11]

He finds that his attainment of the kingship certainly did not get him what he wanted.

> And that which should accompany Old-Age,
> As Honor, Love, Obedience, Troopes of Friends,
> I must not looke to have. [2241–43]

Other characters might simply have wished for the crown in order to obtain power, but Macbeth's orientation is clear enough. He meets his impending downfall with a purely military stance, cursing his men for cowardice and showing none himself. If critics have seen a reintegration of Macbeth's character toward the end, what they have observed is perhaps the peace of truth. It is soldiership toward which he aspires, and while he has been misled, he now at least knows what he is about. For him the issue is military, and one can easily fight on a battlefield to the end.

> Yet I will try the last. Before my body,
> I throw my warlike Shield: Lay on, *MacDuffe*,
> And damn'd be him, that first cries Hold, enough. [2473–75]

Even though the appalling news about MacDuff led him to say "I'll not fight with thee," MacDuff's apparently impossible demand, "yield thee, coward," precipitated those, Macbeth's last lines of the play.

We also have observed how, "in process," as it were, Hamlet may be unable to decide on adequate objectification, thereby likening himself to Aaron, Cassius, Edmund, Iago, and Richard III. But the fact that Hamlet is presented with a real rather than

fancied problem pushes him to the excesses of a Richard II, for
unlike Cassius, who tentatively assumes only a few roles, Hamlet
is forced by Shakespeare to experiment to such an extent that he
becomes involved on a purely verbal level. Moving from malcontent to court fool, to lover, to suicide, to avenger of God, to Machiavelli, to play producer, even to out-Osricing Osric, his inability to perform decisive action is a function of his inability to
commit himself to an objectification of himself. While he delays
his decision to kill, he also remains undecided as to whether or
not to kill. In his effort to avoid becoming Iago, this Iago-like
character tries on so many self-objectifications that his speeches
are often like Richard's, especially the "What a rogue and peasant
slave am I" soliloquy in which he attempts to sound like an
avenger and contemplates the paradox of the actor who can easily
assume any role he wishes, and with real tears. In fact, Hamlet's
central problem, once the ghost establishes it, determines the action. How does one conclude that one loved one's father; how
does one prove it? This is a role in which one must convince oneself that one feels an emotion. But trying to be a father-lover by
verbalizing and thinking is rather like trying to be a king in Richard II's sense. Although Hamlet aspires to the transcendental figure of his father, he is more complicated than Othello because
Shakespeare merely makes Hamlet's particular relation to the
transcendental the strongest of a number of potential stances,
suggesting to us that the complexity of Hamlet may be a complexity of experimentation with many character types in one
figure.

A theory of tragic character can never be a close description of
specific figures in a given drama. It is only the basis upon which
structures are built, just as a theory of solid geometry may explain
something about houses in a given era but does not account for
every dwelling built according to such general principles. To take
our rest in theory would be to have described Shakespeare as a
psychologist, perhaps, and even as a transcendentalist philosopher,
but not as a dramatist. For us to proceed further would thus not
be to attempt to discover facets of a characterization in order to
make them fit into our general theory but to observe the traits of

some specific character in order to ask whether they can lead us to a concept of a whole construct in which all traits may be accounted for by reference to elements of our general theory. Only then might we glance back to determine whether any of Shakespeare's tragic heroes may be regarded as sophisticated variations of that configuration of ideas which has been the subject of our study. The difference between the analyses of drama and philosophy obviously lies in the emphasis of the former upon a different order of relationships. To analyze a philosophic treatise is not the same thing as to determine and establish the set of facts which, by definition, constitute the fabric of a consciously fashioned work of fictive art.

It is with such a statement that our study should terminate, and we attempt, in conclusion, to rectify any imbalanced emphases with such recapitulation as may describe finally the nature and some limits of the foregoing inquiry.

Our primary interest has been in tracing the lineations of the idea of personality in Renaissance thought, eschewing as often as possible any concept of the term "character" which might subject discourse to the relativities of differing critical presuppositions. Whether or not certain ideas might be specifically realized in dramatic offerings, we have reminded ourselves that concepts of character in the art of any period are inevitably subject to the cultural particularizations of some general philosophical system. The general principle of transcendentalist thought, for example, admits to many possible conceptualizations: there is no reason why the transcendental Entity—and these are clichés of anthropology —may not be some vast mountain or some ideal ocean. The transcendentalism of much Western thought and its traditions during the English Renaissance conceptualized this Entity as a humanoid personality, and the significance of this maneuver for our own interests cannot be overemphasized. When transcendental Being emerges as the figuration of a person, the grammar of thinking about purely human psychology is not only related to but implicitly revealed by such a societal gesture.

In other kinds of transcendentalist projections, for example, a mountain, an ocean, or a storm may serve as the conceptualized Entity, but humans can be "like" these things only in limited and symbolic senses. However, when Proclean concepts predominate, when human selfhood must be like, must relate to, must find true unity with an Entity which is itself conceived of as humanoid, then teleology becomes an important aspect of any cultural approach to psychological theory. This is as much as to say that a civilization formally committed to transcendentalist epistemology of the kind to which we have alluded will tend to issue formal dicta for the optimum in mental attitudes. The attributes of humanoid Entity will be prescribed by the dominant social group, which will generate a code of ethics describing that psychological organization requisite for the individual attainment of *enosis* with Supreme Being. Such a paradoxical attempt to legislate psychology, to establish rules for emotion, is exemplified in the codification dialectics of the English Renaissance, where theories of love were complemented with ideas of order. The concept of order enjoined obedience to the promulgated rules for psychological attitudes, while love alluded to the emotional result, that indescribable ecstasy which was the reward of obedience, of conformity to order. It was, of course, this very concept of the ineffable which ultimately buttressed the logic of the code, for the inevitable failure to comprehend the incomprehensible was, by definition, a failure to conform to order.

But if the ineluctable modality of the invisible served those who, without any necessarily sinister aims at the control of thought, would write, preach, command, or believe in these matters, it could also serve as a point of departure for those who might wish to probe the dilemmas of human nature. The indescribable ecstasy of love might seldom be experienced by man, but if the dialectical rejoinder was to remind him that knowing charity or love was precluded for him by his innate defects, such a dialogue at least provided a language of exploration. After all, man's inability to know, to see, to comprehend true Being was an issue which would inevitably lead to inquiries into perception, for the failure to "know" in such terms was actually a failure to attain those symbological sophistications which are the bases of transcendentalist thought in the first place. Even though sophistry is one result of sophistication, and even though we have observed that, in dialectical fact, codified Renaissance transcendentalism required the acceptance of symbols as signs, the general bent of such an epistemology introduces the problem of symbol awareness into the language of theorizing about human personality.

The historian of ideas will, of course, be aware that notions of hypothetical "personality" in any given culture will not necessarily account for all shades possible in the total spectrum of human psychology. Actually, societal concepts as to optimal traits are no more accurate in describing humans than those theories which have formulated them. Because some civilization might have no intellectual basis upon which to formulate the terms of an abnormal psychology, the "madman" can be rejected or evaded by theory as nonhuman, for example, despite any more pertinent conclusions that might be drawn by a few contemporary pragmatists. Cultural presuppositions, even in their overemphases, may define, yet they seldom restrict the interests of art. Renaissance transcendentalist assumptions that there was in man a proneness to conceptualize at a level lower than the transcendental, to construct personal symbol which might offer the illusion of ontological apprehension and consequent satisfaction, were more fertile for the realization of that dimension in personality theory which we might term "characterization" than the techniques of the fifteenth-century morality would seem to imply. This emphasis on perception establishes intellectual parameters for a structuring of personality in dramatic figurations that might intentionally collocate, for instance, Hamlet's assumption regarding the significance of the ghost's merely physical resemblance to his father with his insistence that his mother's sexuality constitutes the dimension and total definition of her "sin."

These suggestions, finally, are not prescriptive ones: to seem to have argued for the formulaic would be to have failed in our intent to intimate in Renaissance dramatic characterization a complexity deserving the critical caution that is more often brought to the study of later literature. Conversely, if we quite rightly hesitate to rationalize the complexities of twentieth-century fiction by reducing it to the status of mere Freudian, Jungian, or Kierkegaardian tractate, even though one can trace many realization and self-discovery processes in the modern hero back to such general conceptual heritages, we must also argue for a similar restraint of bivalued orientation toward the analysis of Renaissance dramatic art. If the ideological milieu of a Shakespeare emphasized the existence in man of an unrealized and often unconscious drive for unity with a higher condition of Being, the result was not necessarily biblical drama. Rather, Shakespeare's ideological backgrounds may have sensitized his imaginings about character, about some profound dilemmas implicit in the human sense of identity, and may have given him a language of thought with which to approach the complexity and ambivalence of human drives toward self-realization in this life. While some dramatists might not ultimately have agreed with Montaigne's conclusion to the "Apologie of Raymond Sebond," they were certainly familiar with the conceptual structure which would have shaped those final words.

To make the handfull greater than the hand, and the embraced greater then the arme; and to hope to straddle more then our legs length; is impossible and monstrous: nor that man should mount over and above himselfe or humanity; for, he cannot see but with his owne eyes, not take hold but with his owne armes. He shall raise himselfe up, if it please God extraordinarily to lend him his helping hand. He may elevate himselfe by forsaking and renouncing his owne meanes, and suffering himselfe to be elevated and raised by meere heavenly meanes. It is for our Christian faith, not for his Stoicke vertue to pretend or aspire to this divine Metamorphosis, or miraculous transmutation. [II. xii. 326]

INDEX

ARTIFICIAL PERSONS was designed by
Robert L. Nance. Body type is Linotype Electra;
display, Delphian Open Title. The book has been
printed letterpress on a paper of extraordinary lon-
gevity, Warren's University Text, which has been
watermarked with the Press emblem. Composition, printing, and binding were done by
Kingsport Press, Inc.